The Essential
PARLEY P.
PRATT

The Essential
PARLEY P.
PRATT

FOREWORD BY

PETER L. CRAWLEY

SIGNATURE BOOKS
SALT LAKE CITY
1990

Cover Design: Randall Smith Associates

∞Printed on acid free paper.

13   12   11   10   09   2008   7   6   5   4   3

LIBRARY OF CONGRESS CATALOGING-IN-PUBLICATION DATA

Pratt, Parley P. (Parley Parker), 1807–1857.
    [Selections. 1990]
    The essential Parley P. Pratt / with an introduction by Peter L. Crawley.
       p.   cm.
    ISBN: 0-941214-84-2
    1. Mormon Church—Apologetic works.   2. Mormon Church—Doctrines.
3. Church of Jesus Christ of Latter-Day Saints—Apologetic works.
4. Church of Jesus Christ of Latter-Day Saints—Doctrines.
5. Pratt, Parley P. (Parley Parker), 1807–1857.   I. Title.
BX8609.P478   1990
230′.9332—dc20   89-27568
                                                              CIP

Contents

Publisher's Preface

Parley Parker Pratt was born on 12 April 1807 in Burlington, western New York, to Jared Pratt and Charity Dickinson. He was third in a family of five sons which included his younger brother, Mormon apostle and theologian Orson Pratt.

Parley's childhood was marked by extreme poverty. His father, an unsuccessful farmer, moved his family frequently as he struggled to provide for them. The Pratts belonged to no particular religious sect, considering themselves to be non-conformist Christians. Parley's education was cut short at age fifteen when he was obliged to help support his family by working for other farmers. Despite these obstacles, Pratt pursued learning on his own, studying the Bible and other books, developing the literary and rhetorical skills for which he later became famous.

At seventeen, Parley and his older brother William set out to purchase a farm on credit. About this time Parley joined the Baptists but later claimed that he remained discontented with their version of Christianity. The Pratt brothers improved their farm, working it for a year, but were required to give it up when they were unable to meet the payment, a failure they believed resulted from depressed market conditions. William returned home, while Parley went to frontier Ohio where he lived for a year, building a cabin in the wilderness near the settlement of Cleveland and subsisting by hunting. For Pratt, the time he spent in Ohio was a period of spiritual retreat and searching. At twenty he made up his mind to pursue a calling as a minister and returned home to make the necessary arrangements.

Once home, Parley went to the house of Thankful Halsey with the intention of marrying her. Thankful, a widow nearly ten years Pratt's senior, had known Parley from his youth. Thankful reportedly did not remarry after the death of her husband because she loved Parley and was waiting for his return. Parley shared with her his hopes of becoming a preacher and asked that she accept his calling as well.

The couple married and moved to Pratt's property in Ohio which Parley was able to improve with the help of his bride's dowry. They built a frame house to replace the log cabin, cleared fifty acres, and planted gardens and orchards. While in Ohio, Parley met and joined Sidney Rigdon, a preacher who had broken off from Alexander Campbell's primitive gospel movement.

ix

Because of Parley's desire to preach, he sold his estate, clearing only about ten dollars, and set out with Thankful to New York by steamer in August 1830. Thankful's health was fragile and Parley arranged for her to stay with friends in Buffalo while he disembarked at Rochester to begin preaching.

It was at this time that Parley discovered the Church of Christ, later the Church of Jesus Christ of Latter-day Saints (Mormon), founded by Joseph Smith only five months earlier in upstate New York. Pratt borrowed a copy of the Book of Mormon from a Baptist deacon and read it in one evening. Excited by his discovery, he went directly to Palmyra, New York, to seek the Mormon prophet. He found that Joseph Smith had moved to Pennsylvania, but that Joseph's older brother Hyrum was there. Pratt was taught and soon baptized.

The next month Joseph Smith called Pratt and other early converts on a proselytizing mission to the American Indians on the Missouri frontier. On his way to Missouri, Pratt passed through Ohio and succeeded in converting his former minister, Sidney Rigdon, and over one hundred of Rigdon's followers in the Kirtland, Ohio, area. It was in part Pratt's successful missionary work that brought Smith and church headquarters to Kirtland.

Despite hostility from federal Indian agents and local clergy in Missouri, Pratt returned from his mission and reported that Missouri would make an ideal gathering place for the Mormons. Thankful, who joined the church while her husband was in Missouri, had not gone with the other Saints to Kirtland, deciding instead to remain with friends in the east. Pratt returned to Missouri without his wife, where Smith declared that the Saints must gather to build the New Jerusalem in preparation for the second coming of Jesus Christ.

In February 1832, Pratt resolved to bring Thankful to Missouri, even though she was ill. The journey was financed with sixty dollars Thankful had earned in the east. Also, a member of the church sent money with Parley to assist in establishing a farm but soon became dissatisfied and demanded his money returned, leaving Pratt destitute. Meanwhile Pratt was called on another church mission, this time to Illinois.

Returning from his mission, Pratt began to prosper, as the Saints gathered in Jackson County, Missouri. But mounting persecution from neighbors forced him and Thankful to escape to neighboring Clay County. Pratt left for Ohio in the winter of 1834 to alert Joseph Smith and other Mormon leaders to the problems the Mormons were facing in Missouri. Pratt joined the Zion's Camp expedition mustered by Smith to liberate the Saints and punish their persecutors. Disease weakened the camp members, and the Mormon settlement in Jackson County was abandoned.

In 1835, Smith called Pratt to the original Quorum of Twelve Apostles and sent him to Canada, a mission that garnered the conversion of John Taylor, who subsequently became third president of the Mormon church. During this mission, Thankful gave birth to a son, Parley Jr., but she died soon after.

Pratt returned to Kirtland in 1837 to rampant economic and spiritual crisis. Leading Mormons, Pratt included, became angry with Joseph Smith over failed business ventures Smith had endorsed. Pratt, leading the dissent, accused Smith of false prophecy. Smith countered by calling a church court to excommunicate the dissenters. Pratt and others successfully challenged the court's jurisdiction, and before another court could be convened Pratt made a partial confession thereby escaping excommunication. Smith sent Pratt on a mission to New York where, on 9 May 1938, he married his next wife, Mary Ann Frost, a widow with one daughter.

Following the collapse of the Mormon economy in Kirtland, Pratt left New York in April 1838 to meet the Saints who were gathering in northern Missouri. Soon he was embroiled in the same kind of troubles with non-Mormon neighbors he had fled four years earlier. In October, he was arrested and imprisoned along with Smith, Rigdon, and other Mormons for treason, murder, and other crimes. They were never brought to trial but were moved from jail to jail. After eight months imprisonment Pratt escaped to join the Mormons gathering this time in Nauvoo, Illinois.

Pratt was now called with others of the Twelve on successive missions to the eastern states and England. In Philadelphia, he learned from Joseph Smith the doctrine of plural marriage. He visited the cities of Detroit, Washington, D.C., and New York in the company of Brigham Young, Orson Pratt, and other colleagues from his quorum. In England, Pratt was busy organizing the emigration of Latter-day Saints to Nauvoo and printing works such as the *Latter-day Saints' Millennial Star*. He arrived back in Nauvoo on 12 April 1843, serving as a member of the Nauvoo City Council from 1843 to 1845.

In the spring of 1844, Pratt left again for the eastern states on a mission. During his absence Joseph and Hyrum Smith were assassinated on 27 June. Pratt hurried to Nauvoo where he and others of the Twelve worked to keep the church united against various claims of presidency. He then returned to New York where he spent the first half of 1845 as president of the Eastern States Mission.

Pratt had secretly married Belinda Marden on 20 November 1844 and travelled with her to New York. His first wife, Mary Ann, who remained in Nauvoo, knew nothing of her husband's plural marriage. Also unknown to Mary Ann were three other marriages to Elizabeth

Brotherton in 1843 and to Mary Wood and Hannette Snively in 1844. Returning to Nauvoo, Belinda joined Pratt's household as a maid. She became pregnant that winter.

In January 1846, Parley and Orson Pratt publicly argued in the newly completed Nauvoo temple over accusations Parley had made against Orson's wife, Sarah. Orson and Sarah had quarreled with church officials ever since Joseph Smith reportedly approached Sarah in 1842, while Orson was in England, with a proposal of plural marriage. Shortly before Parley's and Orson's dispute, Sarah had informed Mary Ann of Belinda's and Parley's relationship. Mary Ann confronted Belinda and, after learning the truth, left Parley. They formally divorced seven years later.

In the temple Parley accused Sarah of "ruining and breaking up his family," as well as of being an apostate. Parley's and Orson's argument became so intense that Orson was voted out of the temple. The next day Orson wrote to Brigham Young, president of the Twelve, defending his attack on Parley. He denied responsibility for Mary Ann's knowledge of Parley's polygamous marriages and told Young he was willing to repent of anything that would keep him out of good standing. But, he declared, Parley was now his "avowed enemy." The two brothers did not reconcile until seven years later in 1853.

Temple-related activities in Nauvoo, including plural marriages, ceased early in 1846 when the Saints moved to Iowa on their way to the Rocky Mountain Great Basin. Despite Brigham Young's prohibition, Parley and Apostle John Taylor married additional wives in the temple. Young accused both men of adultery.

Pratt left the Saints at Winter Quarters, Iowa, to serve another mission in England and returned in time to accompany them on the western trek, arriving in the Salt Lake Valley in September 1847. He was active in the organization of the territory of Deseret and served twice as delegate to unsuccessful Utah statehood conventions in 1849 and 1856. He also fulfilled missions in California and South America from 1850 to 1852.

Pratt left for California in 1854 to oversee the church's Pacific Mission headquartered in San Francisco. There he met Eleanor McLean, who had joined the Mormons but whose husband, Hector, had remained antagonistic to Mormonism. Eleanor gave Pratt food and cared for his domestic needs while his wife was ill; Pratt gave Eleanor advice on her apparently unhappy homelife. After an unsuccessful attempt to claim her children in New Orleans, where Hector had sent them to live with relatives, Eleanor decided to leave her husband and move to Utah where Pratt employed her as a teacher to his children. Within a month of her arrival, Eleanor married Parley, his tenth and last plural wife. She had not been divorced from Hector.

On 10 September 1856, Parley was called to assist the church in Virginia. Eleanor asked to go with him, hoping to get her children and bring them back to Utah. They reached St. Louis in November, and Eleanor continued to New Orleans where she professed to relatives that she was leaving Mormonism. Thus she succeeded in finally taking her children with her. Hector was immediately alerted and left for New Orleans to track them down.

When Hector arrived in St. Louis, Parley was warned and fled. Hector swore out a warrant against Parley and Eleanor both. They were subsequently located and arrested. A trial was held in Van Buren, Arkansas, where they were acquitted. On 13 May 1857, Parley was given his horse and allowed to leave. But before he traveled far, Hector caught up with and killed him. Parley was secretly buried in Fine Springs, Arkanas, late the next day.

In preparing the following texts of Parley P. Pratt's writings for publication, a note should be made about presentation. Care has been taken to present them exactly as they were first printed. The only exception to this is the correction of obviously unintentional typesetting errors such as letter transpositions and repeated words. Archaic, variant, and idiosyncratic spelling, usage, and grammar remain as they are found in the original, with no attempt made to correct or resolve occasionally ambiguous constructions and meanings.

The inclusion of Pratt's autobiography is problematic since it is apparent from the internal style and statements from associates that other writers besides Pratt contributed to its writing. These include his son, Parley Pratt, Jr., John Taylor, and George Q. Cannon. Still, enough of Pratt's unmistakable hand is evident to justify its republication here.

Finally, Pratt's writings occasionally evince a bombastic, confrontational tone which some readers might find offensive. Much of Pratt's polemicism can be attributed to his environment and self-education. Although not a schooled theologian, Pratt was one of early Mormonism's most original thinkers and influential writers. While some of his spirited, opinionated writing seems quaint or antiquated today, it struck deep, familiar chords with his disenfranchised, independent-minded frontier contemporaries. For this reason, Parley P. Pratt's writing serves today as an unembellished window to the concerns, motivations, fears, and aspirations of early Mormons, even if it does not in every aspect conform with contemporary LDS teachings or sensibilities.

Foreword

Peter L. Crawley

To measure the contribution to Mormonism of Parley Parker Pratt (1807–57), it may be helpful to review the circumstances surrounding the writing of his first books. This begins with some mention of the so-called primitive gospel movement, a part of the religious milieu in which the Church of Jesus Christ of Latter-day Saints was born.

The primitive gospel movement was a collection of diverse, independent movements which arose in New England, the South, and the West between 1790 and 1830 in response to the religious revivalism and sectarian conflict that characterized evangelical Protestantism. Certain attitudes tended to be shared by the various groups, among them a biblicist point of view; a rejection of Calvinist predestination; an anticipation of mass conversions foreshadowing an imminent Second Advent; a belief that the established churches were corrupt departures from the original, primitive Christian faith; and the belief that religion should be more personal, more independent of organized, hierarchical institutions. One other attitude is especially pertinent. Primitive gospelers tended to be *anticreedal*. Deploring the disunity and conflict among the established churches resulting from widely differing interpretations of the Bible, they attacked this problem, not by imposing an authoritarian statement of doctrine, but by eschewing any dogma beyond the most fundamental principles enunciated in the scriptures.[1]

Primitive gospel leanings are clearly discernible in Joseph Smith's parents and grandparents as well as in those who surrounded him during Mormonism's earliest months. David Whitmer's account of the birth of the Mormon church describes a loosely organized, anticreedal group of religious "seekers" in which Joseph Smith was distinguished only by his "call" to translate the gold plates. Whitmer, who probably reflected the most apparent primitivistic orientation, felt that the church was as organized as it needed to be during the eight months preceding its formal organization on 6 April 1830, that in this embryonic state it was closer to the primitive ideal than at any other time in its history.[2]

Mormonism differed from most other primitive gospel movements, however, in a number of ways. It rejected the infallibility of the Bible and accepted the Book of Mormon as a new volume of scripture. More fundamental, this loosely organized, anticreedal group of seekers centered on a man who spoke with God. Virtually all other primitive gospelers—the Vermont lay preacher Elias Smith for example—began their ministries as a result of personal visions. Joseph Smith, on the other hand, continued to receive revelations throughout his life. As new converts were drawn into the fold and Joseph Smith's revelations multiplied, his stature in the new church inevitably grew to a position of preeminence, and his revelations took on the weight of scripture and became part of an expanding body of dogma.

In an anticreedal church, a growing body of dogma produces fundamental tensions. And a significant part of the history of Mormonism's first decade can be viewed as the ebb and flow of these tensions which ultimately were resolved only by the excommunication of early Mormon stalwarts such as David and John Whitmer, Oliver Cowdery, and Martin Harris in 1838 and the church's move to Commerce (later Nauvoo), Illinois, the next year.³ Moreover, the anticreedalism of the early church insured that little of the developing theology would be openly discussed or written about until the church settled in Nauvoo. Although Mormonism began with a book, few others were published during this first decade that dealt with any aspect of Mormon theology.⁴ On the two occasions when the church attempted to print the revelations to Joseph Smith in book form, internal stresses broke into the open.⁵ The preface of the 1835 Doctrine and Covenants alludes to these tensions and to the reluctance of early Mormons to solidify the gospel in print: "There may be an aversion in the minds of some against receiving any thing purporting to be articles of religious faith, in consequence of there being so many now extant; but if men believe a system, and profess that it was given by inspiration, certainly, the more intelligibly they can present it, the better. It does not make a principle untrue to *print* it, neither does it make it true not to print it."

It was against the backdrop of these attitudes that Parley Pratt, an ordained apostle of the new church since 1835, journeyed to New York City in July 1837. The Mormon economy in Kirtland, Ohio, was in a state of collapse; dissension was rife following the demise of the Kirtland Safety Society. Parley himself had been touched by the rampant apostasy. And in an act of renewal he fled to New York to preach the gospel and purify himself. Few New York doors opened to him, so impelled by the literary instincts within him, he retired to his room to write. In two months he produced the most important of all noncanonical Mormon books, the *Voice of Warning*.⁶

This was not the first Mormon tract or the first outline of the tenets of Mormonism. A year before Orson Hyde had published his single-sheet broadside *Prophetic Warning* in Toronto which enumerated the judgments to accompany the Second Advent—but avoided any mention of the Latter-day Saints. Two years before that, Oliver Cowdery, one of

Joseph Smith's closest associates, had published a one-page outline of the beliefs of the Mormons in the first issue of the Kirtland *Messenger and Advocate*. But Cowdery's guarded outline could have represented any evangelical Christian sect and seems to have been written to underscore the similarities between Mormonism and other Christian denominations. *Voice of Warning* emphasized the differences. More significant, it erected a standard for all future Mormon pamphleteers by setting down a formula for describing Mormonism's basic doctrines and listing biblical prooftexts, arguments, examples, and expressions which would be used by others for another century. It was, finally, the first use of a book other than the standard scriptural works to spread the Mormon message.

Three months after *Voice of Warning* was published, the proselytizing effort in New York City was bearing fruit. A growing congregation of Latter-day Saints met in a room outfitted for them by a local chairmaker, David W. Rogers, and a few copies of *Voice of Warning* were in circulation around the city. The inevitable response by local clergy came quickly. La Roy Sunderland, editor of the Methodist *Zion's Watchman*, attacked the Mormons in an eight-part article (13 January – 3 March 1838), basing much of his information on Eber D. Howe's influential exposé *Mormonism Unvailed* (Painesville, Ohio, 1834). Sunderland also quoted freely from the Book of Mormon, Doctrine and Covenants, and *Voice of Warning*. When Howe's *Mormonism Unvailed* was first published, the Mormons all but ignored it. One finds only four or five passing references to it in the entire three-year run of the *Messenger and Advocate*. But in New York City, away from the main body of the church, feeling the power of the press and seeing his own work attacked in print, Parley Pratt responded in kind. In April 1838, just before he left New York for the new Mormon colony at Far West, Missouri, he published his fiery rebuttal to Sunderland, *Mormonism Unveiled: Zion's Watchman Unmasked, and Its Editor Mr. L. R. Sunderland, Exposed: Truth Vindicated: the Devil Mad, and Priestcraft in Danger!* This 47-page pamphlet marks another bibliographical milestone: it is the first of a vast number of tracts written in response to anti-Mormon attacks. And like *Voice of Warning*, it established a formula that would be followed by Mormon pamphleteers for another century, balancing a defense of Mormonism's sacred books and its doctrines with an unrelenting assault on the religion of the attacker.[7]

Pratt reached Far West, Missouri, in the spring of 1838. There he found the Mormon colony wracked by the same dissension from which he had fled the year before in Kirtland, Ohio. Within six months anti-Mormon violence had driven the Latter-day Saints from Missouri, and some of its leaders, including Joseph and Hyrum Smith, Sidney Rigdon, and Parley Pratt, were beginning terms of many months in Liberty and Columbia jails.

For Pratt the months of solitude in Columbia Jail meant time to write. Before he escaped on 4 July 1839, he produced a number of hymns and two significant essays. The first of these essays is an account of the violence in Missouri, which he published in Detroit in October 1839 while en route to a church mission in Great Britain, as an 84-page pamphlet entitled *History of the Late Persecution*.[8] Three months later he re-published it in New York City as a hardback book with the title *Late Persecution of the Church of Jesus Christ of Latter Day Saints*. The second edition incorporates an introduction, not included in the first, which gives some of the early history of Mormonism as well as a summary of its most fundamental beliefs. None of the doctrinal concepts appearing in this introduction were new to the printed record. All are discussed, for example, in *Voice of Warning*. What was new was the concise formulation of the concepts in a few pages. In February 1840 Pratt reworked the doctrinal portion of this introduction into a four-page pamphlet entitled *An Address by Judge Higbee and Parley P. Pratt . . . To the Citizens of Washington and to the Public in General*. This was the first short missionary tract outlining the fundamentals of Mormonism. Immediately after he reached England in April 1840, Pratt reprinted his four-page address, slightly rewritten for a British audience, with the title *An Address by a Minister of the Church of Jesus Christ of Latter-day Saints to the People of England*. During the next three years it was reprinted twice more in England and three times in the United States.[9]

Pratt's second prison essay is the more interesting of the two. Entitled "A Treatise on the Regeneration and Eternal Duration of Matter" and printed in his *Millennium and Other Poems* (New York, 1840), it was the first writing to deal with the truly distinguishing doctrines of Mormonism. Earlier articles such as Sidney Rigdon's three serial pieces, "Millennium," "Faith of the Church," and "The Gospel," begun in *The Evening and the Morning Star* and continued in the *Messenger and Advocate*, could just as well have been published in the magazine of any Christian denomination. Even the "Lectures on Faith," printed first in the 1835 Doctrine and Covenants, treat only the most general Christian principles. Just a single distinctive idea — that God and Jesus Christ are separate beings — appears in them, in the fifth lecture. "A Treatise," on the other hand, put in print for the first time such radical ideas as: matter and spirit can neither be created nor annihilated; the world was not created *ex nihilo* but organized out of existing matter; and God is bound by certain overriding laws. In short it announced that the "omnis" of traditional Christianity did not apply to Mormonism. Four years later the ideas in "A Treatise" were amplified in a pair of essays, "Immortality of the Body" and "Intelligence and Affection," both included in Pratt's *An Appeal to the Inhabitants of the State of New York* (Nauvoo, 1844). These two essays express the most optimistic view of humanity in any Mormon printed source. They establish, in my opinion, a high-water mark in Mormon theological writing.

The year 1840 marked the confluence of several streams of events which changed the course of Mormon intellectual history. During the two years following its appearance in 1837, the *Voice of Warning* demonstrated the usefulness of the press in spreading the Mormon message, and by the fall of 1839, the first edition of 3,000 was sold out and Pratt was preparing a second edition. At this same time others turned to the press to advertise the Mormon expulsion from Missouri, while Joseph Smith journeyed to Washington, D.C., to seek redress from the U.S. Congress for the Mormon losses there.[10] Free from the inhibiting anticreedal influence of David Whitmer and others, Joseph Smith now began to openly discuss the unique doctrines of Mormonism which before had only been whispered of in Kirtland.[11] These public teachings, in turn, drew attacks from outside clergy.[12] In addition, by the spring of 1840 nine of the Quorum of Twelve Apostles were arriving in Great Britain, and this massing of activity brought further attacks from British clerics. Thus the stage was set for a flowering of Mormon pamphleteering. Where only three polemical tracts were published during the nine years 1830–38, eighteen were published by Mormons in 1840, eight by Pratt.[13] Before the death of Joseph Smith in 1844, Mormon writers produced more than seventy works, twenty by Pratt.[14]

These ephemeral pamphlets fundamentally changed Mormonism. For as they multiplied, the tenets of the church, bit by bit, were identified in print. In the absence of an official statement of doctrine, the ideas printed in these missionary tracts came to serve as the church's confession of faith. And thus was Mormonism transformed from an anticreedal religion to one identified with a number of distinguishing doctrines.

By the early 1850s essentially all of Mormonism's beliefs had been discussed somewhere in print, but no single comprehensive treatment had yet been written. Again it fell to Parley Pratt to produce the first book of this kind. In San Francisco in August 1851, just prior to leaving for his mission to Chile, he began work on his *Key to the Science of Theology*. Sixteen months later the next-to-last chapter, Chapter 16, was printed in the *Deseret News*; and in March 1855 the first edition was offered for sale.[15]

Key to Theology is Mormonism's earliest comprehensive synthetical work. Its scope is complete. Beginning with a definition of theology, it traces the loss of the true gospel among the Jews and the gentiles; then in linking chapters it discusses the nature of the godhead, the origin of the universe, the restoration of the gospel, the means by which men and women regain the presence of God, the resurrection, the three degrees of glory, and the ultimate position of exalted men and women as pro-creative beings. Unlike the writings of Orson Pratt, Parley's younger brother, which are definitive, almost dogmatic, *Key to Theology* is poetic, allusive, at times ambiguous. It is a masterly book. It is also Pratt's last major work, published just two years before his assassination in Arkansas in 1857 by the husband of a woman he had been courting.

There are other "firsts" to Pratt's credit. During his mission with the Twelve to the eastern states in the summer of 1835, he stopped in Boston to publish *The Millennium, a Poem. To Which is Added Hymns and Songs*, the first book of Mormon poetry.[16] Again in Boston nine years later, he took a day off from campaigning for Joseph Smith's presidency and wrote "A Dialogue Between Joe Smith and the Devil," which was printed in the *New York Herald* and later reprinted in pamphlet form. Although written to make a point — that modern Christendom was corrupt and Mormonism was the only true Christian faith — *A Dialogue Between Joe Smith and the Devil* is the earliest work that can be classified as Mormon fiction.[17]

Just prior to leaving San Francisco for Chile in September 1851, Pratt composed *Proclamation to the People of the Coasts and Islands of the Pacific* and handed the manuscript to fellow missionary Charles W. Wandell for publication. Two months later, immediately upon reaching Sydney, Australia, Wandell arranged for the printing of *Proclamation*.[18] This was the first Mormon book published outside of North America and Western Europe, the first book associated with that extraordinary effort that sent Mormon missionaries in the early 1850s to Africa, India, China and Australia.

While in Chile, Pratt wrote *Proclamacion Extraordinaria Para Los Americanos Espanoles*, which he published in San Francisco after his return in May 1852. Soon after it appeared, a San Francisco newspaper attacked this tract and questioned the practice of polygamy among the Mormons. Not until 28 August 1852 would the Latter-day Saints first publicly acknowledge what had been a fact for more than ten years, that polygamous families existed among them.[19] But six weeks before this announcement and two months before it was put in print, Pratt replied to the newspaper attack with his broadside *"Mormonism!" "Plurality of Wives!"* in which he outlined a defense of plural marriage that, with various amplifications, would be repeated for another fifty years.

Parley Pratt's contribution goes beyond merely producing "first books," however. Although most of his works are now virtually unknown, much of what was printed in them has survived. The early Mormon pamphleteers thought little of borrowing from one another, and many of Pratt's arguments and ideas flowed into the works of others and thus were perpetuated as a permanent part of Mormonism's gospel tradition. A few examples from publications by missionaries will illustrate this process.

Chapter 3 of *Voice of Warning* deals with the kingdom of God and is based on the following outline: the kingdom has (1) a king, (2) officers, (3) laws, (4) subjects; (5) faith, repentance, baptism by one with authority, and the gift of the Holy Ghost are requisite for entrance into the kingdom; (6) the kingdom must embrace apostles, prophets, pastors, teachers, etc.; (7) its members must enjoy the "gifts of the spirit." Benjamin Winchester used this outline in the second number of his *Gospel Reflector* (Philadelphia, 1841) and again in the *History of the Priesthood* (Philadelphia, 1843). William I. Appelby followed it in his tract, *A Dissertation on Nebuchadnezzar's Dream* (Philadelphia, 1844), at one point quoting Pratt directly — without attribution. And the first number of David Candland's *Fireside Visitor or Plain Reasoner* (Liverpool, 1846) borrowed Pratt's treatment of the necessity of baptism. But the most important use of this chapter was by Parley's brother, Orson.

Orson Pratt arrived in Liverpool, England, in August 1848 to assume the presidency of the church's British mission. Enjoined to "print, publish, and superintend the emigration,"[20] he wrote sixteen tracts during the next two-and-one-half years which were published and republished by the tens of thousands and formed the basis of the missionary work in Great Britain. Early in 1851 these tracts were bound together with a title page and table of contents, forming a book which eventually came to be known as *Orson Pratt's Works*. This was an extremely influential book. It was published at a time when the British mission was producing its most converts. For many of these new converts, Orson's tracts provided the first contact with published Mormon theology. Orson was a towering figure in the British mission, loved and admired as "the St. Paul of Mormondom," the "Gauge of Philosophy." With the onset of the Utah War in 1857, Mormon book writing almost totally ceased, and for the next twenty years virtually no new books were printed.[21] What this meant was that those books which were in print before the Utah War continued to exert their influence for another generation, especially *Orson Pratt's Works* which simply outnumbered all others by many thousands. When LDS books began to be published again after the death of Brigham Young, *Orson Pratt's Works* was reprinted three times (1884, 1891, 1899). Two more editions have been published in our century. More important, *Orson Pratt's Works* was a principal point of departure for Mormonism's twentieth-century writers, such as B. H. Roberts, James E. Talmage, and John A. Widtsoe.

Orson Pratt's Works includes a series of four tracts, *The Kingdom of*

God (1848–49), which treats, as the title suggests, the same subject as the third chapter of *Voice of Warning*. It is constructed on an outline of seven topics essentially identical to Parley's outline in *Voice of Warning*.

Anticipating the claim of the non-Mormon clergy that the Bible contains all sacred writings, Parley listed, in the fourth chapter of *Voice of Warning*, a number of sacred books mentioned in the Bible but not included in it. Expanded and accompanied by the biblical citations, this list was printed in his tract *Plain Facts, Showing the Falsehood and Folly of the Rev. C. S. Bush* (Manchester, 1840). A few months later John Taylor included Parley's list in his *Truth Defended and Methodism Weighed in the Balance and Found Wanting* (Liverpool, 1840). Benjamin Winchester reprinted the list and citations in his *Gospel Reflector*, and Lorenzo D. Barnes incorporated it in his *References to Prove the Gospel in its Fulness* (Philadelphia and Nauvoo, 1841). It was printed again in Erastus Snow and Benjamin Winchester's *An Address to the Citizens of Salem and Vicinity* (Salem, 1841). Finally, Orson Pratt used half of Parley's list together with the accompanying argument in the first installment of his six-part *Divine Authenticity of the Book of Mormon* (1850–51), also a part of *Orson Pratt's Works*.

The concluding section of *Mormonism Unveiled: Zion's Watchman Unmasked* attacks the doctrines of the Methodists, particularly their concept of a God without body, parts, or passions. Parley expanded this in his unsigned pamphlet *The True God and His Worship Contrasted with Idolatry* (Liverpool? 1842?) which argues that a belief in a God without body, parts, or passions is equivalent to a belief in a God that does not exist — a belief, the tract declares, that is nothing short of atheism. John Taylor quotes Parley's attack on the Methodists in *Truth Defended*, and W. I. Appleby incorporates it in *Dissertation of Nebuchadnezzar's Dream*. The idea that those who believe in a God without body or passions are atheists is one of the central ideas in Orson's *Absurdities of Immaterialism* (1849), an important pamphlet in *Orson Pratt's Works*.

As mentioned above, Parley's *An Address by a Minister of the Church of Jesus Christ of Latter-day Saints to the People of England* was derived from the doctrinal part of his introduction to *Late Persecution*. *An Address* is quoted in part — with a citation — in Snow and Winchester's *Address to the Citizens of Salem and Vicinity*. It is reprinted in full — without citation — in John E. Page's *Slander Refuted* (Philadelphia? 1841?); and its discussion of authority is evident in Moses Martin's *A Treatise on the Fulness of the Everlasting Gospel* (New York, 1842). But again it is Orson Pratt who makes the most intriguing use of this text. In Edinburgh in the fall of 1840 Orson published his *Interesting Account of Several Remarkable Visions and of the Late Discovery of Ancient American Records*. This is a signal book, the first printed account of Joseph Smith's 1820 vision. Reprinted in 1848 with the title *Remarkable Visions*, it was included in *Orson Pratt's Works*. The last seven pages of *Interesting Account* contain "a sketch of the faith and doctrine" of the church which is generally considered to be the precursor of the thirteen Articles of Faith. It is clear, however, that Orson's "sketch of the faith and doctrine" was written with Parley's introduction to *Late Persecution* in view; at one point a paragraph from the introduction is quoted directly — again without credit.

The most egregious case of borrowing is by George J. Adams in his *A Letter to His Excellency John Tyler, President of the United States, Touching the Signs of the Times, and the Political Destiny of the World: By G. J. Adams* (New York, 1844). This is nothing more or less than a faithful reprint, including typographical errors, of Parley's *Letter to the Queen of England* (New York? 1841). Adams supplied only a short concluding paragraph and acknowledged the source of his text in a grudging and disingenuous postscript: "It is but justice for me to add, that I am indebted to Elder P. P. Pratt for many truths contained in the foregoing letter."

If Parley P. Pratt was the inventor of Mormon book writing, why is his name not remembered as prominently as B. H. Roberts, Orson Pratt, James E. Talmage, and John A. Widtsoe? The answer lies in the accidents of history as well as in the nature of Mormon theology itself.

Even though it is a "revealed" religion, Mormonism is all but creedless — an inheritance from its primitivistic beginnings. While certain doctrines are enunciated in the standard works and some doctrinal issues have been addressed in formal pronouncements by the LDS First Presidency, there is nothing in Mormonism comparable to the Westminster Confession of Faith or the Augsburg Confession. Few of the truly distinctive doctrines of Mormonism are discussed in "official" sources. It is mainly by "unofficial" means — Sunday school lessons, seminary, institute, and Brigham Young University religion classes, sacrament meeting talks, and books by church officials and others who ultimately speak only for themselves — that the theology is passed from one generation to the next. Indeed it would seem that a significant part of Mormon theology exists primarily in the minds of the members.

The absence of a formal creed means that each generation must produce a new set of gospel expositors to restate and reinterpret the doctrines of Mormonism. As one looks back at the flow of LDS doctrinal exposition, one sees, beginning in the 1850s, this process of restatement occurring roughly every thirty years.[22] The books that are now best remembered are the great synthetical books that came out of these periodic restatements. Here the names of Widtsoe, Talmage, and Roberts come to mind.

John A. Widtsoe (1872–1952) was the most prominent gospel writer of the period near the Second World War. His three-volume *Evidences and Reconciliations* (1943–51) discussed Mormonism with an eye to the prevailing notions of science and history. B. H. Roberts (1857–1933) and James E. Talmage (1862–1933) were the preeminent Mormon writers of the period just after the turn of the twentieth century. Roberts's *Mormon Doctrine of Deity* (1903), *Seventy's Course in Theology* (1907–12), his edited seven-volume *History of the Church* (1902–32), and his six-volume *Comprehensive History* (1930) are still in print and still read, as are Talmage's monumental books *Articles of Faith* (1899) and *Jesus the Christ* (1915).

Roberts, whose *The Gospel* was first published in 1888, actually spanned two generations, as did Orson Pratt (1811–81). After Parley's death in 1857, Orson lived another twenty-five years, a period when almost no other Mormon books were written and most of the Latter-day Saints had a copy of *Orson Pratt's Works* on their shelves. His reputation as the great nineteenth-century Mormon intellectual was greatly enhanced by his lectures and articles on science and mathematics in the *Deseret News*, published in Salt Lake City, and the *Latter-day Saints' Millennial Star*, published in England; his bettering of John P. Newman, chaplain of the U.S. Senate, in a debate on polygamy; and his conflicts with Brigham Young over doctrinal matters.[23]

Except for *Voice of Warning* and *Key to Theology*, Parley's books were ephemeral missionary tracts printed in small editions. And it is tempting to conjecture that the Latter-day Saints preferred more direct, unambiguous books such as Orson Pratt's series *True Faith, True Repentance*, etc. (1856–57), John Jaques's *Catechism for Children* (1854), Charles W. Penrose's *"Mormon" Doctrine Plain and Simple* (1882), and Franklin D. Richards and James A. Little's *Compendium* (1882) to the poetic *Key to Theology*—in spite of the fact that in spirit and approach *Key to Theology* is more faithful to the informal, idiosyncratic nature of Mormon theology.

Nevertheless *Voice of Warning* and *Key to Theology* are still in print and still affectionately read by a few twentieth-century Mormons. Parley grew prophetic when he wrote in the preface of the 1847 edition of *Voice of Warning*, "And should the author be called to sacrifice his life for the cause of truth, he will have the consolation that it will be said of him, as it was said of Abel, viz, 'He, being dead, yet speaketh.'"

NOTES

1. Marvin S. Hill, "The Role of Christian Primitivism in the Origin and Development of the Mormon Kingdom, 1830–1844," Ph.D. diss., University of Chicago, 1968, 6–36. See also Dan Vogel, *Religious Seekers and the Advent of Mormonism* (Salt Lake City: Signature Books, 1988); and Marvin S. Hill, *Quest for Refuge: The Mormon Flight from American Pluralism* (Salt Lake City: Signature Books, 1989).

2. See Hill, "Christian Primitivism," 37–60. Peter Crawley, "The Passage of Mormon Primitivism," *Dialogue: A Journal of Mormon Thought* 13 (Winter 1980): 26–37. David Whitmer, *An Address to All Believers in Christ* (Richmond, MO, 1887), 28–33, 45–48.

3. Crawley, "Passage of Mormon Primitivism," 26–37.

4. Just three polemical tracts were published before 1839: Orson Hyde, *Prophetic Warning* (Toronto, 1836); Parley P. Pratt, *Voice of Warning* (New York, 1837); and Parley P. Pratt, *Mormonism Unveiled: Zion's Watchman Unmasked* (New York, 1838). Virtually all of the early Mormon tracts were self-published, including most of those cited herein.

5. Crawley, "Passage of Mormon Primitivism," 29–32.

6. Peter Crawley, "A Bibliography of the Church of Jesus Christ of Latter-day Saints in New York, Ohio, and Missouri," *Brigham Young University Studies* 12 (Summer 1972): 516–18. Apart from its importance in the intellectual history of Mormonism, *Voice of Warning* was probably the most effective nineteenth-century Mormon missionary tract. Before 1900 the Utah church printed twenty-four editions in English as well as editions in Danish, Dutch, French, German, Icelandic, Spanish, and Swedish.

7. Leroy Sunderland, born in 1804 in Rhode Island, founded *Zion's Watchman* in 1835. He was an impassioned advocate of temperance, abolition, mesmerism, phrenology, and spiritualism. Following his 1838 exchange with Parley Pratt, he established the Wesleyan Methodist Church, attended the World Anti-slavery Convention in London, founded the first spiritualist newspaper in the United States (*The Spiritual Philosopher*), and published at least eight books, ranging from *Pathetism; with Practical Instruction* to *The Trance and Correlative Phenomena*. He died in Massachusetts in 1885. See Leslie A. Shepard, *Encyclopedia of Occultism and Parapsychology* (Detroit: Gale Research Co., 1985), 1305.

8. Crawley, "Bibliography of the Church," 535–37.

9. Two editions were published in Manchester, England, in 1840; a third was published in Bristol, England, in 1841. Two editions were published in New York City in 1841; a third American edition was published in Philadelphia in 1843.

10. See, for example, John P. Greene's *Facts Relative to the Expulsion of the Mormons* (Cincinatti, 1839); and John Taylor's *A Short Account of the Murders, Roberies [sic], Burnings, Thefts, and Other Outrages* (Springfield, 1839).

11. Crawley, "Passage of Mormon Primitivism," 34.

12. Caleb Jones, a Methodist preacher, published two tracts under the pseudonym Philanthropist which were responded to by Samuel Bennett and Erastus Snow. H. Perkins, a Presbyterian, delivered an anti-Mormon lecture which brought a response from Benjamin Winchester. See note 12.

13. The three early tracts are cited in note 4. In addition to the works of Parley Pratt listed below, those works published in 1840 include: Samuel Bennett, *A Few Remarks by Way of Reply to an Anonymous Scribbler* (Philadelphia, 1840); Orson Hyde, *A Timely Warning to the People of England* (Manchester, 1840); Orson Pratt, *Interesting Account of Several Remarkable Visions* (Edinburgh, 1840); Sidney

Rigdon, *An Appeal to the American People* (Cincinnati, 1840); Erastus Snow, *E. Snow's Reply to the Self-Styled Philanthropist of Chester County* (Philadelphia, 1840); three tracts by John Taylor — *An Answer to Some False Statements and Misrepresentations Made by the Rev. Robert Heys* (Liverpool, 1840); and two tracts by Benjamin Winchester — *An Examination of a Lecture Delivered by the Rev. H. Perkins* (n.p., 1840), and *The Origin of the Spaulding Story* (Philadelphia, 1840).

14. Chad J. Flake, *A Mormon Bibliography 1830–1930* (Salt Lake City: University of Utah Press, 1978).

15. Parley P. Pratt, *Autobiography* (New York, 1874), 433. (It is uncertain how much of Pratt's autobiography was written by Pratt himself and how much of it reflects the involvement of his son, Parley Jr., John Taylor, and George Q. Cannon.) *Deseret News*, 8 Jan. 1853. *Latter-day Saints' Millennial Star* 17 (31 March 1855): 208.

16. Crawley, "Bibliography of the Church," 498–99.

17. Pratt, *Autobiography*, 376; *New York Herald*, 25 Aug. 1844.

18. Peter Crawley, "The First Australian Mormon Imprints," *Gradalis Review* 2 (Fall 1973): 38–51.

19. *Deseret News Extra*, 14 Sept. 1852.

20. *Latter-day Saints' Millenial Star* 10 (15 Aug. 1848): 241.

21. Flake, *A Mormon Biliography*.

22. The first synthetical books include Orson Spencer, *Letters Exhibiting the Most Prominent Doctrines of the Church of Jesus Christ of Latter-day Saints* (Liverpool, 1848); John Jaques, *Catechism for Children* (Liverpool, 1854); *Key to Theology* (Liverpool, 1855); Orson Pratt's series of eight tracts, *True Faith, True Repentance . . .* (Liverpool, 1856–57); and Franklin D. Richards, *Compendium* (Liverpool, 1857). In the 1880s this restatement occurred with such books as John Taylor, *Items on Priesthood* (Salt Lake City, 1882), and his *Mediation and Atonement* (Salt Lake City, 1882); John Nicholson, *The Preceptor* (Salt Lake City, 1883), and B. H. Roberts, *The Gospel* (Salt Lake City, 1888). After the turn of the century it occurred again through such works as B. H. Roberts, *Mormon Doctrine of Deity* (Salt Lake City, 1903) and his *Seventy's Course in Theology* (Salt Lake City, 1899), and James E. Talmage's *Jesus the Christ* (Salt Lake City, 1915). In the mid-twentieth century this process of restatement was repeated through the writings of John A. Widtsoe, Joseph Fielding Smith, Lowell Bennion, and others.

23. Thomas Edgar Lyon, "Orson Pratt — Early Mormon Leader," M.A. thesis, University of Chicago, 1932, 86–134; Gary James Bergera, "The Orson Pratt-Brigham Young Controversies: Conflict Within the Quorums, 1853 to 1868," *Dialogue: A Journal of Mormon Thought* 13 (Summer 1980): 7–49. Orson Pratt's reputation greatly extended beyond the facts; he was certainly not "one of the world's greatest scientists." Lyon, 2.

"The Kingdom of God"

(from *A Voice of Warning and Instruction to All People,
Containing a Declaration of the Faith and Doctrine of
the Church of the Latter Day Saints, Commonly Called Mormons*
[New York: Printed by W. Sandford, 1837])

"Seek first the Kingdom of God," was the command of the Saviour while on the earth, teaching the children of men.

Having taken a general view of the Prophesies Past and Future — we will now proceed to fulfil this command, and search out the kingdom of God. But before we proceed, I would again caution the reader not to proceed with me in this research, unless he is prepared to sacrifice every thing, even to his good name, and his life itself, if necessary, as a sacrifice for the truth; for if he should once get a view of the kingdom of God, he will be so delighted as never to rest satisfied short of becoming a citizen of the same. And yet it will be so unlike every other system of religion now on earth, that he will be astonished that any person with the Bible in his hand, should ever have mistaken any of the systems of men, for the kingdom of God. Now there are certain powers, privileges, and blessings, pertaining to the kingdom of God, which are found in no other kingdom, nor enjoyed by any other people. And by these things it was ever distinguished from all other kingdoms and systems, insomuch that the inquiring mind, who is seeking the kingdom of God, being once acquainted with these peculiarities concerning it, need never mistake or be at a loss to know when he has found it. But before we proceed any farther in our research, let us agree upon the meaning of the term, or the sense in which we will use it; for some apply this term to the kingdom of Glory above, and some to the individual enjoyments of their own souls, while others apply it to his organized government on the earth. Now, when we speak of the kingdom of God, we wish it to be understood as speaking of his organized government on the earth.

Now reader, we launch forth into the wide field before us, in search of a kingdom. But stop, let us consider what is a kingdom? I reply that four things are required in order to constitute any kingdom, in Heaven or on earth: Namely, first, a king; second, commissioned officers duly qualified to execute his ordinances and laws; thirdly, a code of laws, by which the citizens are governed; and fourthly, subjects who are governed. Now, where these exist in their proper order and regular authority, there is a kingdom, but where either of these cease to exist, there is a disorganization of the kingdom; consequently an end of it, until re-organized after the same manner as before. Now in this respect, the king-dom of God is like all other kingdoms: wherever we find officers duly commissioned and qualified by the Lord Jesus, together with his ordi-nances and laws existing in purity, unmixed with any precepts or com-mandments of men; there the kingdom of God exists, and there his power is manifest, and his blessings enjoyed as in days of old.

We shall now take a view of the commencement of the setting up of the kingdom of God in the days of the Apostles. The first intimation of its near approach was by an angel to Zachariah, promising him a Son, who should go before the king to prepare his way. The next man-ifestation was to Mary, and finally to Joseph, by an holy angel, promis-ing the birth of the Messiah; while at the same time the Holy Ghost manifested unto Simeon in the temple, that he should not die until he had seen the Saviour. Thus, all these, together with the shepherds and the wise men from the east, began to rejoice with a joy unspeakable and full of glory, while the world around them knew not the occasion of their joy. After these things, all seemed to rest in silent expectation, un-til John had grown to manhood, when he came bounding from the wil-derness of Judea with a proclamation strange and new; crying, repent ye, for the kingdom of heaven is at hand, baptizing unto repentance, telling them plainly that their king was already standing among them on the point of setting up his kingdom. And while he yet ministered, the Messiah came, and was baptized and sealed with the Spirit of God, which rested upon him in the form of a dove; and soon after, he began the same proclamation as John, saying, "Repent ye, for the kingdom of heaven is at hand." And soon, after choosing twelve disciples, he sent them forth into all the cities of Judea, with the same proclamation—the kingdom of heaven is at hand; and after them he sent seventy, and still another seventy, with the same news, so that all might be well warned and prepared for a kingdom, which was soon to be organized among them. But when these things had produced the desired effect, in caus-ing a general expectation, more especially in the hearts of his disciples, who daily expected to triumph over their persecutors, by the corona-tion of this glorious personage, while they themselves were hoping for a reward of all their toil and sacrifices made for his sake, by being ex-alted to dignity near his person—what must have been their disappoint-ment, when they saw their king taken and crucified, being mocked, de-rided, ridiculed, and finally, overcame and triumphed over both by Jew and Gentile? They would gladly have died in battle, to have placed him upon the throne. But tamely to submit without a struggle, to give up all their expectations, and sink in despair, from the highest pitch of enthusiasm to the lowest degradation, was more than they could well endure. They shrunk back in sorrow, and turned every man to his net, or to their several occupations, supposing all was over; probably with reflections like these: is this the result of all our labours? was it for this we forsook all worldly objects, our friends, our houses, and lands, suffering persecution, hunger, fatigue, and disgrace? — and we trusted it should have been he, who would have delivered Israel; but alas, they have killed him, and all is over. For three years we have awakened a general expectation through all Judea, by telling them the kingdom of heaven was at hand, but now our king is dead, how shall we dare to look the people in the face. With these reflections, each pursuing his own course, all was again turned to silence, and the voice had ceased to be heard in Judea, crying, repent ye, for the kingdom of heaven is at hand. Jesus slept in the arms of death; a great stone with the seal of state secured the tomb where he lay, while the Roman guard stood in watchful silence, to see that all was kept secure; when suddenly from the regions of glory, a mighty angel descended, at whose presence the soldiers fell back as dead men, while he rolled the stone from the door of the sepulchre, and the Son of God awoke from his slumbers, burst the bonds of death, and soon after appearing to Mary, he sent her to the disciples, with the joyful news of resurrection, and appointing a place to meet them. When, after seeing him, all their sorrow was turned into joy, and all their former hopes were suddenly revived, they were no longer to cry, the kingdom of heaven is at hand, but were to tarry at Jerusalem, until the kingdom was established, and they prepared to unlock the door of the kingdom, and to adopt strangers and foreigners into it as legal citizens, by administering certain laws and ordinances, which were invariably the laws of adoption; without which no man could ever become a citizen. Having ascended up on high, and having been crowned with all powers in heaven and on earth, he again comes to his disciples and gives them their authority, saying unto them, "Go ye into all the world, and preach the gospel to every creature; he that believeth and is baptized shall be saved, but he that believeth not shall be damned. And these signs shall follow them that believe: in my name shall they cast out devils; they shall speak with new tongues; they shall take up serpents; and if they drink any deadly thing, it shall not hurt them; they shall lay hands on the sick and they shall recover." — Mark xvi., 15, 16, 17, 18. Now, I wish the reader never to pass this commission, until he understands it, because, when once understood, he never need mistake the kingdom of God, but will at once discover those peculiarities, which were forever to distinguish it from all other kingdoms or religious systems on earth: and lest he should misunderstand, we will analyze it, and look at each part carefully in its own proper light: — first, they were to preach the gospel, (or in other

3

words, the glad tidings of a crucified and risen Redeemer) to all the world; second, he that believeth, and is baptized, shall be saved; third, he that did not believe what they preached, should be damned; and fourth, these signs shall follow them that believe — first, they are to cast out devils; second, to speak with new tongues; third, to take up serpents; fourth, if they drink any deadly thing, it shall not hurt them; fifth, they were to lay hands on the sick, and they should recover.

Now, it is wilful blindness, or ignorance of the English language, that has ever caused any misunderstanding here. For some do tell us that those signs were only to follow the apostles; and others tell us that they were only to follow believers in that age. But Christ places the preaching, the believing, the salvation, and the signs that were to follow, all on an equal footing; where one was limited, the other must be; where one ceased, the other died. And if the language limits these signs to the apostles, it limits faith and salvation also to them. And if no others were to have these signs follow them, then no others were to believe, and no others were to be saved: again, if the language limits these signs to the first age or ages of Christianity; then it limits salvation to the first ages of Christianity; for one is precisely as much limited as the other; and where one is in force, the other is — and where one ends, the other must stop. And as well might we say preaching the gospel is no longer needed; faith is no longer needed; salvation is no longer needed; they were only given at first to establish the gospel: as to say these signs are no longer necessary, they were only given to establish the gospel. But says the astonished reader, have not these signs ceased from among men? I reply, prove that they have ceased, and it will prove that the gospel has ceased to be preached, and that men have ceased to believe and be saved, and the world without the kingdom of God; or else it will prove that Jesus Christ was an impostor, and his promises of no effect.

Now, having analyzed and understood this commission, let us pursue the subject of the organization of the kingdom of God, in the days of the apostles. The Saviour having given them their authority, commands them to tarry, and not undertake their mission, until they were endowed with power from on high. But why this delay? because no man was ever qualified, or ever will be, to preach that gospel, and teach all things whatsoever Jesus commanded them, without the Holy Ghost; and a very different Holy Ghost too, from the one now enjoyed by men who are not inspired: for the Holy Ghost of which Jesus spake, would guide into all truth, bring all things to remembrance, whatsoever he had said unto them, and show them things to come — not to mention that it would enable them to speak in all the languages of the earth — Now a man who preaches needs that Holy Ghost very much; first, to guide into all truth, that he may know what to teach; second, to

4

strengthen his memory, lest he might neglect to teach some of the things which was so commanded them; and third, he needs to know things to come, and that would constitute him a prophet, that he might forewarn his hearers of approaching danger. From this, the reader may see how careful Jesus was, that none should preach his gospel without the Holy Ghost. And he may also learn how different the Spirit of Truth is, from the spirits now abroad in the earth, deceiving the world, under the name of the Holy Ghost. If the churches of the present day have the Holy Ghost, why are they so much at a loss to understand truth? why do they walk in so many different ways and doctrines? And I inquire, why do they need whole libraries of sermons, tracts, divinities, debates, arguments and opinions, all written by the wisdom of men, without even professing to be inspired? Well doth the Lord complain, saying, "their fear towards me is taught by the precepts of men." But to return — the apostles tarried at Jerusalem, until endowed with the power, and then they commenced to proclaim the gospel.

Here we have discovered several things towards a kingdom; 1st. we have found a king, crowned at the right hand of God; to whom is committed all power in heaven and on earth; 2nd. we have found officers commissioned, and duly qualified to administer the laws and ordinances of that Kingdom; 3rd. the laws by which they were to be governed, were, all things whatsoever Jesus had commanded his disciples to teach them.

And now if we can find how men became citizens of that kingdom, I mean as to the rules of adoption, then we have found the kingdom of God in that age, and shall be very much dissatisfied with every thing in our own age, professing to be the kingdom of God, which is not according to the pattern.

It happened that there were no natural born subjects of that kingdom; for both Jew and Gentile were included in sin and unbelief; and none could be citizens without the law of adoption, and all that believed on the name of the king, had power to be adopted; but there was but one invariable rule or plan by which they were adopted; and all that undertook to claim citizenship in any other way whatever, were counted thieves and robbers, and could never obtain the seal of adoption. This rule was laid down in the Saviour's teaching to Nicodemus, namely, "Except a man be born of water (that is, baptized in water) and of the Spirit, (that is, baptized with the Spirit,) he cannot enter into the kingdom of God."

Now to Peter were given the keys of the kingdom; therefore it was his duty to open the kingdom to Jew, and also to Gentile. We will therefore carefully examine the manner in which he did adopt the Jews into the kingdom, at the day of Pentecost.

Now, when the multitude came running together on the day of Pentecost, the apostle Peter standing up with the eleven, lifted his voice and reasoned with them from the Scriptures, testifying of Jesus Christ, and his resurrection and ascension up on high—insomuch that many became convinced of the truth, and inquired what they should do. Now understand, these were not Christians; but they were people who were that moment convinced that Jesus was the Christ, and because they were convinced of this fact, they inquired, what shall we do? Then Peter said unto them, "repent and be baptized, every one of you, in the name of Jesus Christ, for the remission of sins, and you shall receive the gift of the Holy Ghost; for the promise is unto you and to your children, and to all that are afar off, even as many as the Lord our God shall call." But, kind reader, do you understand this proclamation? if you do, you will see that this gospel is not preached by any of the priests of this day. Let us therefore analyze and examine it, sentence by sentence. You recollect they already believed, and the next thing was for them to repent: first, faith, second, repentance, third, baptism, fourth, remission of sins, fifth, the Holy Ghost, was the order of the gospel. Faith gave the power to become sons or citizens; repentance and baptism in his name, was the obedience through which they were adopted; and the Holy Spirit of promise was the seal of their adoption, and this they were sure to receive if they would obey. Now, reader, where do you hear such preaching in our day? Who teaches that those who believe and repent, should be baptized, and none others? Perhaps the reader may say the baptists do; but do they call upon men to be baptized as soon as they believe and repent? Be assured, kind reader, they do not: and moreover, do they promise them the remission of sins, with the gift of the Holy Ghost? Recollect now, what effect the Holy Ghost has upon people who receive it. It will guide them into all truth, strengthen the memory, and show them things to come. And Joel said, it would cause them to dream dreams, to see visions, and prophesy. O! my reader, where do you find a gospel like this preached among men? Would men go mourning for weeks upon weeks, without the forgiveness of sins, or the comfort of the Holy Spirit, if Peter stood among us, to tell precisely how to get such blessings? Now what would you think of a camp-meeting, where three thousand men should come forward to be prayed for? and one of the ministers should (Peter-like,) command them every one to repent and be baptized for the remission of sins, promising that all who obeyed, should receive the remission of sins, and the gift of the Holy Ghost, which should cause them to dream dreams and prophesy; and then should arise with his brethren of the same calling, and the same hour commence baptizing, and continue until they had baptized them all; and the Holy Ghost should fall upon them, and they begin to see visions, speak in other tongues, and prophesy. Would not the news go abroad far and wide, that a new doctrine had made its appearance, quite different from any thing now practised among men? O yes, says the reader, this to be sure would be something new, and very strange to all of us. Well, strange as it may seem, it is the gospel, as preached by Peter on the day of Pentecost: and Paul declares that he preached the same gospel that Peter did; and he has also said, "though we, or an angel from Heaven, preach any other gospel, let him be accursed." Now, the reader need no longer be astonished to see that these signs do not follow them that believe some other gospel or doctrine, different from that preached by the apostles.

But now let us return to the kingdom of God organized in the days of the apostles; you discover that three thousand persons were adopted into the kingdom the first day the door was opened. These, together with the numerous additions which were afterwards made, were the subjects of this kingdom; which being fitly framed together, grew unto a holy temple in the Lord. Thus we have cleared away the rubbish of sectarian tradition and superstition, which arose in heaps around us; and having searched carefully, we have at length discovered the kingdom of God, as it existed at its first organization, in the days of the apostles; and we have seen that it differs widely from all modern systems of religion, both in its officers, ordinances, powers, and privileges, insomuch, that no man need ever mistake the one for the other.

Having made this discovery, we shall proceed to examine the progress of that kingdom, among Jew and Gentile; and what were its fruits, and what were its gifts, and blessings enjoyed by its citizens — soon after the organization of the kingdom of God at Jerusalem? — Philip came to Samaria, and there preached the gospel; and when they believed Philip, they were baptized both men and women, and had great joy. And afterwards Peter and John came from Jerusalem, and prayed, and laid their hands on them, and they received the Holy Ghost. Mark here, they first believed, and then were baptized, having great joy, and yet had not received the Holy Ghost. But that was given afterwards, by the laying on of hands and prayer, in the name of Jesus. Oh, how different from the systems of men! Witness Paul's conversion while on his journey to Damascus; the Lord Jesus appeared to him in the way; but instead of telling him, his sins were forgiven, and pouring the Holy Ghost upon him, he sent him to Damascus, telling him that it should there be told him what he should do. And coming to Damascus, Ananias being sent, commanded him not to tarry, but said unto him, "arise and be baptized, and wash away thy sins, calling on the name of the Lord:" then he arose, and was baptized, and was even filled with the Holy Ghost — and straightway preached that Jesus was the Christ.

Again, witness Peter going to Cornelius, a gentile of great piety, whose prayers were heard, whose alms were remembered, and who had even attained to the ministering of an angel; yet with all his piety, and the Holy Ghost poured out upon him, and his friends, before they were baptized, yet they must be baptized, or they could not be saved. Why? because the Lord had commanded the apostles to preach to every creature, and every creature who would not believe, and be baptized, should be damned, without one exception. Witness the words of the angel to Cornelius. "He, (Peter) shall tell you words, whereby thou and all thy house shall be saved." Now, query, could Cornelius have been saved without obeying the words of Peter? if so, the angel's errand was in vain. Recollect, Peter commanded them to be baptized. Now methinks that a minister who should find a man as good as Cornelius was, would say to him, go on brother, you can be saved, you have experienced religion, you may indeed be baptized to answer a good conscience, if you feel it your duty, or if not it is no matter, a new heart is all that is really necessary to salvation, &c. As much as to say, that the commandments of Jesus are not absolutely necessary to salvation; a man may call him Lord, Lord, and be saved, just as well as to keep his commandments. O vain and foolish doctrine; O ye children of men, how have you perverted the Gospel; in vain do ye call him Lord, Lord, and do not obey his commandments.

Next, we call to mind the Jailor, and his household, who were baptized the same hour they believed, without waiting for the day. And Lydia and her household, who attended to the ordinance, the first sermon they heard on the subject.

Also, Philip and the Eunuch, who stopped the chariot, at the first water they came to, in order to attend to the ordinance, while a few minutes before was the first he had heard of Jesus. Now, I gather from all those examples of ancient days, and from the precepts laid down in them, that baptism was the initiating ordinance, by which all those who believed and repented were received and adopted into the church or kingdom of God, so as to be entitled to the remission of sins, and the blessings of the Holy Ghost; indeed it was the ordinance through which they became sons and daughters; and because they were sons, the Lord shed forth the Spirit of his Son into their hearts, crying Abba, Father. It is true, the Lord poured out the Holy Ghost upon Cornelius and his friends, before they were baptized; but it seemed necessary in order to convince the believing Jews, that the Gentiles also had part in this salvation. And I believe, this is the only instance in the whole record, of the people receiving the Holy Ghost, without first obeying the laws of adoption. But, mark! Obeying the laws of adoption would not constitute a man, an heir of the kingdom, a citizen entitled to the blessings,

8

and gifts, of the Spirit, unless these laws, and ordinances, were administered, by one who had proper authority, and was duly commissioned from the King; and a commission given to one individual, could never authorize another, to act in his stead. This is one of the most important points to be understood, as it brings to the test every minister in Christendom; and questions the organization of every church on earth, and all that have existed since direct inspiration ceased. Now, in order to come at this subject in plainness; let us examine the constitution of earthly governments, in regard to the authority and laws of adoption. We will say, for instance, the President of the United States writes a commission to A. B.; duly authorizing him, to act in some office in the government, and during his administration; two gentlemen from Europe, came to reside in this country, and being strangers, and foreigners, wishing to become citizens, they go before A. B., and he administers the oath of allegiance in due form, and certifies the same, and this constitutes them legal citizens, entitled to all the privileges of those of natural-born citizens, or subjects.

After these things, A. B. is taken away by death, and C. D. in looking over his papers, happens to find the commission given to A. B., and applying it to his own use, assumes the vacant office; mean time, two foreigners arrive and apply for citizenship, and being informed by persons ignorant of the affairs of government, that C. D. could administer the laws of adoption, they submit to be administered unto by C. D., without once examining his authority; C. D. certifies of their citizenship, and they suppose they have been legally adopted, the same as the others, and are entitled to all the privileges of citizenship. But by and by, their citizenship is called in question, and they produce the certificate of C. D.; the President inquires who is C. D., I never gave him a commission to act in any office, I know him not, and you are strangers and foreigners to the commonwealth, until you go before the legally appointed successor of A. B., or some other of like authority, who has a commission from the President, direct in his own name. In the mean time, C. D. is taken and punished according to law, for practising imposition, and usurping authority, which was never conferred upon him. And so it is with the kingdom of God.

The Lord authorized the apostles and others by direct Revelation, and by the spirit of Prophecy; to preach and baptize, and build up his church and kingdom; but after a while they died, and a long time passed away, and men reading over their commission, where it says to the eleven apostles; "Go ye into all the world and preach the Gospel to every creature, &c." — they have had the presumption to apply these sayings as their authority, and without any other commission, have gone forth professing to preach the Gospel, and baptize, and build up the church and kingdom of God; but those whom they baptize never receive the same blessings, and gifts, which characterized a saint or citizen of the kingdom, in the days of the apostles. Why? Because they are yet foreigners and strangers, for the commission given to the apostles, never commissioned any other man to act in their stead. This was a prerogative the Lord reserved unto himself. No man has a right to take this ministry upon himself, but him that is called by Revelation, and duly qualified to act in his calling, by the Holy Ghost. But the reader inquires with astonishment — what! is none of all the ministers of the present day called to the ministry, and legally commissioned? Well, my reader, I will tell you how you may ascertain from their own mouths, and that will be far better than for me to answer; go to the clergy and ask them if God has given any direct Revelation, since the New Testament was finished; inquire of them whether the gift of prophesy ceased with the early age of the church; and in short ask them if revelations prophets the ministering of angels, &c.; are needed or expected in these days, or whether they believe that these things are done away, no more to return to the earth; and their answer will be, the Bible contains sufficient, and since the Canon of Scripture was full, Revelation has ceased, the Spirit of Prophecy has ceased, and the ministering of angels have ceased, because, no longer needed; and in short they will denounce every man as an impostor who pretends to any such thing and when you have obtained this answer, ask them, how they themselves were called and commissioned to preach the gospel, and they will be at a loss to answer you, and will finally tell you the Bible commissioned them; saying, go ye into all the world, &c. Thus you see, all who have no direct revelation from the King of Heaven to themselves, neither by angels, nor by the voice of God, nor by the Spirit of Prophesy: are acting under authority which was given to others, who are dead, and their commission stolen, and their authority usurped; and the king will say, Peter I know, and Paul I know, I commissioned them, but who are you? I know you not, I never spoke to you in my life, indeed you believed it was not necessary for me to speak in your day. Therefore you never sought in faith for any Revelation, and I never gave you any, and even when I spoke to others you mocked them, and called them impostors, and persecuted them, because they testified of the things I had said unto them; "Therefore depart from me ye cursed, into everlasting fire, prepared for the Devil and his angels, for I was an hungered, and ye fed me not, I was naked, and ye clothed me not, I was a stranger, and ye took me not in, sick and in prison, and ye visited me not." Ah! Lord, when did we fail in any of these things? Inasmuch as you have not done it unto the least of these, my brethren (taking them for impostors, because they testified of the things which I had revealed unto them,) ye have not done it unto me.

But to return; having examined the kingdom of God, as to its offices, authorities, laws and ordinances, and having discovered the only means of being adopted into it, let us examine more fully, what are the blessings, privileges, and enjoyments of its citizens. You have already seen, that they were to cast out devils, speak with new tongues, heal the sick by the laying on of hands in the name of Jesus, as well as to see visions, dream dreams, prophesy, &c.

But let us look at the kingdom in its organized state, and see whether these promises were verified to Jew and Gentile, wherever the kingdom of God was found in all ages of the world.

Paul, writing, first, to the church of God at Corinth; second, To them that are sanctified in Christ Jesus; third, To them who are called to be saints; and fourth, To all that in every place call on the name of Jesus Christ our Lord both theirs and ours. — He says to them all, in 1 Cor. xii. 1.; "Now, concerning spiritual *gifts*, brethren, I would not have you ignorant." And then continuing his instructions a few verses farther on, he says, "But the manifestation of the Spirit is given to every man to profit withal. For to one is given by the Spirit the word of wisdom; to another, the word of knowledge by the same Spirit; to another, faith by the same Spirit; to another, the gifts of healing by the same Spirit; to another, the working of miracles; to another, prophecy; to another, discerning of spirits; to another, divers kinds of tongues; to another, the interpretation of tongues: but all these worketh that one and the self-same Spirit, dividing to every man severally as he (Christ) will. For as the body is one, and hath many members, and all the members of that one body, being many, are one body; so also is Christ. For by one Spirit are we all baptized into one body, whether we be Jews or Gentiles, whether we be bond or free; and have been all made to drink into one Spirit. For the body is not one member, but many. If the foot shall say, because I am not the hand, I am not of the body; is it therefore not of the body? And if the ear shall say, because I am not the eye, I am not of the body; is it therefore not of the body? If the whole body were an eye, where were the hearing? If the whole were hearing, where were the smelling? But now hath God set the members every one of them in the body, as it hath pleased him. And if they were all one member where were the body?" I reply it would not exist. "But now are they many members, yet but one body. And the eye cannot say unto the hand, I have no need of thee: nor again, the head to the feet, I have no need of you. Nay, much more those members of the body, which seem to be more feeble, are necessary: and those members of the body, which we think to be less honourable, upon these we bestow more abundant honour; and our uncomely parts have more abundant comeliness. For our comely parts have no need: but God hath tempered the body together, having given more abundant honour to that part which lacked: that there should be no schism in the body; but that the members should have the same care one for another. And whether one member suffer, all the members suffer with it; or one member be honoured, all the members rejoice with it. Now ye are the body of Christ, and members in particular. And God hath set some in the church, first apostles; secondarily prophets; thirdly teachers, after that miracles, then gifts of healings, helps, governments, diversities of tongues. Are all apostles? are all prophets? are all teachers? are all workers of miracles? Have all the gifts of healing? do all speak with tongues? do all interpret? But covet earnestly the best gifts. And yet shew I unto you a more excellent way." From the 13th verse of the above chapter, we learn that the Apostle is still speaking to the whole church in all ages, whether Jew or Gentile, bond or free, even all who should ever compose the body of Christ, and showing that Christ's body consisted of many members, baptized by one Spirit into one body, possessing all these different gifts, some one gift, and some another; and then expressly says, that one member possessing one gift, should not say to another member possessing another gift, we have no need of thee.

And having shown that it required apostles, prophets, evangelists, pastors, and teachers; together with the gifts of Prophesy, miracles, healing, and all other gifts, to compose the church, or body of Christ, in any age, whether Jew or Gentile, bond or free; and having utterly forbidden any of the members ever to say, of any of these gifts; we have no need of thee; he declares the body never could be a perfect body, without all of them, and that if they were done away, there would be no body, that is, no church of Christ in existence. Having shown all these things clearly, he exhorts them to covet earnestly the best gifts. And in the 13th chapter exhorts them to faith, hope, and charity, without which all these gifts would avail them nothing; and in the 14th chapter repeats the exhortation, "Follow after charity, and desire spiritual gifts, but rather that ye may Prophesy." Again, in the Ephesians, i. 17, Paul prays, that the Lord would give unto the church the Spirit of wisdom and of revelation, in the knowledge of God. Again, Ephesians iv. He tells, them, there is one body and one Lord, one Spirit, one Faith, and one Baptism; and that Christ ascended up on high, led captivity captive, and gave gifts to men. And he gave some Apostles, and some Prophets, and some Evangelists, and some Pastors, and Teachers. And if the reader inquire what their gift or offices were for, let him read the 12th verse; "For the perfecting of the saints, for the work of the ministry, for the edifying of the body of Christ." And if we inquire how long these were to continue, the 13th verse says, "Till we all come in the unity of the faith, and of the knowledge of the Son of God, unto a perfect man, unto the measure of the stature of the fullness of Christ." And if he still inquires what further object Christ had in giving these gifts? let him read the 14th verse, "That we henceforth be no more children, tossed to and fro, and carried about with every wind of doctrine, by the sleight of men, and cunning craftiness, whereby they lie in wait to deceive."

Now, without these gifts and offices, first, the saints cannot be perfected; second, the work of the ministry cannot proceed; third, the body of Christ cannot be edified; and fourth, there is nothing to prevent them from being carried about with every wind of doctrine. Now, I boldly declare that the cause of all the division, confusion, jars, discords, and animosities; and the reason of so many faiths, lords, baptisms, and spirits; yea, the reason the understanding being darkened; and of men being alienated from the life of God, through the ignorance that is in them, because of the blindness of their hearts; is all because they have no Apostles, and Prophets, and other gifts, inspired from on high, to whom they give heed; for if they had such gifts and would give heed unto them, they would be built up in one body, in the pure doctrine of Christ, having one Lord, one Faith, and one Baptism, one hope of their calling; yea, they would be edified, perfected, built up unto Christ in all things, in whom the whole body fitly joined together, would grow into an holy temple in the Lord.

But so long as the cunning craftiness of men can persuade them that they have no need of these things, so long they can toss them about, with every wind of doctrine, just as they please.

Now reader, I have done our examination of the kingdom of God, as it existed in the apostles days; and we cannot look at it in any other age, for it never did, nor ever will exist, without Apostles and Prophets, and all the other gifts of the Spirit.

Were we to take a view of the churches, from the days that Inspiration ceased, until now, we should see nothing like the kingdom which we have been viewing with such admiration and delight. But instead of apostles and prophets, we should see false teachers whom men had heaped to themselves, and instead of the gifts of the Spirit, we should see the wisdom of men; and instead of the Holy Ghost, many false spirits; instead of the ordinances of God, commandments of man; instead of knowledge, opinion; guess work, instead of Revelation; division, instead of union; doubt, instead of faith; despair, instead of hope; hatred, instead of charity; a physician, instead of the laying on of hands for the healing of the sick; fables, instead of truth; evil for good, good for evil; darkness for light, light for darkness; and in a word, anti christ instead of Christ; the powers of earth, having made war with the saints and overcome them, until the words of God should be fulfilled. O my God, shut up the vision, for my heart sickens while I gaze; and let the day hasten on when the earth shall be cleansed by fire, from such awful pollutions; but, first, let thy promise be fulfilled, which thou didst make by the mouth of thy servant John; that thou wouldst call thy people out of her; saying, come out of her my people, lest ye partake of her sins, and receive of her plagues; and then, O Lord, when thou hast called thy people out from the midst of her, by the fishers and hunters, which thou hast promised to send in the last days, just in time to gather Israel; yea, when thine everlasting covenant has been renewed and thy people established thereon; then let her plagues come in one day, death, mourning, and famine, and let her be burned with fire; that thy holy apostles and prophets, and all that fear thy name, small and great, may rejoice, because thou hast avenged the blood of thy saints upon her. I ask these things in the name of Jesus Christ. Amen.

Mormonism Unveiled: Zion's Watchman Unmasked, and Its Editor, Mr. L. R. Sunderland, Exposed; Truth Vindicated; The Devil Mad, and Priestcraft in Danger!

(New York: Printed for the Publisher, 1838)

"And all liars, shall have their part in the lake which burneth with fire and brimstone; which is the second death." — Rev. xxi:8.

"And there shall in no wise enter into it any thing that defileth, neither whatsoever worketh abomination, or maketh a lie." — Rev. xxi:27.

"For without are dogs, and sorcerers, and whoremongers, and murderers, and idolaters, and whosoever loveth and maketh a lie." — Rev. xxii:15.

When the public are overwhelmed with lying slanders of every description concerning the Church of the Latter Day Saints. The inquiry often arises, why do the Elders of the Church hold their peace, instead of contradicting the various falsehoods, which are published concerning them and their principles? The answer is, it would require a standing army of writers, and printers in constant employ; for no sooner are our enemies detected in one falsehood, than a thousand more are put in circulation by them: and there are many who love a lie so much more than the truth, that we are quite willing they would enjoy their strong delusion; because, they believe not the truth, but have pleasure in unrighteousness; and we know, that those who are seeking for truth, will judge for themselves, by an examination of our books, and not allow our opposers to judge for them. What ideas would be formed of the Bible, by one who had never read the book himself; but who trusted altogether to the statements of Thomas Paine, and other Infidel writers concerning it? We propose in this work, to prove to every candid mind, that whether our principles be true or false, Mr. Sunderland is guilty of the most glaring falsehoods, misrepresentations, and lying slanders, that ever disgraced humanity; and that he has palmed upon his deluded readers, such wilful and barefaced imposition, that he is justly ranked among dogs, sorcerers, whoremongers, murderers, and idolaters; and no longer fit to fill any place in civilized society; much less to stand at the head of a paper, under the sacred title of "Zion's Watchman." If his readers do not dismiss his paper immediately, after coming to a knowledge of his wickedness, they will be set down as partakers of his evil deeds; and if they hold him any longer in fellowship either as a christian or a member of society, the proverb will be fulfilled upon them, "that a man is known by the company he keeps."

We will now proceed to an examination of "Mormonism," as published by him in the "Zion's Watchman."

First he enquires, "What is Mormonism?" then proposes to answer, by an appeal to the books, which they have published concerning themselves. First, the Book of Mormon, published 1836, printed by Grandin. Now, Mr. S., the book to which you refer, was published, and dated 1830; making a difference of six years. You say, first, "All Mormons profess to act under the infallable inspiration of God; and to have power to work miracles, such as the interpretation of languages they have never learned; healing the sick, and raising the dead." And you attempt to prove it by a quotation from the "Voice of Warning," by P. P. Pratt, pages 118 and 119. Now Mr. Sunderland, you verily know, that raising the dead, is not mentioned in the "Voice of Warning," in connection with the spiritual gifts, bestowed upon the members of the Church, Ancient or Modern. And that, raising the dead, is not included in the spiritual gifts, mentioned by the Apostle, in his writings to any of the Churches; neither is raising the dead included in the signs, which the Saviour promised should follow them that believe, Mark, c. 16: v. 17, 18; consequently, we must think, you intended to misrepresent, and that you are possessed of a lying spirit. It is true, there are a few instances of raising the dead, mentioned in Scripture, but nowhere included among the spiritual gifts enjoyed by the members of the Church; and you know too that the "Voice of Warning" does not argue, that every member should possess all the gifts, but that the Church should have all the gifts distributed among them, dividing to them severally as Christ will, and that God is the author of that principle, and not Mr. Pratt.

2d. Says Mr. Sunderland, "they profess to have intercourse with the angels of God, and affirm that they frequently see them, and have messages from God thro' them." Very good, Mr. S. this is what the Saints professed in all ages of the world, in every country, among every nation, and under every dispensation of God to man, whether Patriarchal, Mosaic, or Christian; and one who does not believe in such enjoyments, is an infidel, and not a believer of revelation in any shape.

3d. Mr. S. says, "They claim to be the only true Church, all other churches are of Anti-Christ, and exposed to God's eternal displeasure." Pray, Mr. Sunderland, how many churches, or doctrines, and religious systems, has the spirit of truth instituted among men? How many systems did the Apostles acknowledge among men? I reply one, and only one, and that one, was a system of direct Inspiration, which put men in possession of the gifts, and power of God.

All others were false religions. How many systems do the Latter Day Saints acknowledge to be true? I answer, only one, and that one is a system, which puts men in possession of the gifts, and power of God; and of course, God is not well pleased with any other.

Mr. S. further quotes, "The only true and living Church upon the face of the whole earth," "with which I, the Lord, am well pleased; speaking unto the Church collectively, and not individually." Doctrine and Covenants, Sec. I. Now, Mr. S. why did you stop so short with the word *earth*, in this quotation? Why not finish the sentence, so the idea might be conveyed, which the author intended? Does it not amount to a falsehood, for you to quote half an idea, so as to leave a wrong impression on the mind of your readers, and thus delude them? Again, "they say," says Mr. S. "that God has sent down from Heaven, a city, called the New Jerusalem, and located it in the Western boundaries of Missouri, where he requires all his true followers to go, under pain of his wrath." As proof of this, Mr. S. quotes, Voice of Warning, page 197, which reads thus, "America is a chosen land of the Lord above every other land; it is the place of New Jerusalem, which shall come down from God out of Heaven, upon the earth," "*when renewed.*" Now, Mr. S. why did you omit the words, *when renewed*, in your quotation of this page? And why did you lie again, by converting the word *shall* into *has*, in the conclusion you draw from the quotation on this subject? The one expresses something future, which will happen upon the new earth, when time is no longer. The other conveys an idea of a city, which has already descended, which is perfectly ridiculous; and none but the most abandoned and hardened of liars, could possibly have so misrepresented another's statement. And again, says Mr. S. "where he requires all his true followers to go, under pain of his wrath." What wrath, Mr. S.? I know of no requirement, in any of our books, which compels men to go there or any where else, under pain of any wrath, except the troubles of a temporal nature, which shall befal the Nations. And, if God has provided the great West for a refuge, from such wrath, it is no more than he has done for his saints in former ages. Think of Noah, Lot and many others, who received revelations, directing them to a temporal refuge, from the calamities which befel the wicked: and remember, it must be LIKEWISE in the days of the coming of the Son of man. Indeed, our revelations are backed by the political papers of the Eastern cities. They give the same advice now which the Lord gave seven years ago, namely, that those who are in distress flee to the West, and even advise that those who are unable to go should be assisted in going.

Mr. S. makes three other quotations from our books on the subject, which all go to prove something future, concerning a New Jerusalem, and not at all favoring the lie which he states concerning a city which has come down.

Pray Mr. S. what delusion is there in moving West, and building a city, called "Zion," or "New Jerusalem," with a Temple or Sanctuary in the midst? when it is an event which all the Prophets have predicted. — But, says Mr. S. the cruelty of requiring all to go there. But here you are at war with the 60th chapter of Isaiah, which declares concerning a city of Zion, not only that nations and kings should be gathered unto it; but the nation and kingdom which will not serve THEE, shall perish and be utterly wasted.

But again, Mr. S. why did you break off in the middle of the subject, concerning the sheding of blood! — Thus sir, you are likely to be an instrument, by your lying and deception, to cause our blood to flow, in fulfilment of this revelation. Had you quoted the whole subject, it would have forbidden us to shed blood, and foretold that our enemies would shed ours; which has actually been fulfilled; be the revelation true or false.

"They affirm," says Mr. S. that "their books, preaching, pretended prophecies, and revelations, are Scripture, and of equal authority with the Bible." — This is another falsehood, for we lay no stress of PRE-TENDED prophecies or revelations; but rely on *real ones*. Now, I ask, if the word of the Lord, spoken by the Holy Ghost, is not equal in authority with the Scriptures? Or, what authority has the Scripture more than that? "They pretend," says Mr. S. "to have power to give the Holy Ghost to those on whom they lay their hands for this purpose." What fault can be found with that ordinance, more than with baptism or any other duty? seeing it is according to the New Testament pattern. Which is the best, Mr. S. to do according to the pattern, or to cry, Lord, Lord, while we teach for doctrines, the commandments of men?

Mr. S. finds fault, because all are condemned, who reject the message which God has sent us to preach. — But, I enquire, did God ever send a man to preach the gospel and baptize; and then save those who would not obey it?

Mr. S. remarks, that Mormonism, Mahommedism, the French Prophets, the Shakers, Swedenborg, and others, have a kind of family likeness, and have equal claims to divine origin. But wherein are they alike? Says, Mr. S. they all pretend to receive revelations, prophecies, ministering of angels, &c. Well, Mr. S. you may include all the Prophets and apostles, both true and false, which ever made their appearance among men, and all that ever will come, in this family likeness. Paul and Peter are just like the rest in this respect. All, both true and false, have these peculiar characteristics, namely, they pretend to prophecies, visions, revelations, &c.; therefore, your rule of judging is this — beware of false prophets; you shall know them by their fruits; all who have visions, prophecies, revelations, angels, &c. are false; and I would add, all who do not have any of them are false of course. And so, between us both, nothing would be left but atheism. But I like the old rule best, I mean the rule given by John: "whosoever transgresseth, and abideth not in the doctrine of Christ, hath not God," "He that abideth in the doctrine of Christ, hath both the Father and the Son." Now, by this rule, I reject Mahomet, first, because he had no testimony but his own; and secondly, because his doctrines agree not with the Law and the Testimony. I reject the French Prophets, for the same reason, as to doctrine; and because their predictions were unscriptural, and did not come to pass.

I reject Ann Lee, first, because God never sent a dispensation by a woman. Second, she forbid to marry. Third, she pretended Christ had come the second time according to promise, in her person. Fourth, she denied the resurrection of the body. Fifth, she laid aside all the ordinances of the gospel.

I reject Swedenborg, because he mistifies the Scriptures, and does away the ordinances of the gospel; and lastly, I reject Methodism, and other systems, because they do away the power and gifts of God, and change the ordinances of the gospel.

But when I come to Mormonism, it sets in order in their ancient purity, all the ordinances, gifts and powers, and thus restores the pure doctrine of Christ. — This, Mr. S. proves in his various quotations, and references to our doctrine, ordinances, &c. notwithstanding his endeavors to throw a shadow of darkness over them.

Mr. Sunderland speaks of the power of imagination over the nervous system, in regard to the healing of diseases; and as many in the city of New-York and other places, have been healed by faith in the name of Jesus, and the laying on of hands; I am pleased that imagination has such power. For my part, if I can persuade people to imagine themselves well, it answers every purpose necessary to their bodily comfort, and this power of imagination has been many times manifested in this city of late; even in the persons of infants of from three to eight months old. But probably, Mr. S. would call them impostors, who were so interested in Mormonism, that they only pretended to be healed, in order to palm off a deception.

Mr. S complains of the Mormonites professing to be inspired, and placing themselves on a level with the Apostles; this, we acknowledge of course, for they were men of Adam's fallen race, just like every body else by nature; and all they did was by faith in Jesus Christ through the grace of God given; and I know of nothing but equality in the Church of Christ, for one is their Master, and they are all brethren.

Mr. Sunderland seems to hold forth two kinds of inspiration; the one he calls Plenary Inspiration. The other is that by which sinners are converted, the heart changed, &c. This last he seems to think is liable to mistakes or errors, and is not above the light of nature. As to Plenary Inspiration, I know of no such term in the Scriptures: and as to the other kind, it is no where to be found in the Scripture or any where else, except in the imagination of modern sectarians. — What! Mr. Sunderland, has it come to this at last that you hold forth a kind of inspiration that gives no certainty, no knowledge, no light above that of nature? Pray, what benefit would such inspiration be to any person? The inspiration of the Holy Ghost reveals to those who enjoy it, the knowledge of the truth. — And the Bible knows no other. And this inspiration is for all the Saints. And indeed no man can even be a Saint without it. However, we will suggest a couple of terms which will distinguish Mr. Sunderland's two kinds of inspiration more clearly. I would say, inspiration of the spirit of truth, and inspiration of the spirit of error, that the one guides into all truth, and the other into all the divisions of modern sectarians.

"Miracles," says Mr. Sunderland, "are for the proof or evidence of some particular doctrine, or in attestation of the Divine Mission, of some particular person." Now, hear what the Apostle says on this subject, first, Cor. c. 12, and Eph. c. 4, and other places. He says "gifts were for the work of the ministry; for the perfecting of the saints; for the edifying of the body of Christ." Now, if we believe Paul instead of Mr. Sunderland, we must believe that gifts and miracles are for a different purpose, from what he would represent, and that they were to continue as long as the gospel ministry itself; and as long as there were Saints, who were to be perfected or edified. But if they were given only to establish some particular doctrine or mission; then the Scripture concerning Jesus should read thus: Jesus did more mighty miracles in his native place, than any where else, because of their unbelief. Again, a certain text should read, God hath given them ears, but they hear not; eyes but they see not; hearts that understand not, that they might be converted, and healed, because of unbelief. And again, faith comes by miracles. And again, without faith it is possible to please God so as to be healed.

Mr. Sunderland complains of scores of miracles recorded in the Book of Mormon, as performed on the most trifling occasions; but can give but one instance of the kind, namely, the Lord showing his finger to the brother of Jared; "and it was *as* the finger of a man like unto flesh and blood." But, Mr. Sunderland was careful to omit the word AS, in order to make a false and ridiculous statement appear in the Book of Mormon, where there is none. For of course, the Lord's finger appears AS the finger of a man appears; or man could not be created after His image and likeness. — Mr. Sunderland, just remember the fingers of God that the impious Belshazzar saw writing on the wall.

Mr. Sunderland intimates that the Bible records no instances of mir-

acles being performed, or revelations given, except on great and important occasions. Now, in the first place, we challenge Mr. Sunderland, or
any other man, to produce instances where miracles are introduced in
the Book of Mormon on any occasion, except for great and important
ends; ends worthy the exertion of the power of God. We challenge any
man to produce a single instance in that book of an angel's visit without
an errand worthy their attention. And, secondly, we will proceed to
notice, a few of the great and important objects, which called forth angels, revelations and miracles, in the Bible. Exo. c. 33, v. 22 and 28. "And
it shall come to pass, while my glory passeth by, that I will put thee in
the cleft of the rock; and will cover thee with my hand, while I pass by:
and I will take away my hand, and thou shalt see my back parts; but my
face shall not be seen." Now, Mr. Sunderland, what would you say to
this, if it were in the Book of Mormon, that the Lord put Jared in the
cleft of the rock, and placed his hand over it to keep Jared from seeing
his face, but after he had gone past, he took his hand off, and suffered
Jared to see his back parts? See also, Deut. c. 23, v. 1 and 13, concerning
who was to come into the congregation of the Lord, and concerning the
paddle. Now, Mr. Sunderland, you say there is a vast difference between
the two books in this respect. I wish you to bring a few parallel cases
from the Book of Mormon, for an offset against the above sublime truths.

Also, see Deut. c. 25, v. 9, "then shall his brother's wife come unto
him, in the presence of the elders, and loose his shoe from off his foot;
and spit in his face," &c. Verse 10, "and his name shall be called in
Israel, the house of him that had his shoe loosed." See also, Deut. c. 22,
v. 6 and 7, concerning the bird's nest, — "But thou shalt in anywise let
the dam go, and take the young to thee; that it may be well with thee,
and that thou mayest prolong thy days." I should like to see something
brought forward from the Book of Mormon, that will compare with
the above examples; and with the great occasion of the Lord's turning
water into wine, that they might drink a little more, after they had well
drunk.

Mr. Sunderland says, "Mr. Smith pretended to be three years trans-
lating the book." This is not so. — The plates containing the record, was
obtained Sep. 22, A.D. 1827, and appeared in print in March, 1830, making two years and a half; much of which time, was spent in laboring
with his hands for his support & much was spent in fleeing from place
to place on account of persecution, and of course much was spent in
printing, &c.. Mr. S. further says, "No person ever saw one of their
miracles, but themselves." How do you know that, Mr. Sunderland?
Or, by what authority do you speak? Have you been with all our elders,
in all their travels? I have only to say, your assertion is false; for it is a
noted fact, that there are many in this city, who have been healed, who

did not belong to the church; and these things are done publicly, and this we are prepared to prove by good witnesses, both in the church and out of the church. Mr. Sunderland further says, that "public monuments must be set up, and some outward actions also, must be perpetuated in memory of the miracles thus publicly wrought." Now, I ask, what monuments or ordinances, are standing proof of the thousands of miracles and gifts, wrought by the Apostles and members of the ancient church? O my soul, has it come to this at last, that men cannot go to the true and living God, in the prayer of faith, and learn the truth for themselves? but must depend on certain monuments of antiquity for all the knowledge they have, either of God or religion. May the Lord pity such a graceless and ungodly generation. But I acknowledge, that such abominable liars, as La Roy Sunderland, need something before their eyes to put them in mind of a God, for I am sure there is no place for the witness of the spirit of truth in their hearts.

He further says, "The existence of the Plates, is not vouched for by any disinterested person." But in the name of common sense, I ask who would be a disinterested person? If all christendom should see the plates, and be convinced of the truth of the record, every person would be as interested in the same, as those who first witnessed it. Who ever heard of God's choosing a disinterested witness of his resurrection, or any other truth? Or, would Mr. Sunderland have a witness who would say, the thing is true, but does not concern me, I purpose never to obey it myself; but go down to hell, for the sake of giving others a disinterested testimony of its truth?

Let christians blush at the ignorant and impotent objections of the editor of the Zion's Watchman; for I am satisfied that even infidels never advance objections, so foolish and unreasonable!

Concerning Prophesy, he remarks that "it cannot be proved that one prediction, in that book, which is not taken from the Bible, was written before the event said to be described." Again he says, "there are no predictions, peculiar to this book, yet to be fulfilled, no names of persons or places, or periods of time, are referred to, by which any thing definite can be known, as to what is meant by the jargon of Mormon Prophets." Now, Mr. La Roy Sunderland, we will prove to the world, that this is one of the most barefaced falsehoods, ever uttered by man. The Book of Mormon contains many Prophecies, yet future, with names, places and dates so definite, that a child may understand; indeed it is one of the peculiar characteristics of the Book of Mormon, that its predictions are plain, simple definite, literal, positive, and very express, as to the time of their fulfilment. Notice a prediction of Nephi, page 125, second edition. "For after the book, of which I have spoken, shall come forth, and be written unto the Gentiles, and sealed up again unto the

Lord; there shall be many, which shall believe the words which are written and they shall carry them forth, unto the remnant of our seed, (the Indians,) and then shall the remnant of our seed know concerning us; how that we came out from Jerusalem; and that they are the descendants of the Jews; and the gospel of Jesus Christ, shall be declared among them; wherefore they shall be restored unto the knowledge of their fathers; and also to the knowledge of Jesus Christ, which was had among their fathers; and then shall they rejoice for they shall KNOW, that it is a blessing unto them, from the hand of God. And their scales of darkness shall begin to fall from their eyes; and many generations shall not pass away among them; save they shall be a white, and delightsome people. And it shall come to pass that the Jews which are scattered, also shall begin to believe in Christ; and they shall begin to gather in upon the face of the land; and as many as shall believe in Christ, shall also be a delightsome people; and it shall come to pass, that the Lord God shall commence his work among all nations, kindreds, tongues, and people, to bring about the restoration of his people upon the earth. . . . For the time speedily cometh, that the Lord God shall cause a great division among the people, and the wicked will he destroy, and he will spare his people."

Also, page 121, 2d edition. "Behold that great and abominable Church, the whore of all the earth, must tumble to the earth, and great must be the fall thereof: for the kingdom of the devil, must shake; and they which belong to it must needs be stirred up unto repentance, or the devil will grasp them with his everlasting chains, and they be stirred up to anger, and perish; for behold at that day shall he rage in the hearts of the children of men, and stir them up to anger against that which is good."

Also, page 122, 2d edition. "Woe unto all those who tremble and are angry, because of the truth of God; for behold he that is built upon the rock, receiveth it with gladness: and he that is built upon a sandy foundation, trembleth, lest he shall fall." Also, page 123, 2d edition. "Woe be unto the Gentiles, saith the Lord God of Hosts; for notwithstanding I shall lengthen out my arm unto them from day to day, they will deny me." See also page 514, and read the fate of our nation, and the fate of the Indians of America; in the day that the Gentiles should reject the fullness of the Gospel. — (The Book of Mormon.) See also, page 526, where a sign is given, and the time clearly set for the restoration and gathering of Israel from their long dispersion, namely, the coming forth of the Book of Mormon, should be the sign; and in the day this work should come forth, should this great event commence among all nations. Also, p.527, where all who will not hearken to the Book of Mormon, shall be cut off from among the people; and that too, in the day it comes forth to the Gentiles and is rejected by them. And not only does this page set the time for the overthrow of our government and all other Gentile governments of the American continent, but the way and means of this utter destruction are clearly foretold, namely, the remnant of Jacob will go through among the Gentiles and tear them in pieces, like a lion among the flocks of sheep. Their hand shall be lifted up upon their adversaries, and all their enemies shall be cut off. This destruction includes an utter overthrow, and desolation of all our Cities, Forts, and Strong Holds—an entire annihilation of our race, except such as embrace the Covenant, and are numbered with Israel.

Now, Mr. Sunderland, you have something definite and tangible, the time, the manner, the means, the names, the dates; and I will state as a prophesy, that there will not be an unbelieving Gentile upon this continent 50 years hence; and if they are not greatly scourged, and in a great measure overthrown, within five or ten years from this date, then the Book of Mormon will have proved itself false. And furthermore, as Mr. La Roy Sunderland has lied concerning the truth of Heaven, the fulness of the Gospel; and has blasphemed against the word of God, except he speedily repent, and acknowledge his lying and wickedness, and obey the message of eternal truth, which God has sent for the salvation of his people. God will smite him dumb, that he can no longer speak great swelling words against the Lord; and a trembling shall seize his nerves, that he shall not be able to write; and Zion's Watchman shall cease to be published abroad, and its lies shall no longer deceive the public; and he will wander a vagabond on the earth, until sudden destruction shall overtake him; and if Mr. La Roy Sunderland enquires, when shall these things be? I reply, it is nigh thee—even at thy doors; and I say this in the name of Jesus Christ. Amen.

I hope Mr. Sunderland, will no more complain of the jargon of the Mormon Prophets being unintelligible or indefinite.

Mr. S. says, "admitting the 29th Chapter of Isaiah was a prediction of the existence of the Book of Mormon, it does not predict that, that book would be a good one." Now I am more, and more astonished at the perfect weakness of your cause. What! the deaf hear the words of the Book, the meek increase their joy in the Lord, and the poor rejoice; the house of Jacob be glad in the Holy One of Israel; they that err in spirit come to understanding, and they that murmur learn doctrine.— And all this brought about by the means of a Book, and that Book not a good one? You say, "the text speaks of a book being presented to a person unable to read it."—Here you mistake again: the text speaks of the WORDS of a book being delivered to the learned who could not read them; but of the Book itself being delivered to the unlearned, thus making a distinction. The words or characters being copied from the Plates and delivered to the learned who could not read them, while the Book was delivered to the unlearned; thus fulfiling the words of the text.

Mr. S. further says, "the text speaks of a Book—it says nothing about Brass Plates." But I reply, the text says nothing about parchment, tables of stone, papyrus, bark, paper, or any thing else on which this Record was to be written; consequently, it must not be written on any thing, according to your logic. But as you are learned, please define what materials may be written on, in order to constitute a book; and what materials may not be used; and what name we may give to a Record on Plates, as they would not constitute a book.

Mr. S. says, "Mormonism is directly opposed to the Holy Scriptures. 1st.—The New Testament informs us, that if we believe what is written in that book, of the Son of God, we shall be saved.—John, c. xx: v.31. While the Book of Mormon says, if we don't believe that also, in addition to the old and new Testament, we must be eternally damned; hence Mormonism is a lie." Stop, stop, don't be so fast; John makes no allusion to the New Testament, in the text you have quoted, but refers to the Book he was then writing now called the Gospel according to St. John. For the book called the New Testament, did not exist at that time neither is it at all probable that he had any book before him at the time, to which he alluded, except the testimony, or gospel, which he was then in the act of finishing; consequently, you will please relinquish all claim to faith in any other book of the New Testament, and set them down for lies, as you have Mormonism. Because John wrote his book that you might believe on the Son of God, and that believing you might have life through his name; therefore, according to your own logic, you are bound to reject all others as lies. 2d. — You say, "God has imperatively forbidden any addition to what was written in the Old and New Testaments. Deut. c. iv: v. 2: and Rev. c. xxii: v, 18." Here you are too fast again, Mr. Sunderland. These two texts say nothing concerning the Old and New Testaments at all; the one speaks of Moses's writings only; not at all including the writings of the Prophets, for they were not the commands of Moses, and were not in existence when Moses wrote. And the other speaks exclusively of the "words of the Prophesy of this book," (the book of the Revelation of St. John,) which was not then compiled with any other book under heaven. Thus, Mr. Sunderland, in destroying the Book of Mormon, you destroy every book in the Bible. By your application of the first text, you destroy every book except John's Gospel; not excepting Moses nor the Revelation of St. John. — Then by your application of the other two texts, you destroy the Gospel of St. John and all the other books except Moses and the Revelation of John. Thus if you gain the victory over the the Book of Mormon by these texts, you gain an equal victory over all the other books. It is not Mormonism alone, that is struggling for existence beneath your infidel thrust; but it is the whole truth of Heaven, which was ever revealed to man, or ever will be. Indeed your logic would shut Heaven, seal up the mouth of Jehovah, forbid the ministry of Angels, deprive men of the Holy Ghost, (the spirit of Prophesy and Revelation,) close all communication between man and his Maker, and leave the world in Atheism. First, by destroying the Bible, and all other ancient Records which are sacred. Secondly, by forbidding mankind ever to receive any more. Thirdly, you say, "the Holy Scriptures are sufficient as a rule of our faith and practice," and you make many quotations to prove it. And you further say, "the doctrine taught in these passages, Mormonism denies;" and to establish the accusation, you quote our Doctrines and Covenants, Sect. 5th, "In cases of difficulty respecting doctrine or principle, when there is not a sufficiency written to make the case clear to the minds of the Council; the President may enquire and obtain the mind of the Lord by revelation." You make it read thus, "if not sufficiently written," thus giving a false quotation. Now, sir, you are a false accuser, for our doctrine and covenants, in this text, perfectly agree with the rules of faith and practice, laid down in the Bible. See James, c. i, v. 5: "If any of you lack WISDOM, let him ASK OF GOD, who giveth to ALL MEN liberally, and upbraideth not, and it SHALL be given him." And again, the Apostle prays that God will enrich the disciples "in the Spirit of WISDOM and REVELATION in the KNOWLEDGE of God." Now Mr. Sunderland, wherein does Mormonism differ from the rules of faith and practice just quoted from the Bible? And if desired, I pledge myself to produce a thousand precepts and examples of a similar kind; all being rules of faith and practice, which we fulfil or live according to, in fulfiling that one rule of our "Doctrine and Covenants." Indeed, if the scriptures were given for our rule of faith and practice, then are we continually to receive Revelation, Prophecies, Visions, Angels, &c.; for this is according to all the precepts, examples, rules, faith, and practice of Scripture, and you, sir, in opposing this part of Mormonism, are in opposition to all the rules which you yourself have brought forward from Scripture. — Thus, like Haman, you receive that punishment, which you prepared for others.

"Christ born of Mary, at Jerusalem, the land of our forefathers." — Book of Mormon, page 240, 2d edition. This you say, is a contradiction of his being born in Bethlehem, (a little place, six miles from Jerusalem,) but mark the local difference in the places where each was spoken. One prophet stands in the vicinity where the thing was fulfilled, and points out the exact location, (Bethlehem.) The other stands on the other side of the globe, from Jerusalem, and addresses a people who knew but little concerning the localities of the various towns and villages of Judea. The prophet speaks in general terms concerning a thing which should transpire in the land of Jerusalem, as they had a general idea of the great capitol city and country, from whence they sprang, rather than a distinct idea of all its villages. This is in perfect accordance with all the circumstances under which they wrote, and a great proof in favour of the Book of Mormon; because an imposter, in forging a book, would have said Bethlehem; for every school boy knows, that Bethlehem is the place where the Lord was born.

And Mr. Sunderland, you say, "the Book of Mormon gives numerous instances of persons ordained to the *Mosaick* Priesthood, who were of the tribe of Joseph," but I know of no *Mosaick* Priesthood. But if you mean the Aronic, I deny the assertion, for the Aronic Priesthood is no where pretended to in the Book of Mormon. The Josephites claim the Priesthood after the Order of Melchisidek; which had power over all things — the Aronic Priesthood not excepted for they paid tithes to this greater Priesthood, according to Paul. This Priesthood was after the power of an endless life, without beginning of days, or end of life; and holds the keys and authorities over all the other offices of the Church, in all ages of the world. The book claims no Ark of the Covenant, no temple service, as to the Holy of Holies, or any thing that pertained exclusively to the Aronic or Levetical Priesthood. But says Mr. S., "the Jews were not allowed to offer Burnt Offerings in any other place after the Temple was built, except Jerusalem. — Deut. c. xii: v. 1 13, 14. The reason of this prohibition was, the holy fire could be obtained in no other place. — Lev. c. x: v. 1."

I have examined both of these texts. The first does not mention the Temple, but only the place which the Lord should choose. — See verses 10, 11, of the same Chap. WHEN they dwelt in the land, the other side of Jordan, and had rest from their enemies, and WHEN they dwelt there in safety, THEN there should be a place for them to bring their burnt offerings and sacrifices. THEN they were to take heed not to offer sacrifices in every place, but in the place which the Lord should choose. Now I ask, if Lehi, who left Jerusalem just in time to escape the Babalonish Captivity, or his children who lived in America, were dwelling in the land of Canaan, the other side of Jordan, in peace, at the same time they were roaming the wilderness as outcasts from the land of their fathers? If so, then the restriction concerning sacrifices, applies to them, if not, it does not apply to them according to verses 10 and 11 of that chapter. Lev. c. x: v. 1, says nothing concerning Jerusalem or the fire obtained there, any more than it does of the flood. And why it is quoted by Mr. Sunderland on that subject, I am unable to guess, unless it was for want of any proof whatever to support the assertion.

I shall now proceed to apply Mr. Sunderland's rule to Elijah, the Tishbite, of the inhabitants of Gilead. 1st Kings, c. 18: where he offered sacrifices on Mount Carmel, near 40 miles south of Jerusalem; and this in the days of King Ahab, a long time after the building of the Temple of Solomon. Consequently, Elijah must share the same fate of all ancient "Mormon" Prophets. Neither did he get his fire from Jerusalem, but from Heaven. This is a more aggravating transgression of Mr. Sunderland's rule, than the Book of Mormon any where records: for this was done in the very country where the Lord had required all to be performed at Jerusalem. Poor old Elijah, what a pity that you did not understand the Law as well as Mr. La Roy Sunderland, Zion's Watchman; for now you are doomed by him to eternal infamy and destruction with us, poor deluded creatures. And it seems your fathers were equally ignorant with yourself, for you only repaired the Altar of God where they had offered their sacrifices before you — and all in the wrong place. And as to others offering sacrifices, who were not of the Aronic priesthood, I refer the reader to Gideon, of the tribe of Manasseh; Judge, c. vi: v. 25. — Manoah, of the tribe of Dan; Judge, c. xiii : v. 16, 19. — Samuel's offering: 1st Sam. v. 7, 9. — David of the tribe of Judah; 2d Sam. c. vi: v. 17, 18. — These all offered sacrifices acceptable to God, and that too, while the Law of Moses was in force, and in a country where the seed of Aaron and Levi were to be found. Now Mr. La Roy Sunderland, you must be looked upon either as a knave, or too ignorant to stand at the head of any paper, much less to be one of "Zion's Watchmen." I have dwelt upon this subject more full, because Mr. A. Campbell, of Virginia, Editor of the "Millennium Harbinger;" Howe, of Painsville, Ohio, publisher of "Mormonism Unveiled." Himes, of Boston, author of a pamphlet on "Mormonism," and Bachelor, with his two horns, cloven foot, and pitchfork, have all raised the same ignorant objections, as to sacrifices and priesthood. All these profess to be very learned, and make a great outcry against Joseph Smith, Jun. and the Mormons in general, for their ignorance. Now how does it come about, that Joseph Smith, and the Elders of the Church, (being unlearned and ignorant men,) should confound and bring to nought, all the wisdom of the wise? Surely the Scriptures are verified, that the weak, the unlearned, and the depised, that God chosen to confound the wise, and bring to nought the understanding of the prudent. Now if this common blunder of theirs, proceeded from ignorance, we shall expect to see a general confession on their part; but if it be the effects of Priestcraft, Knavery, and Imposture, they will signify it by their silence.

Next you say, "the Doctrine and Covenants, Sec. 2, contradicts the Bible by saying, Remission of sins must precede Baptism." This, sir, I deny; it says that the candidate should receive "of the spirit of Christ, UNTO the remission of sins" You further say, "The Voice of Warning, page 22, says the Dreams of Pharaoh were to be literally interpreted.

Thus contradicting what Joseph said of them."—This, sir, is a lie. The "Voice of Warning" says no such thing. But rather says Joseph's Prophesy (to Pharaoh) was to be interpreted literally.—See "Voice of Warning," page 21 and 22.

As to God's repenting and being grieved at his heart because he had been so foolish and shortsighted as to make man, or whether it was Noah that grieved, I leave the candid reader to judge. The one is King James' translation, the other is Joseph Smith's. I suppose if it were written in King James' translation of the Bible, that two and two make twelve, and we should say two and two make four, we should be accused of contradicting the Bible. Thus superstition would make the King's uninspired Translators of far more authority than the God of Truth. You further say, "that God informs us, that the Gospel Covenant is to last forever, and never to be succeeded by another:" and you quote Heb. c. vii: v. 21, 28; c. viii: v. 6, 13; c. vi: v. 13, 20. Now I say God says no such thing in any of the texts, as that the Covenant, Offices and Ordinances of the Gospel, as set in order by the Apostles, would never be broken among men; but these texts speak of the Covenant and Priesthood of the Son of God, how it should last forever; and it will be recollected that he is in Heaven, He is not a priest to administer ordinances here on earth. It is true, Heb. c. viii. from 8th to 13th verse, speaks of a new Covenant to be made with the house of ISRAEL, which Covenant should never be broken, and succeeded by another; but this covenant was to take away THEIR sins, and cause THEM ALL to know the Lord, from the least to the greatest. But this Covenant never took effect in the Apostles' days, nor at any time since, but is yet future, as I will prove by three infallible proofs: first, Roman, c. xi: v. 25 to 31; places that Covenant in future, viz: when God should take away the sins of Israel, and they should obtain mercy, *after the fulness of the Gentiles should come in.* Now I enquire. Are the Jews, together with Israel, now free from sin, & ALL acquainted with the Lord Jesus Christ, their Saviour? The answer is my 2d proof, that, that Covenant is yet future; the Jews are yet scattered in unbelief, blindness, and sin, among all nations. And Mr. La Roy Sunderland dare not say, that the Covenant spoken of in the 8th of Heb. and Rom. 11th, has ever been made with ISRAEL and JUDAH. My 3d proof is, that this Covenant never will take effect with them in their scattered situation, but will take effect with them when they are gathered home from all nations, to their own land. See Ezek. c. xxxvii. Hence the folly of Missionary efforts to bring them to the standards of Sectarianism; when in fact the Gentiles will have to bow to them and their standard, to end their own controversies.

Mr. Sunderland having lied, misrepresented and falsified our Books, and mangled the Scriptures in a most horrid manner, at length cries out, "here is proof positive that these books can never be reconciled, either with themselves or the Scriptures of Truth." When in fact, it is his own blunders and falsehoods, which can never be reconciled with any truth. Mr. S. then proceeds thus, "Mormonism is a system of unrelenting cruelty. To be convinced of this fact, a person has only to read the Book of Mormon, which is one continued history of wars and murders." Pray, Mr. S., is it too cruel to record a faithful history of wars? And again, was the doctrine contained in that book, the cause of the wars recorded in it? or were the wars caused by sin, and opposition to the holy principles contained in it? But, says Mr. Sunderland, "Mormonism is cruel; 1st, in requiring Faith without evidence," and adds, "it is true, eleven men have said it is true." But Mr. S. it is written in the Law, both of God and Man, that the testimony of two men is true. But you say, "ten thousand others can be found who will testify that it is not true." Well, Mr. S., there were twelve to testify that Jesus had risen from the dead, and as many nations to testify he had not risen. But what does this negative amount to, without you first destroy the affirmative? But it seems, some of these witnesses are guilty of being named, Smith and Whitmer. But this is the first time I ever heard of a witness being rejected on account of his name. But I see no cruelty in requiring people to believe anything, true or false, as long as it leaves them at liberty to disbelieve it! But secondly, "Mormonism is cruel in taking from its votaries their property and refusing to restore it again." And then, Mr. S., has heard some literary gentleman say, that he has heard sombody say, that the Mormons in the West, did so and so. Now, Mr. Sunderland, this is proof sufficient against them, although Eleven Men cannot be believed in their favour. Yes, this is quite enough, away with such fellows, crucify them! crucify them! It is not fit that they should live. Now, Mr. S., we do not take any man's property from him, only what is freely donated, in charity to the poor; and we have officers who are bound to see to the distribution of every dollar for the purpose for which it was given. And I ask, if the Abolition, Missionary, Bible, Tract, or any charitable institution, gives back the money donated to them? For instance, if Mr. Sunderland joins the Church of the Latter Day Saints, and gives a certain sum for Colonizing the poor, and this money is expended for the purpose given; the poor eat it up; and Mr. S. apostatises; the officer who handled the money, must go to work and earn the money, in order to replace to Mr. S. what he gave to the poor, otherwise "it is a system of unrelenting cruelty."

Again, Mr. S. says, "its cruelty appears in its requiring its votaries to leave their homes and go to the Western part of Missouri." Now, Mr. S. no "Mormon" has ever gone to that place, except by choice, in order to escape the troubles which God has forwarned us of respecting other countries. And Jesus was equally cruel in telling the disciples to leave Judea, and flee to the mountains, on a certain occasion. I ask, is it cruel to take men from the midst of distress, tribulation, want of employment, starvation, and oppression, and Colonize them where there is land and employment enough, with provisions in abundance, and very cheap?!! But, says Mr. S., "its monstrous cruelty appears again, in its pretending to send all to hell who do not believe it. But I reply, that every dispensation that God ever sent, is equally cruel in this respect; for God sends all to hell who reject any thing that he sends to save those that believe. And I add, if Methodism be true, God will send every man to hell who rejects it. And a man must be very inconsistent, to come with a message from God, and then, tell the people that they can be saved just as well without, as with it. But he complains of its consigning to hell, all who persist in the doctrine of Infant Baptism. But pray, Mr. Sunderland, is Infant Baptism any part of the pure Gospel which Paul preached? If not, it is a perversion of the Gospel: and Paul has been so cruel as to agree with Mormon, in pronouncing a curse upon all those who pervert the Gospel. Says Mr. Sunderland, "the writings of the Mormonites, are replete with nonsense and blasphemy." He then gives several specimens: first, it is impious blasphemy to teach that the Lord suffered for the sins of the world, and bled at every pore; and that sinners must repent, or suffer for their own sins, as he has suffered for them. And, indeed, (says he) "it would be difficult to find ONE passage in *any* of their writings, that we have seen, which conveys ANY THING LIKE GOOD SENSE." Then follows another specimen. Our Doctrine and Covenants, say God is the light of the Sun, Moon and Stars, and the power by which they are made, and that God is in them. This seems to be nonsense and blasphemy when found in Mormon writings. But let the Bible say, he is in all things; that he is the light of every man that comes into the world; or let a Methodist Priest say that God is Omnicient, and Omnipresent, i. e. that he is in the Sun, Moon and Stars, and every where else, and it *then* becomes good sense, and a pious saying. Now, let the reader mark, that it is writing these things in a Mormon Book, that makes "nonsense and blasphemy" of them. Under the head of nonsense and blasphemy, he quotes the following from the "Doctrine and Covenants." "Through the redemption which is made for you, is brought to pass the Resurrection of the dead, and the spirit and the body, is the soul of Man, and the Resurrection from the dead, is the redemption of the soul."

This "nonsense and blasphemy," becomes good sense the moment it is found in the other Scriptures. Instance, in Gen. where God formed *Man* of the dust of the earth, and breathed into his nostrils the *breath of life*, and man became a living SOUL. Here, the earthly part, animated by the Spirit of Life, is called *Man*, and is also called a living SOUL. Now, this is "nonsense and blasphemy," in "Mormonism," but in the Bible it becomes sublime truth. Or has the Ignoramus never read the Bible? But another specimen of Mormon nonsense and blasphemy is quoted by him. "And the Saints shall be filled with glory, and be EQUAL with Him," (Christ.)—"Doctrine and Covenants." This nonsense and blasphemy, becomes truth when found in the Bible. As to this equality of Christ and his people, see the prayer of Christ, recorded by John, concerning his saints, becoming ONE with him and the Father, as they are ONE—and certainly they are *equal*. And again, the saints are *joint heirs* with Him. And again, "he that overcometh, shall sit down with Christ in his Throne, as he has overcome and sit down with the Father in his Throne." And again, the spirit should guide his saints into all truth, and if it does guide his saints into all truth, God is in possession of *all truth*, and *no more*: consequently, his saints will *know* what *he knows*: and it is an acknowledged principle, that "knowledge is power;" consequently, if they have the *same knowledge that God has, they will have the same power*. And this will fulfil the Scripture, which saith, "Unto him that believeth ALL THINGS ARE POSSIBLE." And I am sure God can do no more than *all things*: consequently there must be *equality*. That is, the redeemed return to the fountain, and become *part* of the great *all*, from which they eminated. Hence the propriety of calling them "GODS, even the *sons of God*." In fact it was this doctrine of *equality*, that constituted blasphemy in the minds of the Jews, and brought down their malice and vengeance upon the head of our dear Saviour.

The next specimen of "nonsense and blasphemy," is quoted by Mr. Sunderland from "Doctrine and Covenants," Sec. 7th. It is a clause from a Revelation, rebuking the Church for the idleness of some of its members, and the wickedness of their children, together with their covetousness and neglect of prayer and devotion. But this is the first time, that speaking against such evils amounted to "nonsense or blasphemy." Indeed, I now understand why he uttered that sweeping declaration, that it would be difficult to find one passage of good sense in all of our books; it is because they are taken up mostly, in speaking against sin, which amounts, in his mind, to nonsense and blasphemy, therefore, our books are filled with "nonsense and blasphemy," because they are filled with warnings against sin; and because they hold forth repentance and redemption, through the blood of Christ, the resurrection of the dead, and a fulness of glory at the right hand of our blessed Redeemer.

Another specimen from the Book of "Doctrine and Covenants," Sec. 27, is brought forward by this lying deceiver, but he could not make nonsense of it without altering it for the worse in three places. "Let my servant, Sidney Gilbert plant himself in the HOUSE (the revelation reads, "in this place," instead of *house*, and establish a Store, that he may sell goods without fraud, that he may obtain money to buy lands for the good of the Saints." This provision for colonizing the poor has become "nonsense and blasphemy." — Although the Lord could once send Peter to catch a fish in order to get a little money to pay taxes, without blaspheming; but perhaps Mr. S. would say, that was in the days of humility and simplicity, when he was poor, and had not where to lay his head, but since he had got in possession of so many fine Temples, Chapels, Livings, Honours, Titles, Salaries, &c., his mind could not stoop to hear the cries of the poor. But he quotes still further: "Let my servant, W. W. Phelps, be planted in *the house*, (the Revelation reads, "*in this place*," instead of the house,) and let him be established as a Printer to the Church, *and let all the world receive his writings*." Surely this would be nonsense; for all the world cannot read — all the world have not conveyances by mail, and all the world includes more than three thousand languages and dialects; and all the world would keep our Printing Establishment very busy to print *four or five hundred millions* of a monthly paper, in the several thousand different tongues. But it is Mr. S. who makes nonsense, by his lying, (the passage reads thus, "and inasmuch as the world receive his writings, let him obtain all he can obtain in righteousness, for the good of the Saints.") The truth of the matter is this, that we planted a Colony in Missouri, and to that Colony was attached a Mercantile and Printing Establishment, the profits of which, were to be devoted to the purchase of lands, for the purpose of Colonizing the poor, who were unable to buy lands for themselves. The fact is, this speculating, lying hypocrite, not only falsifies almost every passage he quotes, but is continually converting the most benevolent institutions among the Saints, into nonsense, blasphemy, and money making, whereas, it is his own Order, and not Ours, that is guilty of moneyed plans, and priestcraft. Indeed, I have often heard the members of the Methodist Church complain, that the great cry of their Priests, was money, money, give, give. Indeed, whoever will read their Discipline, will find it abounding with moneyed plans; making a regular provision for the support of their hireling Priests. And whoever will read our Book of "Doctrine and Covenants," will find no provision for the support of Preachers, except to go forth without Purse or Scrip, or Two Coats, taking no thought for the morrow; freely giving and freely receiving such things as the people see fit to give. Indeed, I have preached in this city more than six months, many times a week, besides visiting the poor, the sick, &c.; and I have not mentioned money, money, nor give, give, for the support of the Gospel; neither has such a thing ever been named in any of our meetings, except by way of condemnation. But the Gospel I preach has power to fill those who receive it with charity, and it

33

opens their hearts, so that my necessities are supplied. But nature's wants are few, I dispense with those extravagances most of the Priests are guilty of. I have preached the Gospel from Maine to Missouri, for near eight years, and all I ever received, during my whole ministry, would not amount to the yearly salary of one of the lazy, extravagant loungers, who under the name of priests, are a nuisance to the whole country.

But to return to another specimen of "nonsense and blasphemy," "Behold I command you [Hiram Smith] that you need not suppose that you are called to preach until you are."

This "nonsense and blasphemy," if put in practice in all christendom, would rid the world of Popes, Right Reverend Fathers in God, Lord Bishops, D.D's. Rabbies, &c. which ever were a curse to it: yes, it would rid the world of all the hirelings, and of all the uninspired men, which have so long been a burden to society.

He next complains of Mrs. Smith, being called an "elect lady." The ignorant clown, verily thinks the term "lady" in America, amounts to a title of nobility paramount with "lord," and intimates, that we shall soon have "Lord Joseph." Why, Mr. Sunderland, if ever you had been in good society in this country, you would have perceived that ALL females of respectability are called "ladies," as a matter of common courtesy; that it does not imply a title of nobility; however, you are to be pardoned for this stupid blunder, for I judge it was through ignorance you committed it; but the female part of the community will think you rather clownish. But this "nonsense and blasphemy," becomes sublime truth, the moment John makes use of the same term in the Bible, or perhaps John was so much of a pope, in your estimation, that he had power to confer titles of nobility.

Mr. S's next specimen of "nonsense and blasphemy," is quoted from the book of "doctrine and covenants," sect. 66, giving the word of the Lord to J. Smith, Jun. and S. Rigden, appointing them a mission to Missouri; yet, he says "the Scriptures are for our rule of faith and practice." Well, Mr. S if this is "nonsense and blasphemy;" then of course, the word of the Lord to Philip, that he should go towards the desert, and to the chariot of the Ethiopian, is condemned by the same rule; and also the word of the Lord to Paul, directing him in his mission: or, have the Scriptures ceased to be a rule or pattern for us to follow? Come, Mr. Sunderland, throw off the cloak of religion — come out open infidel, for surely you have as good reason to condemn the Former Day Saints, as the Latter Day Saints, in this respect, unless you worship a changeable God: who condescended to speak in old times; but has now become dumb, from misdemeanor or through old age! For shame, why worship a God who has no ears, mouth nor eyes, whose arm is shortened that he cannot save and has no power to deliver? It is true, I am not much in the habit of ridiculing, but really, if Isaiah, or Elijah were here, they would hold you in derision, and your God too. And I am sure, the living God would laugh at as well as mock both you and your God. It seems at last, I have discovered what Mr. S. means by our revelations being blasphemy. Who ever will read the first article of religion in the doctrines and "discipline" of the Methodist Episcopal Church, will find a description of their God: a God without body or parts of course then he has neither eyes, ears, or mouth, and can neither see, hear, nor speak. Well now, Mr. Sunderland, we acknowledge that all the revelations we have ever received from Israel's God, was direct blasphemy against yours. But let it be understood distinctly, that we do not love, serve, nor fear your God; and if he has been blasphemed, let him speak and plead his own cause: but this he cannot do, seeing he has no mouth. And how he ever revealed his choice of La Roy Sunderland, as a "Watchman" for his Zion, I am at a loss to determine. But we worship a God, who has both body and parts; who has eyes, mouth, and ears, and who speaks when he pleases — to whom he pleases, and sends them where he pleases. And he always did blaspheme other Gods, and hold them up to ridicule and contempt; and so did his followers; and as Mr. Sunderland is unacquainted with our God, and has been worshiping an imaginary God all his days, I take this opportunity of declaring the true God to him; and I hope if ever he is brought to a knowledge of Him, he will become a man of truth; for our God is a God of truth.

Mr. S. quotes numerous typographical errors in the Book of Mormon, many of which are corrected in the second edition; but he takes advantage of these errors of language, by saying the Book was PRINTED under Infallible Inspiration. By this we are to understand that Mr. Grandin, a Job Printer, at Palmyra; a man who makes no pretentions to religion, is inspired to set his type all just right. This is too ridiculous to come from a man of common sense; and deserves no reply, only a remark, that Mr. S.'s skull must be rather thick, or he is partially deranged.

Mr. S. proceeds to quote numerous phrases from the Book of Mormon, which are found in the other Scriptures, and thinks it strange and incredible, that God who is the Author of both, should have made use of the same phrases in both countries. Or that he knew some truths a little too early. He seems to think, that all who can believe that the Spirit of God is acquainted with modern phrases, or phrases which his spirit selected, and made use of in another country or ages, must be prepared to believe any thing, however shocking or absurd. He seems to think, the Spirit of God in America, has been guilty of literary theft, in imitating its own likeness, as manifested in other writings, and in other ages and countries. He says, "a very large proportion of this Book, (the

Book of Mormon,) is made up of base, and bungling attempts to imitate the Scripture style; and to quote ONE of a HUNDRED of these attempts, we should have to transcribe SEVERAL HUNDRED pages." Astonishing!!! The Book of Mormon, according to this statement, would consist of at least, TWENTY THOUSAND pages. Surely this would compare with the mammoth. One would suppose of a truth, as he has said, it would take three years to write and print a book so large. But this statement is about as near the truth as he is in the habit of speaking.

CONTRADICTIONS

Under this head, Mr. Sunderland says, "in the Book of Mormon, page 149, and throughout the Book, the Plates on which it is said to have been engraved, were Brass. But the eight witnesses say they had the appearance of Gold." This is Mr. S.'s BLUNDER, and NOT a contradiction in the Book. The Plates on which the Book of Mormon was written, are nowhere called brass, but the Plates brought from Jerusalem to America, containing the writings of Moses and the Jewish Prophets, are called Brass; and the distinction is kept so plain throughout the whole Record, that a blunder or mistake on this point, on the part of Mr. S., is inexcusable. And from his general proceedings in this matter, we feel justified in calling it a lie. Mr. S. also says, "it speaks of a Compass, five or six hundred years before Christ." But he does not tell us the fact as the Book does, in relation to the invention of this Compass. The Book says it was prepared by the hand of the Lord; but perhaps Mr. S. thinks the Lord could not have invented a Compass in that early age of Arts and Sciences: but some scientific men profess to trace the knowledge of the compass back to very early ages. Indeed, some show reasons for believing it was invented in Egypt, in the days of her glory — but be this as it may; our God is just as good at mechanical inventions, architecture, tayloring, smithing, stone working, &c. &c., as at any other business. For proof of this, we refer the reader to the Tables of Stone, not only written on by the finger of God, but the first tables were made by Him. — Also, the plans of the Tabernacle, Temple, Aaron's Garments, &c.; as well as the workers in Gold and Silver, &c., were all inspired of God, according to Moses.

Again, he says, "on page 440, it is said the Sun does not move at all." — This is another lie. It only speaks of the principle of lengthening out the day, and gives us to understand that the Earth rolls back on its Axes, to cause this phenomena, instead of the Sun moving for this purpose. He further says, page 431, ten years before Christ, a writer pretends to quote the following passage: "they that have done good

36

shall have everlasting life; and they that have done evil shall have everlasting damnation:" but he adds, "no such Scripture was written at that time." I reply, no such Scripture is now written, except in the Nephite records, of which the Book of Mormon is not one hundreth part and Sunderland knows not what was written among them; therefore, he cannot judge; he knows not but the Scriptures referred to, was written 40 times over, in some of their former Records; therefore, he has made a presumptuous assertion.

He quotes, Book of Mormon, page 65: "Adam fell that man might have joy." This does not read so, but says, "Men are, that they might have joy." But I am tired of noticing his lies. He says, "The Voice of Warning, page 37, says the Nile now has Seven Mouths." But the "Voice of Warning," page 37, says no such thing, not even naming the Nile, its streams or mouths. Mr. S. proceeds to reject the 11th Chapter of Isaiah, because from the construction of the Lion's Jaws. — He cannot chew the cud like the ox. Now, Mr. Sunderland, you begin to come out like a man; you no longer act under a cloak of religion, you have turned Infidel at last, and cannot believe the Bible one whit sooner than the "Book of Mormon." And the "Book of Mormon" says, if we believe one we will believe the other. But he pleads an excuse for his unbelief by saying, the passage referred to cannot be taken literally. Pray, Mr. S., permit me to suggest a rule of interpretation, that will just suit your views of this passage. That little N-O-T, which the tempter made use of, in his quoting Scripture to Eve, then it would read thus: "The Lion shall N-O-T eat straw like the ox." You further say, "according to the representation on page 540 of the Book of Mormon, there was an insect called in the reformed Egyptian language, a Honey Bee." This is another falsehood; the original language, there calls it "Deseret," which is by interpretation, a Honey Bee. Again, you find fault with page 542, for speaking of windows so long before the invention of glass. But here you are at war with the Bible, which mentions windows as early as Noah's Ark, and the Flood. You complain of a certain book being written among the Josephites, in the language of their Fathers, (Hebrew,) and yet the book professes to be reformed Egyptian. Well, what contradiction in all this? The Brass Plates brought from Jerusalem were in Hebrew; and the abridgement that Mormon made [now called the "Book of Mormon,"] was written in the "Reformed Egyptian." But you say, "the Reformed Egyptian was never spoken by any person." But how do you know what was done in America? The writers in the "Book of Mormon" say it was called *among them*, "Reformed Egyptian," being handed down and altered by *them*, according to *their* manner of speech.

One would certainly judge you to be acquainted in ancient America, when you make an assertion like the foregoing. But again;

you say, "Let any 'Mormonite' produce a specimen of such a language if he can." This I agree to do, when you produce a man acquainted with all the ancient languages. Again, you say, "a hero in the Book of Mormon, page 529, is made to say, that his ten thousand warriors, whom he was leading into battle, were killed. But in the very next page he is represented as leading them in the front of battle again, after they were hewn down." I say boldly, this is a gross misrepresentation: and now, let the public read the two pages, and judge for themselves.

Again; you say the "Book of Mormon," page 48, mentions the *Mariners'* Compass. I say it does not mention the *Mariners'* Compass; but a Compass prepared by the hand of God, as you may read particularly in the "Book of Mormon."

Mr. S. says, "The Book of Mormon purports to have been originally engraven on Brass Plates." Now Mr. La Roy Sunderland, why do you lie again? Why not continue to add lie to lie, to make the "Book of Mormon" appear false? The "Book of Mormon" nowhere purports to have originally been engraven on "Brass Plates." [I am more, and more, ashamed of the living lie; whose falsehoods I am unveiling;] the Book says "Gold Plates."

But you say, "Now, admitting there were as many plates as there are pages in the Book; and that each plate weighed not less than one pound each; these plates must have weighed not less than five hundred and fifty pounds." Here we see another mark of a confused and shattered brain. Why! Mr. S., there is only half as many leaves in a book as there are pages for one leaf makes two pages; as you may learn by examining Mr. Webster's Spelling Book. Besides, a thin gold plate, about 7 by 8 inches, and about the thickness of tin, would not weigh a pound: and you should know that the "Egyptian" is a much shorter language than the English. You say, "probably Smith knew very well that the traditions of the Natives would not countenance the "Book of Mormon." In answer to this, I will quote a few of their Traditions.

First, says Mr. Boudinot, "It is said among their principal or beloved men, that they have it handed down from their ancestors, that the Book which the white people have, was once theirs: that while they had it they prospered exceedingly, &c. They also say, that their fathers were possessed of an extraordinary Divine Spirit, by which they foretold future events, and controlled the common course of Nature; and this they transmitted to their offspring, on condition of their obeying the sacred laws, that they did by these means, bring down showers of blessings upon their beloved people; but that this power for a long time past had entirely ceased." Colonel James Smith, in his Journal, while a prisoner among the Natives, says, "They have a tradition, that in the beginning of this Continent, the angels, or Heavenly Inhabitants, as they call them, frequently visited the people, and talked with their forefathers, and gave directions how to pray."

Mr. Boudinot, in his able work, remarks concerning their language: "Their language in its roots, idiom, and particular construction, appears to have the *whole genius* of the Hebrew, and what is very remarkable, and well worthy of serious attention, has most of the peculiarities of that language; especially those in which it differs from most other languages." There is a tradition related by an aged Indian, of the Stockbridge Tribe, that their fathers were once in possession of a "Sacred Book," which was handed down from generation to generation; and at last hid in the Earth, since which time they had been under the feet of their enemies. But these Oracles were to be restored to them again; and *then* they would triumph over their enemies, and regain their ancient country, together with their rights and privileges. Mr. Boudinot, after recording many traditions similar to the above, at length remarks; "Can any man read this short account of Indian Traditions, drawn from Tribes of various Nations; from the West to the East, and from the South to the North, wholly separated from each other, written by different authors of the best character, both for knowledge and integrity, possessing the best means of information, at various and distant times, without any possible communication with each other; and yet suppose, that all this is the effect of chance, accident, or design, from a love of the marvellous, or a premeditated intention of deceiving, and thereby ruining their well established reputation? Can any one carefully, and with deep reflection, consider and compare these traditions with the Ten Tribes of Israel, without at least, drawing some presumptive inferences in favour of these wandering Natives being descended from the Ten Tribes of Israel?"

Mr. S. says, "In the Book of Mormon, page 550, a man is spoken of who was the Father of 32 children!" I reply, this was almost half as many as Ahab had sons—2d Kings, c. x.: v. 6; where his 70 sons are mentioned, and no doubt he had some daughters. But this Bible statement can be spiritualized and so avoid the marvellous.

But, says Mr. S., "it speaks of 'Church' five or six hundred years before Christ." I reply, the Bible speaks of "Church" as early as Moses. But, says he, "this Book speaks of the Paradise of God, 500 years before Christ;" but I ask, (if there was no such place till invented by modern Priests,) where did Adam dwell, when first created? and did the Saviour add a new term, as well as idea, to the Hebrew, when he told the Thief on the Cross concerning Paradise?

Mr. S. says, "the Jews never kept any of their records on Plates of Brass." But I inquire, how does he know? In fact he seems to be perfectly acquainted with every thing that ever transpired in every age and country. Pray, Mr. S., who are you? "This Book," says Mr. S., "countenances murder for opinions' sake; it also countenances deception and theft; page 12 and 13." I say it does not countenance murder for opinions' sake; the circumstances recorded on these pages, was the slaying of Laban, who had robbed them, and sought their lives. Therefore, this is another lie, Mr. S. And as to deception and theft, it was taking a record from a robber, who had robbed them of an immense property. But Mr. S., why not condemn the Bible? look at Moses slaying the Egyptian, and concealing him in the sand, and running away to escape justice. Look at the Israelites, borrowing of the Egyptians and not paying them. Look at Jacob's deception of his Father, Isaac; and his deception of his Father-in-law, with the pealed rods. And at Rachel, stealing the Images; and of Samuel slaying Agag; and at David's deception, feigning himself crazy, by letting his spittle run down on his beard. And when you have looked at all these, you shall have as many more. — But yet, in your estimation, the Bible is unerring truth, and the "Book of Mormon," a deception. Oh! what an impartial judge.

You say, "it speaks of the Lamb of God; and of the Gospel of the Lamb; the Apostles of the Lamb; the Holy Ghost; the Mother of God; of priestcraft; of the Crucifixion of Christ, and his Baptism by John; of the Roman Catholic Church; and of immersion: — long before the advent of Messiah." I reply, it does not use the term "Roman Catholic," nor "Christians," nor "immersion," in the place to which you refer; and only speaks of the other events, as some thing future, shown to Nephi in a Vision, and made known to him by an Angel; and if this is a mark of "fraud," then it is a mark of fraud for Christ to be as a Lamb, slain from the foundation of the World: or for God to have foreknowledge; or for Isa to speak of the Mother of God — "Behold, a Virgin shall conceive." You say, "on page 236, Christ is represented as the grandson of God, he is called 'The Son *of* the only begotten of the Father,' " Here, Mr. S., you have taken advantage of a Typographical error; the word *of* being inserted where it should not, and is corrected in the second edition. Are you so foolish as to think, this was really the sentiment of any people? No: you know better. — It was through malice, you did it. You say the Book admits, that men are liable to mistakes; so it does, and you admit it too; why then take advantage of men's mistakes? But you say, on page 538, we are *commanded* to give thanks to God, that he hath made manifest *its* imperfections. — This, sir, is not so. But Moroni exhorts, rather than *commands*, that we would give thanks unto God, that he had made manifest *his* (not *its*,) imperfections and the imperfections of those who had written before him, that we might learn to be more wise than that which they had been. Now, if you take advantage of such humble acknowledgements, then why not take advantage of David's imperfections, so clearly made manifest in the Psalms, and in his history? Why not take advantage of all wise and good men? for they have all been guilty of some imperfections. And I highly esteem those who are most willing to acknowledge their own, and to forgive those of others, when they are acknowledged in a humble manner: and God loves them too. Yes, Mr. Sunderland, I could take even you, by the hand, and forgive you of your lies, mistakes, blunders, and hard speeches, if you would humbly acknowledge them, and repent: and I am sure God would forgive you too. Your Seventh Number on "Mormonism," is not worthy of any reply, being made up of all manner of evil spoken against us falsely, because of the word of our testimony; and this too, taken from a book falsely called, "Mormonism Unveiled:" — a work got up not only by a most determined enemy, but by one, whose character is so disgusting to every decent, respectable person who knows him, that the Book never had any weight at all in the West, where it was published. — However, I will gather much from your last number in favour of "Mormonism." The Saviour says, "blessed are you when men shall revile you, and cast you out of their company, and say all manner of evil against you falsely, for Christ's sake; rejoice ye in that hour and be exceeding glad; for so persecuted their Fathers, the Prophets, which were before you." Now we will see how much it falls short of all manner of evil.

Fortune telling, money digging, juggling, wicked, cheat, liar; profane, intemperate, quarrelsome, not good character, gold bible company, indolent, lying, notoriously bad, wife whipper, destitute of moral character, visionary, addicted to vicious habits; and add to this catalogue, the ridiculous stories that went the rounds of the religious papers concerning the "Angel Caught;" and the walking on the water story; and the murder story; together with "Adultery," and the love tale of Mr. Smith's stealing his wife; and then the all things common; together with doing away with matrimony; and then the Treason against Government; the stiring up of the Slaves against their Masters; the instigating of the Indians to war and bloodshed; together with driving the inhabitants of Jackson County, Missouri, from their houses and lands, and the taking possession of them by force. — And if it does not amount to all manner of evil, then the imagination of the Priests, and the Devil combined, is not fertile enough to fulfil the prediction of the Saviour, for I am sure they have tortured their thinking powers. — Perhaps they might have added the story of eating their own children; and of their having hairy throats, and but one eye, and that in the middle of their foreheads, &c.; as was said concerning the Waldenses, in the North of France; and of the Primitive Christians. But, however, we are willing to give our enemies the Priests, and others, together with his Satanic

Majesty; great credit, for inventive and fertile imaginations, as well as for great credulity; more especially when we remember that, "Mormonism Unveiled," which is now credited by religious editors in this city, was got up by one D. P. Hulburt, (who was cut off from our society for Adultery, and afterwards put under bonds for threatening the life of Brother Smith,) who was assisted by one Deacon Clapp, who, by the by, became so familiar with Hulburt's wife, that he had some hundred dollars to pay; besides endangering his *Deaconship*.

However, Hulburt being so notorious a character, it was thought best (even after he had advertised in the papers, that he was about to publish "Mormonism Unveiled,") to change authors, and publish under the name of Howe, (a printer in Painesville, Ohio,) whose mind had been somewhat chafed, because his own wife and sister belonged to the church of the Saints; so Howe became the adopted father of "Mormonism Unveiled."

But that ridiculous story, (concerning Solomon Spalding's Manuscript Found, converted, by Sidney Rigdon, into the "Book of Mormon,") published at first as a probability, without a shadow of truth; a lie, which never had any credit among the honest and intelligent part of community in the West, has at last been published in the "New-York Evangelist," "Zion's Watchman," and other religious papers, as an established *fact beyond the possibility of a doubt.* Yes, S. Spalding is like to be set down as the author of the "Book of Mormon," and S. Rigdon as the impostor who palmed S. Spalding's Novel upon the World as a "Religious Work." And many are as willing to believe this lie, as the Jews were, that the disciples had come and stolen the body of Jesus, in order to palm a deception upon that age. Thus they have "strong delusion, that they may believe a lie, that they may all be damned, who believe not the truth, but have the pleasure in unrighteousness." All this I am willing they should enjoy, because the Scriptures must be fulfilled. But for the sake of the honest in heart, who love the truth, I here offer my testimony on this subject; as I was a personal actor in the scenes which brought S. Rigdon into an acquaintance with the "Book of Mormon," and into connection with the Church of Latter Day Saints.

About A.D. 1827, Messrs. A. Campbell, W. Scott, and S. Rigdon, with some others, residing in Virginia, Ohio, &c., came off from the Baptists, and established a new Order, under the name of Reformed Baptist, or Disciples; and they were termed by their enemies, Campbellites, Rigdonites, &c. This reformation, as to its Doctrine, consisted principally, of the Baptism of Repentance, for Remission of Sins, &c. And Mr. Rigdon, in particular, held to a literal fulfilment and application of the written word; and by this means he was an instrument to turn many from the false notions of Sectarian Traditions, to an understanding of the Prophecies, touching the great restoration of Israel, and the mighty revolutions of the last days. Many hundred disciples were gathered by his ministry, throughout the Lake Country of Ohio; and many other preachers stood in connection with him in those principles. I was then pursuing an agricultural life, and mostly occupied in converting the wilderness into a fruitful field; but being a member of the Baptist Church, and a lover of truth, I became acquainted with Mr. Rigdon, and a believer in, and a teacher of the same doctrine. After proclaiming those principles in my own neighborhood and the adjoining country, I at length took a journey to the State of New-York, partly on a visit to Columbia Co., N.Y., my native place: and partly for the purpose of ministering the word. This journey was undertaken in August, 1830. I had no sooner reached Ontario Co. N.Y., than I came in contact with the "Book of Mormon," which had then been published about six months, and had gathered about fifty disciples, which were all that then constituted the Church of the Latter Day Saints. I was greatly prejudiced against the book; but remembering the caution of Paul, "Prove all things and hold fast that which is good," I sat down to read it; and after carefully comparing it with the other Scriptures, and praying to God, He gave me the knowledge of its truth, by the power of the Holy Ghost; and what was I, that I should withstand God? I accordingly obeyed the Ordinances, and was commissioned by Revelation; and the laying of hands to preach the fulness of the gospel. Then, after finishing my visit to Columbia Co., I returned to the brethren in Ontario Co., where for the first time, I saw Mr. Joseph Smith, Jr., who had just returned from Pennsylvania, to his father's house, in Manchester. About the 15th of Oct., 1830, I took my journey, in company with Elder O. Cowdery, and Peter Whitmer, to Ohio. We called on Elder S. Rigdon, and *then* for the *first* time, his eyes beheld the "Book of Mormon;" I, myself, had the happiness to present it to him in person. He was much surprised, and it was with much persuasion and argument, that he was prevailed on to read it, and after he had read it, he had a great struggle of mind, before he fully believed and embraced it; and when finally convinced of its truth, he called together a large congregation of his friends, neighbors, and brethren, and then addressed them very affectionately, for near two hours, during most of which time, both himself and nearly all the congregation were melted into tears. He asked forgiveness of every body who might have had occasion to be offended with any part of his former life; he forgave all who had persecuted or injured him, in any manner; and the next morning, himself and wife, were baptised by elder O. Cowdery. I was present, it was a solemn scene, most of the people were greatly affected: they came out of the water overwhelmed in tears. Many others were baptised by us in that vicinity, both before and after his baptism—insomuch, that during the fall of 1830, and the follow-winter and spring, the number of disciples were increased to about 1000; the Holy Ghost was mightily poured out, and the word of God grew and multiplied; and many priests were obedient to the Faith. Early in 1831, M. Rigdon having been ordained, under *our hands*, visited elder J. Smith, Jr. in the state of New-York, for the first time; and from that time forth, rumor began to circulate, that he (Rigdon) was the *author* of the Book of Mormon. The Spaulding story never was dreamed of until several years afterwards, when it appeared in Mormonism Unveiled—a base forgery, by D. P. Hulburt, and others of similar character, who had long strove to account for the book of Mormon, in some other way beside the truth. In the west, whole neighborhoods embraced Mormonism, after this fable of the Spaulding story, had been circulated among them; indeed, we never conceived it worthy of an answer, until it was *converted* by the ignorant and impudent dupes or knaves, in this city, who stand at the head of certain religious papers, into something said to be *positive, certain*, and not to be disputed! Now I testify that the forgers of the Spaulding lie, (concerning S. Rigdon and others,) are of the same description as those who forged the lie against the disciples of old—accusing them of stealing the body of Jesus, &c. And those who love this lie, are no better. I mean the editors of the N.Y. Evangelist, the Zion's Watchman, and all others who are equally guilty, including all who read and believe such a thing. And except they repent they will have their part with drunkards, whoremongers, sorcerers, thieves, murderers, &c., for being guilty of loving or making a lie; and in that day when the secrets of all hearts shall be made manifest: then shall they know, that these things and many others were base falsehoods, put in circulation by the devil and his servants; and that the Book of Mormon, is a record of eternal truth, which speaks from the dust, as a voice from the dead, bearing record of the Gospel of a crucified and risen Redeemer, reproving the sins of the world, and warning them of the things which must shortly come to pass; therefore, repent, all ye ends of the earth, and be baptised for remission of sins, and you shall receive the gift of the Holy Ghost; and signs shall follow those that believe; and this Gospel of the kingdom shall first be preached among all Nations, and *then shall the Son of Man come*. Amen.

METHODISM.—Having unveiled Mormonism, by removing the covering of lies and misrepresentations, which Mr. Sunderland, a Methodist editor, had thrown over it; we shall now proceed to a short examination of Methodism, as taken from their own discipline.

1st. A description of the Methodist God, as found in the second section of their discipline.

1stly. "There is but one living and true God, everlasting, without *body or parts*."

2ndly. In unity of this Godhead, there are *three* persons of one *substance*, power and eternity; the Father, Son, and Holy Ghost.

3rdly. This, "*Christ*, very *God*, and very *Man*, who truly suffered, was crucified, dead and buried."

4thly. "To reconcile his Father to us," &c.

5thly. "Christ did truly rise again from the dead, and took again his *body*, with all things appertaining to the perfection of man's nature, wherewith he ascended into Heaven."

6thly. "And there sitteth until he return, to *judge all men at the last day*."

I must say, that I never saw such a bundle of nonsense, contradiction and absurdity, thrown together before.

1st. A God *without body or parts*, consisting of three persons.

2nd. One of these persons, who is very God, was crucified, dead and buried, (*without body or parts!*)

3rd. The object was to reconcile his *Father* to *us*, instead of reconciling *us* to the Father; thus conveying the idea, that his Father must be *changed* about, and made a *new creature*, in order to be reconciled to poor sinful mortals, who are unchanged.

4th. This God (without body or parts), arose from the dead, and took upon him his *body*, when he had none; but to cap the climax, he has gone to Heaven, there to remain, till He comes to *judge* the world at the *last day*. Thus contradicting the 3rd, 20th and 21st of Acts, where Peter promises that God will send him again, at the times of restitution of all things spoken by the Prophets; this restitution will be a long time before the *last day*; see Rev. c. 20th, and Zech. 14th.

Here then is the Methodist God, without either eyes, ears or mouth!!! and yet man was created after the *image* of God; but this could not apply to the Methodist God, for he has no *image* or *likeness*! The Methodist God, can neither be Jehovah nor Jesus Christ; for Jehovah shewed his *face* to Moses and seventy elders of Israel, and his *feet* too: he also wrote with his *own finger* on the tablets of stone. Isaiah informs us, that his *arm* is not shortened; that his *ear* is not dull of hearing, &c., and that he will proceed to make bare his *arm* in the eyes of all the nations. And Ezek. says, "his fury shall come up in his *face*," and Zech. c. 14, says "his *feet* shall stand in that day, upon the mount of olives," and they which behold shall say, what are these wounds in thy *hands*, and in thy *feet*. &c. Consequently, Methodism is a system of idolatry.

2ndly. THEIR PRIESTHOOD, was handed down from the Wesleys and others, who received their authority from the Church of England, or nowhere; and the Church of England received their Priesthood from the Church of Rome, or from the King and Parliament, or nowhere; and if from the King and Parliament, or the Church of Rome, then it was not from heaven—but of man. For neither the King, Parliament or Pope, had any more authority in conferring Priesthood, than I have to confer the Sceptre of the Chinese Empire upon the American Chief, Blackhawk. But if they received their Priesthood from the Church of Rome, (the mother of harlots,) then is the English Church, a legitimate daughter of the old lady, and Methodism the *grand daughter*; consequently, Methodism is a harlot. But if the Methodists, claim Priesthood by revelation, I deny the claim, for their God is not capable of giving a revelation, having no mouth! and their discipline forbids later revelation than the Scriptures, and the Scriptures know nothing of Methodist Priests.

3rdly. THEIR ORDINANCES.—1st. *Three* kinds of water baptism, are practiced by them. The Bible knows but *one* kind: see Eph. c. 4.

2nd. They baptise infants, whereas the Gospel requires faith and repentance before baptism: see Acts, c. 2, and v. 28; see also, the Saviour's commission to his Apostles.

3d. They neither lay on hands in the name of Jesus, to heal the sick; nor annoint them with oil in the name of the Lord, that they may be healed; thus neglecting to fulfil the Saviour's directions, in the last chapter of Mark. And James' directions in his writings to the Saints.

4th. The gifts of the Spirit, as spoken of in 1st Cor. c. 12: Eph. c. 4, and many other places, are denied by them, and totally set aside—for instance, Apostles, Prophets, Miracles, Healings, Revelations, Visions, Prophesyings, Tongues, Interpretations, &c. &c.; therefore, they have a *form of Godliness*, denying the *power* and *gifts* of God.

4thly. PRIESTCRAFT, MONEYED PLANS, &c.—See Methodist Discipline, section 5: "*Every Preacher*, who has charge of a circuit, *shall* make a yearly collection; and if expedient, a quarterly one, in *every* congregation." "Men and brethren help! was there ever a call like this since you first heard the Gospel sound?" "A public collection shall be made at every annual, and every general conference." "The annual product of the charter fund." "The profits of the Book-concern." Every annual conference, has full liberty to adopt and recommend, such plans and rules, as to them may appear necessary, the more effectually to raise as to them may appear necessary, the more effectually to raise supplies." "It shall be the duty of each annual conference to take measures from year to year, in *every* circuit and station within its bounds." The foregoing are but a few of the moneyed plans of this vast organization. Their cry is money yearly—money quarterly—money monthly—money weekly—money daily,—money at conference meetings—money at circuit—money in congregation—money at class meetings—money for missions; in short it is money when they lay down, and money when they rise up; It is money that will keep their hands from hanging down, and the work of their God from coming to a dead stand. My readers will perceive, that Mr. Sunderland's out cry against the Mormonite moneyed plan, for the support of their poor, comes with a very ill grace.

Having now proved that Methodism is a system of idolatry; a false and perverted Gospel: a daughter of the great mother of harlots — having a form of godliness, denying the power, as well as a system of priestcraft of the deepest dye.

I now call upon every honest Methodist, to come out from such abominations, and receive the TRUTH; *for her sins have reached unto Heaven, and God hath remembered her iniquities, and her judgements slumber not.* Amen!

MR. SUNDERLAND, — *Sir*: If you wish your readers to come at the truth; to read both sides of the question, and judge for themselves; you will doubtless publish my answer, to your papers on Mormonism in full, in the Zion's Watchman; justice, truth and the common principles of humanity require it; not only does justice to an injured, persecuted and inoffensive people, require it — but your readers, who have been deceived and abused by your falsehoods, slanders and misrepresentations, have claims on you, as their editor, to undeceive them; and you will remember too, that there is a still higher authority, to which all men are amenable, and that these things will stare you in the face, in the day of final retribution, if you repent not. Not only is your own welfare at stake, in time and in eternity, but the souls of thousands who read your paper, and who have not our books to compare with your quotations. With these considerations, I hope to see my answer in your paper, should it not appear, I shall conclude that you prefer the dark rather than the light, and that you dare not lay before your readers a statement of facts, and therefore, shall notice it in my next edition.

I am, respectfully,

{3}

"The Regeneration and Eternal Duration of Matter"

(from *The Millennium, and Other Poems:*
To Which is Annexed, A Treatise on the Regeneration
and Eternal Duration of Matter
[New York: Printed by W. Molineux, 1840])

Matter and Spirit are the two great principles of all existence. Every thing animate and inanimate is composed of one or the other, or both of these eternal principles. I say eternal, because the elements are as durable as the quickening power which exists in them. Matter and spirit are of equal duration: both are self-existent, — they never began to exist, and they never can be annihilated. We do not enter upon this boundless subject as a matter of mere speculative philosophy, calculated in its nature merely to charm the imagination — to interest the curious, or to please the learned. So far from this we consider it a subject of deep and thrilling interest to all the human family. A subject equally interesting to Jew, and Christian; Mohammedan and Pagan; the wise and the simple; the learned, and the ignorant — all — all are journeying swiftly through time and are bound to eternity. All are lovers of life and happiness; all are looking forward with inexpressible anxiety to the unexplored regions of futurity.

THE JEW, as he follows his aged parent, his bosom friend, or his tender offspring to the sepulchre of his fathers, while his bosom heaves with anguish, grief and sorrow, is still comforted with sure and certain hope of their being raised from the dead with the whole of Israel's race, and clothed upon with flesh; and of their being restored again to that land which was given to them and their fathers for an everlasting inheritance: while David takes his seat in the holy city and reigns over the twelve tribes forever and ever.

THE MODERN CHRISTIAN when called upon to endure the pangs of grief and sorrow, in following to the grave his nearest friends, is comforted with the hope of a spiritual existence, in a world far distant from his native earth; and far beyond the bounds of time and space, where spirits mingle in eternal joy and everlasting song; and although the body should rise from the dead, yet they suppose that the whole will become spirit unconnected with matter, and soar away to worlds on high, free from all elements of which their nature was composed in this life; and thus enjoy eternal life and happiness, while matter,

Animate and inanimate shall cease to be;

And no more place be found for Heaven, Earth, or Sea.—

THE MAHOMMEDAN is equally subject to all the heart-rendering grief and anguish, which others feel at the loss of friends; but comforts himself with the thoughts of one day gaining a paradise of sensual pleasures; where, with all his faithful friends, he expects to bask forever in all the enjoyments of sensuality. He dreams of trees loaded with delicious fruits, and bending their branches invitingly to his appetite;—and of gardens and pleasure grounds, adorned with pleasant walks—with cooling shades and with blooming sweets which perfume the air; and surrounded with fields of spices more delicious than all the productions of Arabia: while his golden palaces and seraglios are thronged with myriads of delightful virgins, more pure and beautiful than the fairest daughters of Circassia. With these he hopes to spend a life of pleasures forevermore.

THE PAGAN too, in turn, when bowed down with grief and sorrow, finds some relief in anticipation of a future existence—some shady forest filled with game—some delightful prairie of blooming flowers—some humble heaven behind the cloud-topped hill, where he hopes to join his wife, his children, his brothers, his fathers; and in their society to spend a peaceful eternity in all the enjoyments of domestic life, while his faithful horse and dog shall bear him company. These are the hopes and anticipations which serve to dry his tears,—calm his heaving bosom, and to his troubled spirit whisper peace. How desirable then is a just and correct knowledge on this all-important subject. Who does not desire to become acquainted as far as possible with the nature of that eternal state of existence to which we are all hastening? We are dependent alone on the light of revelation and reason, for any just and correct information on this subject. Moses, in his account of the creation, commences thus: [Publisher's note: the Hebrew text is omitted here.]

Which may with propriety be translated thus: "In the beginning God made (or formed) the heavens and the earth, and the earth she was empty and desolate; and darkness upon the faces of the abyss; and the wind of God was brooding over the faces of the waters."

Moses did not see fit to inform us of what kind of materials the Lord formed the earth, and indeed there was no need of revelation to guide us on that subject; for we see for ourselves that it is composed of the common elements which constitute matter in general, and of course this element or matter already existed, and that too in sufficient quantity for the formation of a globe like this. From the Mosaic account of the creation, many have gathered the idea that God created all things out of nonentity,—that solid matter sprung from nothing. But this is for want of reflection, or an exercise of reason on the subject; for instance, when a child inquires of its father, saying, father, who made this house? the father replies, the carpenter made it. Again the child inquires, who made me? the father replies, the Lord made you. Again, the child inquires, who made the earth? the father replies, the Lord made the earth, and all things upon the face thereof. Now the child might suppose that the carpenter created the house without any materials; that he brought it into existence from nothing; and so, with equal propriety, he might suppose that he was formed from nothing; when in fact he was formed of materials which grew out of the earth. And with the same degree of impropriety we might suppose that God made the earth from nothing when in fact he made it out of self-existing element.

It is impossible for a mechanic to make any thing whatever without materials. So it is equally impossible for God to bring forth matter from nonentity, or to originate element from nothing, because this would contradict the law of truth, and destroy himself. We might as well say, that God can add two and three together, and the product will be twelve: or that he can subtract five from ten and leave eight, as to say that he can originate matter from nonentity; because these are principles of eternal truth, they are laws which cannot be broken, that two and three are five, that five from ten leaves five, and that nought from nought leaves nought; and a hundred noughts added together is nothing still. In all these, the product is determined by unchangeable laws, whether the reckoning be calculated by the Almighty, or by man, the result is precisely the same.

Here then, is mathematical demonstration that it is not in the power of any being to orginate matter. Hence we conclude that matter as well as spirit is eternal, uncreated, self-existing. However infinite the variety of its changes, forms and shapes; — however vast and varying the parts it has to act in the great theatre of the universe; — whatever sphere its several parts may be destined to fill in the boundless organization of infinite wisdom, yet it is there, durable as the throne of Jehovah. And ETERNITY is inscribed in indelible characters on every particle. Revolution may succeed revolution, — vegetation may bloom and flourish, and fall again to decay in the revolving seasons — generation upon generation may pass away and others will succeed — empires may fall to ruin, and moulder to the dust and be forgotten — the marble monuments of antiquity may crumble to atoms and mingle in the common ruin — the mightiest works of art, with all their glory, may sink in oblivion and be remembered no more — worlds may startle from their orbits, and hurling from their spheres, run lawless on each other in conceivable confusion — element may war with element in awful majesty, while thunders roll from sky to sky, and arrows of lightning break the mountains asunder — scatter the rocks like hailstones — set worlds on fire, and melt the elements with fervent heat, and yet not one grain can be lost — not one particle can be annihilated. All these revolutions and convulsions of nature will only serve to refine, purify, and finally restore and renew the elements upon which they act. And like the sunshine after a storm, or like gold seven times tried in the fire, they will shine forth with additional lustre as they roll in their eternal spheres, in their glory, in the midst of the power of God.

When in the progress of the endless works of Deity, the full time had arrived for infinite wisdom to organize this sphere, and its attendant worlds, and to set them in motion in their order amid the vast machinery of the universe, — when first the morning stars sang together, and all the sons of God shouted for joy, at the grand occasion of the acquisition of a new system to the boundless variety of his works, all was pronounced very good. The waters, obedient to his word, retired within their respective limits, and filled with the quickening, or life-giving principle, which we call spirit, they produced living creatures in abundance, and very soon the vast deep was found teeming with animal life in countless variety, and in regular graduation, from the monster Leviathan to the shell-fish; or descending down the scale of existence to the minutest speck which is only to be discerned by the aid of powerful glasses. The air swarmed with an almost infinite variety of animal life, from the lofty and aspiring eagle which soars on high, and seems to dip his wing in ether blue, to the humming bird which darts from flower to flower, and hides itself amid the blooming sweets of spring, or descending still, to the puny nations of insects which swarm in clouds of blue on summer breath of morn: all, all the air seemed life and happiness.

THE DRY LAND, organized in its own proper sphere, presented a surface every where well watered, abounded in springs, streams and rivulets, and uninterrupted by any of the rough, broken rugged deformities which now present themselves on every side. Its surface was smooth, or gently undulating, and delightfully varied. Its soul enriched by the dew of heaven, and impregnated with the spirit of animal and vegetable life, soon poured forth a luxuriant growth, not of noxious weeds, and thorns and thistles, but of fruit trees, and herbs, all useful for the food of man or animal, fowl or creeping thing, And soon, too, it brought forth from its bosom every varied species of the animal race, from the ponderous mammoth or the mighty elephant, down to the mole; or descending still in the scale of existence, to the smallest creeping thing that specks the surface of the rock, or mantles the standing pool with varied life.

ITS CLIMATE, free, alike from the noxious vapors and melting heats of the torrid zone, and the chilling blasts of the polar regions, was delightfully varied by the moderate changes of heat and cold which only tended to crown the varied year with the greater variety of productions. Streams of life, and odors of healthful sweets came floating on every breeze. Thus earth so lately a vast scene of emptiness and desolation, burst from its solitude arrayed in its robes of splendor; and where silence had reigned through the vast expanse, innumerable sounds now reverberated on the air, and melting strains of music re-echoing in the distant groves, stole upon the ears of admiring angels, and proclaimed the gladsome news of a new world of animated life and joy.

Thus all was prepared and finished, and creation complete. All save the great masterpiece, the head and governor, who was destined to rule or preside over this new kingdom. This personage, designed as the noblest of all the works of Deity, was formed of earth by the immediate hand of God; being fashioned in the express likeness and image of the Father and the Son, while the breath of the Almighty breathed into his nostrils, — quickened him with life and animation. Thus formed of noble principles, and bearing in his godlike features the emblems of authority and dominion, he was placed on the throne of power, in the midst of the paradise of God, and to him was committed power, and glory, and dominion, and the kingdom, and the greatness of the kingdom under the whole heaven. From the bosom of this noble being, or rather from his side emanated woman. She being composed or fashioned from his bone and from his flesh, and undergoing another process of refinement in her formation she became more exquisitely fine, beautiful and delightsome; combining in her person and features the noble and majestic expression of manhood, with the soft and gentle, the modest and retiring graces of angelic sweetness and purity, as if destined to grace the dignity of manhood, — to heighten the charms of domestic life, — to delight the heart of her lord, and to share with him the enjoyments of life, as well as to nourish and sustain the embryo, and rear the tender offspring of her species, and thus fill the earth with myriads of happy and intelligent beings. O reader, contemplate with me the beauty, the glory, the excellence, the perfection of the works of creation as they rolled from the hand of omnipotent power and wisdom, and were pronounced good — very good, by him whose hand had formed them, and whose eye surveyed them at a single glance. Tell me, O man, which of all these works was formed for decay? and which in themselves possessed the seeds of mortality, the principles of dissolution and destruction? Tell me, was there any curse, or poison, or death inherent in or appertaining to any department of existing matter? Tell me, were any of these works so calculated in their physical construction as to be incapable of eternal duration? Was there any death, or sorrow, pain or sickness, sighing, groaning, tears or weeping? Was there any thing to hurt or destroy in all the holy mountain? The answer to all these questions is plain, positive and definite, if the sacred writings may be relied on as decisive evidence. We are informed in scripture that sin entered into the world, and DEATH by sin. That by one man came death, and that the devil had the power of death. We are also informed that the ground was cursed for man's sake, and its productions materially changed. In short, the great head and ruler, with his fair consort were subjected to many curses and troubles while in life, and with them all the productions of the animal and vegetable kingdoms together with the earth itself were subjected to the dominion of the curse. Thus creation felt the blow to its utmost verge, and has groaned in pain for deliverance until now. From all these declarations of holy writ, and from many other proofs which might easily be adduced, we feel ourselves safe in saying that SIN is the sole cause of decay, or death. If there had been no sin, there would have been no death, no dissolution, no disorganization, no decay, no sorrow and groaning, tears or weeping; neither would there have been any pain, but creation would have continued in the same state to an endless duration. O sin, what hast thou done! Thou hast hurled man from his blissful domain, and hast reduced him from a throne of power and dominion to a state of servitude, where sunk in sorrow and misery, he groans out a wretched existence, which terminates in painful dissolution, and he mingles with his mother earth and is forgotten and lost amid the general ruin.

Thou hast converted a garden of delicious fruits and blooming flowers into a gloomy forest of thorns and thistles. Thou hast transformed a world of life, joy and happiness into the abodes of wretchedness and misery, where sighing, groaning, tears and weeping are mingled in almost every cup. By thee the earth has been filled with violence and oppression; and man, moved by hatred, envy, avarice or ambition, has often imbrued his hands in the blood of his fellow man, by which the fairest portions of the earth have been made desolate, — the abodes of domestic happiness turned to sorrow and loneliness, — the happy wife and tender offspring have become widows and orphans, — the bride has been left to mourn in irretrievable anguish, and the virgin to drop a silent tear over the ruined fragments of departed loveliness. By thee the world has been deluged with a flood of waters, and unnumbered millions swept at once from the stage of action and mingled in the common ruin, unwept and unlamented save by the tears of heaven, or by the eight solitary inhabitants of the ark who alone escaped to tell the news. By thy ravages empires have fallen to ruin, and cities become heaps. The fruitful plains of Shinar, and the splendid palaces of Babylon have been doomed to perpetual waste and irretrieval desolation, never to be inhabited; not even as a temporary residence of the wandering Arab. (And the Arabian shall not pitch tent there. See Isaiah XIII, 20) By thee the cities of Sodom and Gomorrah, and the flourishing country about them, once extremely fertile, and watered as the garden of Eden, have been desolated by fire, and perhaps overwhelmed by a sea of stagnant waters. By thee the land of Edom, once a flourishing empire, possessing a productive and well cultivated soil, and every where adorned with flourishing villages, and splendid cities, has become desolate, without inhabitants; and the Lord has cast upon it the stones of emptiness, and the line of confusion. It has lain waste from generation to generation, as a haunt for wild beasts of the desert, a court for owls, and a place for the cormorant and bittern. On account of thee, the city of Jerusalem has long lain in ruins, the land of Judea is desolate, and their holy and beautiful house where their fathers praised Jehovah is burned with fire; while the Jews have long remained in exile among the nations, in fulfilment of that awful imprecation "his blood be upon us and our children." By thy power the once mighty empires of Greece and Rome have been shaken to the centre, and have fallen to rise no more; and before thy desolating blast, almost innumerable provinces lay in ruin. The waste deserts of burning sand — the sunken and stagnant lakes and miry swamps — the innumerable rockey barrens and mountainous steeps — the desolate and dreary wastes of the polar regions — these all present but so many monuments to thy memory — they speak in language not to be misunderstood, that sin has been there, with its dreadful train of curses, under which they groan in pain to be delivered.

The solid rocks have burst asunder at thy withering touch; they have been rent in twain, and hurled from their firm foundations by thy mighty power: and they lay scattered in broken fragments and ruined heaps as monuments of agonizing nature; and as a testimony of the heaving sighs, the convulsive quakings, and dreadful groanings of the earth itself, while by wicked hands the great Messiah was slain. And what shall I say more? for the time would fail me to innumerate the evils of intemperance, dissipation, debauchery, pride, luxury, idleness, extravagance, avarice and ambition, hatred and envy, priestcraft and persecution, with all their attendant train of troubles, miseries, pains, diseases and deaths; which have all contributed to reduce mankind to a state of wretchedness and sorrow indescribable. The noble and majestic features of manhood have often been transformed by these vices into the frightful and disgusting image of demoniac furies, — the angelic beauties of earth's fairest daughters as often transformed by vice into objects of mingled pity and contempt: but cease my soul, no longer dwell on these awful scenes; my heart is faint, my soul is sick, my spirit grieves within me; and mine eyes are suffused with tears while contemplating upon the scenes of wretchedness and misery which sin has produced in our world. O misery, how hast thou triumphed! O death, how many are thy victories! thrones, and dominions — principalities and powers — kingdoms and empires have sunk beneath thine all conquering arm, —

their kings and their nobles, their princes and their lords, — their orators and statesmen, beneath the blast of thy breath have found one common grave.

The dignity of age, — the playful innocence of youth, or the charms of beauty cannot save from thy cruel grasp, — thou hast swallowed up the nations as water, and thou art an hungered still, — thou hast drunk rivers of blood, and hast bathed in oceans of tears, and thy thirst is still raging with unabating fury. Whither, — ah whither shall I turn for comfort? in what secret chamber shall I hide myself to elude thy swift pursuit? If I would heap up gold as dust I cannot bribe thee. If I would fortify my habitation with the munitions of rocks, thine arrows would pierce them as the spider's web, and find their way to my heart. If I would soar on high as the eagle, or fly to the most secret haunts of the desert, or hide myself in the gloomy thicket with the solitary bird of night; or retire with the bat, to the inmost recesses of the cavern, yet thy footsteps would pursue me, any thy vigilence would search me out. No arguments of the wise — no talents of the eloquent can prevail with thee. The tears of the widow, the cries of the fatherless; or the broken hearted anguish of the lover cannot move thee to pity: thou mockest at the groans and tears of humanity, thou scornest the pure affections of love and tenderness; and thou delightest to tear asunder the silken cords of conjugal affections, and all the tender ties of love and endearment which twine around the virtuous heart, and which serve to cement society, and to administer joy and happiness in every department of life. What mighty power shall check thy grand career, and set bounds o'er which thou canst not pass? Whose mighty voice shall command, saying "thus far, no farther shalt thou go, and here let thy proud waves be stayed?" What almighty conqueror shall lead thee captive — shall burst thy chains — throw open the doors of thy gloomy cells, and set the unnumbered millions of thy prisoners free? — who shail bind up the broken hearted — comfort the mourners — dry the tears of sorrow — open the prison to them that are bound set the captives free — make an end of sin and oppression — bring in everlasting righteousness — swallow up death in victory — restore creation to its primative beauty, glory, excellence, and perfection; "and distroy him who has the power of death, that is the Devil, and deliver those who through fear of death were all their lifetime subject to bondage?" but hark —

> On the plains of Judea me thinks I hear
> The melting strains of the lonely shepherd's
> Midnight song, as it echoes among the hills
> And vales, and dies away in the distance.

Its heavenly melody betokens
A theme of joy such as the sons of earth
Have seldom heard, — some heavenly theme as if
The choirs of angels — mingling their music
With the sons of earth, conspired to celebrate
Some new event — some jubilee of rest —
Some grand release form servitude and woe.
    But see — ah see! the opening heavens around
Them shine; a glorious train of angels bright,
Ascending, fill the air: — it is indeed
A more than mortal theme. But hark again —
Me thinks I understand the words, — they
Celebrate the birth of king Messiah,
The mighty prince who soon shall conquer death
With all his legions, and reign triumphant
Over all, as king of kings, and Lord of lords.
Their chorus ends with peace on earth, good will
To men. O monster death I now behold
Thy conquerer! Jesus of Nazareth —
The babe of Bethlehem — the son of God.

He comes to earth, and takes upon him flesh and blood, — even the seed of Abraham; and this for the express purpose of conquering sin and death, and restoring a lost and fallen world to its former perfection that it may be capable of eternal life and happiness.

"As in Adam all die even so in Christ shall all be made alive." Now let the reader endeavour in particular to understand the precise object of the mission of Jesus Christ into our world; and what was to be accomplished by his death and resurrection. We have already endeavoured to show the effect of Adam's transgression in a physical as well as moral point of view; we have seen that sin materially affected the earth itself, as well as all its animal and vegetable productions. Now the object of a Saviour to bleed and die as a sacrifice and atonement for sin, was not only to redeem man in a moral sense, from his lost and fallen state, but it was also to restore the physical world from all the effects of the fall; to purify the elements; and to present the earth in spotless purity, before the throne of God, clothed in celestial glory, as a fit inheritance for the ransomed throng who are destined to inherit it in eternity. If the question be asked for what Christ died? the answer is first, he died for all of Adam's race. Secondly, for all the animal and vegetable productions of the earth, as far as they were affected by the fall of man. The lion, the wolf; the leopard and the bear; and even the serpent, will finally feel and enjoy the effects of this great restoration, precisely in the same degree in which they were affected by the fall. Thirdly, Christ died for the earth itself, to redeem it from all the effects of the fall, that it might be cleansed from sin and have eternal life. Now this atonement which was made by Jesus Christ was universal, so far as it relates to the effects of Adam's transgression: and this without any conditions on the part of the creature. All that was lost, or in the least affected by the fall of man, will finally be restored by Jesus Christ, — the whole creation will be delivered from its dreadful curse, and all mankind redeemed from death, and all the dreadful effects of the transgression of their first parents; and this without any conditions of faith and repentance; or any act on the part of the creature; for precisely what is lost in Adam's transgression without our agency, is restored by Jesus Christ without our agency. Thus all will be raised from the dead, and the body and the spirit will be reunited, the whole will become immortal, no more to be separated, or to undergo dissolution. This salvation being universal, I am a universalist in this respect, — this salvation being a universal restoration from the fall, I am a restorationer, — this salvation being without works, or without any conditions except the atonement of Jesus Christ, I am in this respect a believer in free grace alone, without works; this salvation, redeeming all infants from original sin, without any change of heart, newbirth, or baptism, and the infant, not being capable of actual transgression, and needing no salvation from any personal sin, is therefore in a state of salvation, and not of depravity; and therefore of such is the kingdom of God: and in their infancy they need no ordinances, or gospel to save them, for they are already saved through the atonement, therefore the gospel and its ordinances are only for those who have come to years of understanding. But while on the subject of redemption, I must not pass without noticing another and very different part of the subject, viz — After all men are redeemed from the fall and raised from the dead, their spirits and bodies being reunited and the whole becoming eternal no more to see corruption, they are to be judged according to their own individual deeds done in the body; not according to Adam's transgression; nor according to sovereign, unconditional grace. Here ends, universalism; here ends Calvinism; here ends salvation without works — here is introduced the necessity of a salvation from actual sin, — from individual transgression, from which no man can be redeemed short of the blood of Jesus Christ applied to each individual transgressor; and which can only be applied on the conditions of faith, repentance, and obedience to the gospel. Now all who neglect to fulfill the conditions of the gospel, will be condemned at the judgment day, not for Adam's fall but for their own sins. But as our subject is more particularly confined to the salvation and durability of the physical world, the renovation and regeneration to a state of eternal and unchangeable purity, we must leave the further prosecution of these often contested points of theology to be perused in their usual channel, and come directly to the merits of the great subject which we have undertaken. Let us now examine, more closely the physical structure and properties of the resurrected, immortal body; endeavour to ascertain in positive, definite terms, whether it does really consist of flesh and bones, — of matter as well as spirit: and if so, endeavour to learn something of its place of residence or final destiny. Christ being the first fruits from the dead, and the only person whose history after their resurrection has come down to us; and he being the great head and pattern of the resurrection, we shall endeavour to ascertain all the particulars which will serve to throw light on the subject, as to the physical nature of his body, both before and after he arose from the dead. His mother was a virgin, a chosen vessel of the Lord, who conceived by the power of the Holy Ghost and brought forth a child, who was composed of flesh and blood; and in his physical organization differing nothing in any respect from the other seed of Abraham. Like other children in their infant state, he no doubt received his nourishment from the breasts of his mother; like all others, he was helpless and dependent for care and protection on his parents, who by the command of God fled into Egypt in order to preserve him from the cruel sword of Herod, who feared a rival in the person of the babe of Bethlehem: like all others he grew in stature by means of the food received into the stomach, and its strength diffused through the physical system; and when grown to manhood his system was composed of the same earthly particles, or the same elements which constitute the human system in general. He was every way subject to the infirmities, passions, pleasures, pains, griefs, sorrows and temptations which are common to the constitution of man; hence we find him sorrowing, weeping, mourning, rejoicing, lamenting, grieving, as well as suffering hunger, thirst, fatigue, temptation, etc. and we also find him possessed of the most refined sensibilities of natural affection, and susceptibilities for close and intimate friendship. This is abundantly illustrated in his close and intimate friendship with Lazarus of Bethany, and his kind-hearted and benevolent sisters, Martha and Mary. He wept with the tears of fond affection over the grave of his departed friend Lazarus, and mingled his tears with the sorrowful and disconsolate sisters, as if to sympathize with them and help to bear their grief, insomuch that the Jews exclaimed, "behold how be loved him." Another striking example of this natural affection is illustrated in his close intimacy with his beloved disciple John. This apostle was at supper; and who was employed to ask questions on subjects in which the others felt a delicacy: he is frequently called "that disciple whom Jesus loved." Now we must think that Jesus loved them all as disciples and followers of the Lamb; but as to a natural affection John was his peculiar favorite; to him he committed his sorrowing and disconsolate mother, as he was about to expire on the cross, and from that time, Mary, the mother of Jesus, became a member of John's family. "He took her home to his own house." Jesus having taken affectionate leave of his sorrowing friends, at length yielded up the ghost, and his disembodied spirit took its rest in paradise; while his lifeless corpse was carefully wrapped in linen and laid in a sepulchre; but for fear of some imposition being practised by his disconsolate and sorrowing disciples, the door of the sepulchre was secured with a great stone, and sealed with the initials of kingly authority, besides a strong guard of Roman soldiers who watched around the door by day and by night. But early on the morning of the third day, an angel descended, at the glory of whose presence the soldiers fell back as dead men. The seal was broken, the great stone rolled away, the door of the sepulchre was opened, and his body re-animated by the returning spirit, awoke from its slumbers and came forth in triumph from the mansions of the dead. Now when his friends and disciples came to the sepulchre and found not his body but saw his grave clothes lying useless, they were troubled, supposing that he had been moved to some other place; but the angel of the Lord said unto them: "He is not here, but is risen," and called them to come and see the place where he had lain. Now let us bear in mind, that it was the same corporeal system—the same flesh and bones, which had yielded up the ghost on the cross, and which had been wrapped in linen and laid in the tomb, that now came forth from the dead, to die no more. Now in order to assist his disciples in understanding this subject, that they might know the difference between disembodied spirits and resurrected bodies, he not only ate and drank with them, but called upon them to handle him and see; for said he, "A spirit hath not flesh and bones as ye see me have." On another occasion, he exhibited his wounded side and hands, and called upon Thomas to put his finger into the prints of the nails, and to thrust his hand into his side, where once the spear had pierced; and finally after being seen of them forty days, he led them out as far as Bethany, and there he was taken up into heaven from their presence, and a cloud received him out of their sight.

Now let us inquire, what was the physical difference between the mortal body of Jesus Christ and his resurrected body? They are both the same flesh, the same bones, the same joints, the same sinews, the same skin, the same hair, the same likeness, or physical features, and the same element, or matter; but the former was quickened by the principles of the natural life, which was the blood, and the latter is quickened solely by the spirit, and not by blood, and therefore is not subject unto death, but lives forevermore. With this glorious body he ascended to the Father, and with this glorious body he will come again to earth to reign with his people. This view of the resurrection is clearly exemplified in the persons of Enoch and Elijah, who never tasted death, but were changed instantaneously from mortal to immortal, and were caught up into the heavens, both body and spirit. This change upon their physical systems was equivalent to death and the resurrection. It was the same as if they had slept in the grave for thousands of years and then been raised and restored to eternal life. When Elijah, for instance, was taken into the chariot of fire, and carried from the presence of Elisha he did not drop his body, but only his mantle; for if he had dropped his body, the sons of the prophets would have attended to his burial, instead of ranging the mountains in search of him. This same subject is made equally plain in the writings of Job, who declares, saying: "I know that my Redeemer lives, and that he will stand in the latter day upon earth: and though after my skin worms destroy this body, yet in my FLESH shall I see God." The Jewish prophets also understood this matter in its clearest light. Isaiah declares, "Thy dead men shall live, — together with my DEAD BODY shall they rise." Daniel speaks plainly of the awaking of them that sleep in the dust. Ezekiel illustrates the subject very clearly in his vision of the dry bones. (See Ezekiel xxxvii.) He not only mentions their being raised from the dead, but the bones, the sinews, the flesh, the skin, and the spirit by which they will be re-animated, are all brought to view in a clear, plain, and positive manner. The writings of the Apostles abound with clear elucidations of the physical nature of the resurrection: for on this one point, depended the whole foundation of the christian system. Hence Paul argues, that if there is no resurrection, then Christ is not risen; and if Christ be not risen, then their preaching was vain; and their faith and joy was vain; they were yet in their sins, and the apostles were false witnesses; and they were of all men most miserable. But there is one view which Paul takes of the subject, that will serve to carry out our present theory in a most conclusive manner. It is this: in opening to his disciples the mysteries of the second advent of the Messiah, and the great restitution of all things spoken by the prophets, he declares, that the saints would not all sleep, (in death,) but that they which were alive and remained until the coming of Christ, should be changed in a moment, in the twinkling of an eye, and be caught up to meet the Lord in the air, and so should be forever with him. Here then, is demonstration, that tens of thousands of the saints, — indeed all the saints who live at a certain period of time will be translated after the pattern of Enoch and Elijah, and their spirits and bodies never be separated by death! Such then is the resurrection; and such the lively views which inspired the prophets, apostles and saints of former times, and having this hope they could with propriety say, "O death, where is thy sting; O grave, where is thy victory?" O, the deep-rooted blindness of early tradition and superstition, how art thou interwoven with all our powers of intellect! and how hast thou benumbed and blunted every faculty of our understanding. From early youth the principles have been instilled into our minds that all must die and moulder to corruption—that Enoch and Elijah were the only persons who were, or ever would be translated without seeing death, when in fact, tens of thousands, as I said before, are yet to arrive by faith to this inconceivable fullness and consummation of eternal life and happiness without tasting death, and without even a momentary separation of soul and body; the transition from mortality to immortality being instantaneous. And yet, strange as it may seem, none will ever attain to this blessing except such as firmly believe in and expect it, for, like all other blessings, it is only to be obtained by faith and prayer. But how shall we believe in and seek for a blessing of which we have no idea? or how shall we believe in that which we have not heard, and how shall we hear without a teacher?

From all these considerations it appears evident that these principles must necessarily be revived so as to become a conspicuous part of modern theology. They must be taught to the people, and the people must believe them; insomuch that every saint on earth will be looking for the great day of the Lord, and expecting to be caught up to meet him in the air; for if the great day of the Lord should come at a time when these principles were neither taught nor believed, surely there would be none prepared for translation: consequently there would be no saints to be caught up to meet the Lord in the air; and if so, the words of the Lord by Paul would become of none effect. I have made the above remarks in order to impress deeply upon the minds of our modern teachers and learners the importance of arousing from the slumber of ages on this subject, and of ceasing to teach and impress upon the youthful mind the gloomy thoughts of death, and the melancholy forebodings of a long slumber in the grave, in order in inspire them with solemn fear and dread, and thus move them to the duties of religion and morality. Experience has proved, in innumerable instances, that this course is insufficient to restrain vice, and to lead to the practice of virtue and religion. The wayward and buoyant spirits of youth feel weighed down and oppressed, when oft reminded of such gloomy and melancholy subjects. All the more cheerful faculties of the soul are thus paralyzed, or more or less obstructed in their operations; the fine toned energies of the mind cease to act with their accustomed vigor, the charms of nature seem clothed in mourning and sackcloth. We conceive a distaste for the duties as well as the enjoyments of life. Courage, fortitude, ambition, and all the stimulants which move man to act well his part in human society, are impaired and weakened in their operations, and the mind, thus soured and sickened, finds itself sinking under deep melancholy and settled gloom, which soon becomes insupportable. He at length sinks in despair,—becomes insane, or groans under various diseases brought upon his physical system by the anguish of his mind; or, with a desperate effort, tears himself from friends and society, and from all the social duties and enjoyments of life, to lead a life of solitude within the walls of a convent, or in the gloomy caverns of the monk. But more frequently the youthful mind when laboring under these gloomy impressions makes a desperate effort to free itself from its dreadful burden, by plunging into all the allurements of vice and dissipation; endeavoring by these means to drive from them the memory all those gloomy impressions, and to lose sight of, or cease to realize, the sure and certain approach of death.

Let us then cease to give lessons on death and the grave to the rising generation, and confine ourselves more exclusively to the proclamation of eternal life. What a glorious field in intelligence now lies before us, yet but partially explored. What a boundless expanse for contemplation and reflection now opens to our astonished vision. What an intellectual banquet spreads itself invitingly to our appetite, calling into lively exercise every power and faculty of the mind, and giving full scope to all the great and ennobling passions of the soul. Love, joy, hope, ambition, faith, and all the virtuous principles of the human mind may here expand and grow, and flourish, unchecked by any painful emotions or gloomy fears. Here the youthful mind may expand its utmost energies, and revel, uncontrolled by remorse, unchecked by time or decay, in the never-fading sweets of eternity, and bask forever in the boundless ocean of delight.

This course of instruction followed out in demonstration of the spirit and of power, would serve to check the allurements of vice, and would greatly tend to lead and encourage the mind in the practise of virtue and religion, and would cheer and stimulate the saint in all the laborious duties of life. It would remove the fear and dread of death. It would bind up the broken hearted, and administer consolation to the afflicted. It would enable man to endure with patience and fortitude all the multiplied afflictions, misfortunes and ills to which they are subject in this momentary life. It would almost banish the baneful effects of fear and gloom, and melancholy from the earth, and thus give new tone and energy to all the various departments of society. The long night of darkness and superstition is now far spent. The truth, revived in its primitive simplicity and purity like the day star of the horizon, lights up the dawn of the effulgent morn when the knowledge of God will cover the earth as the waters cover the sea. With what propriety then, may the rising generation look forward with a well grounded hope, that they or their children may be of that unspeakable happy number who will live to be caught up to meet the Lord in the air, and like Enoch and Elijah, escape the pangs of dissolution, and the long imprisonment of the grave. Or, with still more certainty, they may hope that if they sleep in the dust, it will only be of short duration, and then they will rise again to enjoy the pleasures of life for evermore. Parents, do you love your children? Does it grieve you to see their lifeless bodies laid in the tomb, and shut, as it were, forever from your society? Children, have you ever been called to bid farewell to your beloved and venerable parents, and to grieve with heart-broken anguish, as their bodies were deposited in the cold and silent grave, and you left as orphans upon the dreary world? Husbands and wives, do you love your companions, and often wish that you both might live in the body forever, and enjoy each other's society, without undergoing a painful separation by the monster, death? Be careful, then, to secure a part in the first resurrection, that you, and your friends may live and reign with Christ on earth a thousand years.

O thou broken hearted and disconsolate widow, thou hast been called to part with the bosom friend of thy youth, and to see thy beloved shut from thy presence in the dreary mansions of the dead. Have you ever been comforted with the reflection that the tomb will burst asunder in the morning of the resurrection, — that these once active limbs, now cold in death, — these bones and joints, and sinews, with the flesh and skin will come forth, and be again quickened with the spirit of life and motion; and that this cold and silent bosom will again beat with the most animated and happy sensations of pure love and kindred affection?

Parents and children, husbands and wives, brothers and sisters, have these thoughts sunk deep into your hearts in the hour of sorrow, and served to comfort, to soothe and support your sinking spirits in the hour of keenest distress? or have you imagined to yourselves some spiritual existence beyond the bounds of time and space; some shadow without substance, some fairy world of spirits bright far from earth your native home; and at a distance from all the associations, affections and endearments which are interwoven with your very existence here; and in which were mingled all the sweets of life? No wonder then, that such should cling to life, and shrink from death with terror and dismay: no wonder that such should feel insupportable and overwhelming grief at the loss of friends; for who can bear the thoughts of eternal separation from those lovely scenes with which they have been accustomed to associate from early infancy? Who can endure to be torn from those they love dearer than life, and to have all the tender cords of affection which twine around the heart with mutual endearment, severed and destroyed for ever?

Let us then endeavour to inspire the minds of those who are placed under our care and instruction, with a firm faith in and lively sense of this the most important of all subjects, the resurrection of the body, and eternal life; and thus encourage them with the greatest of all inducements to lead a life of righteousness, such as will secure to them a part in the first resurrection, and a happy immortality in the society and friendship of the ransomed throng who are arrayed in spotless white, and who reign on earth with the blessed Redeemer.

Having now shown clearly that the resurrection of the body is a complete restoration and reorganization of the physical system of man; and that the elements of which his body is composed are eternal in their duration; and that they form the tabernacle—the everlasting habitation of that spirit which animated them in this life; and that the spirits and bodies of men are of equal importance and destined to form an eternal and inseparable union with each other; we must now return to research, as to the final destiny of the earth and its productions of animal and vegetable life.

We have already shown that the earth itself, and all its productions were deeply affected by the fall, and by the sins of the children of men: that the atonement which was made by Jesus Christ was not only for man, but also for the earth and all the fulness thereof: that all things were redeemed from the fall, and would finally be restored from all the dreadful effects thereof; and be regenerated, sanctified and renewed after the pattern, and in the likeness and image of its first creation; partaking of the same beauty, glory, excellence and perfection it had in the beginning. But it is evident that this restitution did not take place at the first advent of the Messiah; and that it has not taken place at any time since: therefore it is yet future, and must be fulfilled at a certain time which is appointed by infinite wisdom. This certain time is called in holy writ, "the times of restitution of all things which God hath spoken by the mouth of all his holy prophets since the world began." Now this restitution is to be accomplished by nothing short of a second advent of the Messiah. He must again descend from heaven to earth in like manner as he ascended. This second advent of Messiah, and the grand events connected with it is a theme which all the prophets and apostles have dwelt on more fully in their writings than they have on any other subject whatever. If I would quote proofs on this subject, I might begin with Enoch the seventh from Adam, who exclaims, "Behold the Lord cometh with ten thousand of his saints," etc. and end with the revelation of Jesus Christ to his servant John, "Behold! he cometh with clouds, and every eye shall see him; and they also which pierced him, and all the kindreds of the earth shall wail because of him." This glorious advent of the Messiah was the comfort of Job in his extreme affliction; he could lift up his sorrowful eyes from the midst of sackcloth and ashes, and exclaim "I know that my Redeemer liveth, and that he will stand at the latter day upon the earth; and though after my skin, worms destroy this body, yet in my flesh shall I see God," etc. This was the solace of Daniel in his captivity. He could exclaim, "I saw in the night, visions and behold, one like the son of man came with the clouds of heaven," etc. This same theme often inspired Isaiah, and David, with an extacy of admiration and delight, and caused them to pour forth their sweetest strains, — their sublimest effusions of poetic inspiration; and this same subject seems interwoven with almost every page of the New Testament writings. Indeed it formed a kind of centre, or rallying point, around which hovered all the hopes, joys, anticipations, and comforts of the former day saints. In bonds or imprisonments, in persecutions and afflictions, in tortures or in flames; they could look forward to the coming of the Lord in joyful anticipation of a resurrection and reward.

It is this glorious advent of the Messiah, and the great restitution connected with it which has ever formed the hope of the Jews; on this one point hangs the destiny of that long dispersed nation, in their final restoration to the favour of God, and to the land of their fathers, and to their beloved city Jerusalem.

This advent is what Paul has allusion to in his writings to the Romans where he said, "As it is written there shall come out of Zion a deliverer, who shall turn away ungodliness from Jacob." This second advent, is what Peter meant when he said to the Jews, (see Acts iii.) "And he shall send Jesus Christ, which before was preached unto you, whom the heavens must receive until the times of restitution," etc. It seems evident then, that Jesus Christ is to come again at the times of restitution; at which time a trump shall sound, at the voice of which the graves of the saints will be opened, and they arise from the dead, and are caught up together with those who are alive and remain, to meet the Lord in the air.

In the mean time the earth will be terribly convulsed; the mountains will sink, the valleys rise, the rough places become smooth; while a fire will pass over the surface of the earth, and consume the proud and all that do wickedly, as the cities of Sodom and Gomorrah were destroyed in the days of Abraham: and thus after the earth is cleansed by fire, from all its wicked inhabitants, as it once was by water, and after its mighty convulsions have restored it to its former shape and surface, it becomes a fit residence for Jesus Christ and his saints. The Jews behold their long-long expected Messiah, and come to the knowledge that he is the Jesus whom their fathers crucified; they are cleansed from their sins through his most precious blood; their holy city Jerusalem becomes a place of holiness indeed, and a seat of government; where will be the tabernacle and throne of Messiah; and where the nations of them that are saved will resort from year to year, from all the adjoining countries to worship the king, the Lord of hosts; and to keep the feast of tabernacles: and thus, there will be one Lord, and his name one; and he will be king over all the earth. "Blessed are the meek for they shall inherit the earth." This promise made by the Saviour while on the mount, will then be fulfilled. (See also, xxxvii Psalm; and also Ezekiel xxxvii.)

The curses which came upon the earth by reason of sin will then be taken off. It will no longer bring forth thorns and thistles, but its productions will be as they were before the fall. The barren deserts will become fruitful, the thirsty land will abound in springs of water, men will then plant gardens and eat the fruit of them, they will plant vineyards and drink the wine of them, they will build houses and cities, and inhabit them, and the Lord's elect will long enjoy the work of their hands. All the earth will then be at rest under one sovereign. Swords will then be beaten into ploughshares, and spears into pruning hooks, and the nations shall learn war no more. The very beasts of prey will then lose their thirst for blood, and their enmity will cease. The lion wil eat herbs instead of preying upon flesh, and all the animal creation will become perfectly harmless as they were in the beginning, while perfect peace will cover the earth, as the waters cover the sea; while all the ancient prophets, apostles, saints and martyrs will be on earth, with their glorified, immortal bodies, to sing the song of victory, and to praise the great Messiah who reigns in the midst of his people. O reader, this is the first resurrection! "Blessed and holy is he that has part in the first resurrection."

O reader, this is the great sabbath of creation; the thousand years of rest and peace; the longexpected Millennium. Wouldst thou live in the flesh, and have part in it? Wouldst thou again enjoy the society of thy friends who were so near and dear to thy heart in this life? Wouldst thou inherit the earth, and be free forever from the grave? Remember — remember, that meekness and holiness of life are the conditions. That it is the meek only who then inherit the earth. That it is the saints who then inherit the earth. That it is the saints only who then possess the kingdom, and the greatness of the kingdom under the whole heaven. In this delightful sabbath of creation, earth and its inhabitants will rest one thousand years from all the pains, and woes, and sorrows they have undergone during the six thousand years of labor, toil and suffering.

After this thousand years is ended, the last resurrection will soon come, together with the judgment day. These grand events will be ushered in by the sounding of the last trump, which will call forth the wicked from their long confinement in the grave, and they will be judged according to their works, and will then depart from the presence of the

Lord to the place appointed for them. At that time the heavens and earth will undergo their last and final change. They die, and rise again from the dead; or, in other words, the elements are changed from their temporal to their eternal state; being renewed, purified, and brought to the highest state of perfection and refinement which it is possible for them to receive.

The earth being thus renewed and purified, is no more to be changed or shaken. It will then roll its eternal rounds amidst the unnumbered systems of the universe; being clothed with celestial glory, and inhabited by immortal and celestial beings who were redeemed from sin and raised from the dead by the blood of Jesus Christ and the power of his resurrection, and who are clothed in white raiment with crowns upon their heads in glory; being kings and priests unto God and to the Lamb with whom they reign on earth for ever and ever; for there will be the holy city, New Jerusalem, the place of his throne; and his tabernacle will be with man, and he will dwell with them and be their God; and he will wipe away all tears from their eyes, and there will be no more death, neither sorrow nor groaning; neither shall there be any more pain, for the old order of things will have passed away and all things will have become new.

Reader wouldst thou leave thy native earth, and soar away to worlds on high, and be at rest thou mayest do so until the great restitution of all things spoken by the prophets; for Christ and the saints have gone to worlds on high, and have entered in before thee. But remember, that in the worlds on high thy stay is short. Jesus and the saints are only there to await the full time for earth to be cleansed and prepared for their reception, and they will all come home again to their native planet; and even while they are in heaven and absent from the earth, they look forward with joyful anticipation to the time of their return to the place of their nativity. The joyful theme of reigning on the earth inspires the music of their heavenly song; for the proof of this the reader is referred to Rev. v. 9, 10, he there records a song which he heard sung by the hosts of heaven, which closes with the following words, "We shall reign on the earth."

If man would enjoy a heaven beyond the bounds of space peopled only by spirits: if he would desire to be for ever free from earth, and absent from the body of his flesh, and from his native planet, he will be under the necessity of embracing the doctrines of the Alcoran, or some of the fables of the heathen mythology, where, in the boundless fields of fancy, or amid the romantic wilds of imagination and fanaticism, the mind roams unchecked by reason, and loses itself from all the realities of rational existence; in a land of shadows, a world of phantoms, from which it will only awake in disappointment by the sound of the last trump, and at last find itself constrained to acknowledge that eternity as well as time, is occupied in realities, and by beings of a physical as well as spiritual existence for the inspired writers, one and all have agreed, that the earth is destined for the eternal inheritance of the saints. The sacred volume opens with a paradise on earth, and closes with a paradise on earth. Moses introduces us to a world of beauty, glory, excellence and perfection in the beginning. And John closes the volume by leaving man in possession of an eternal habitation in his immortal body, in the holy city; and upon the very planet that first gave him being: and this is the end of the matter.

{4}

**"An Address by Judge Higbee and Parley P. Pratt,
Ministers of the Gospel, of the Church of Jesus Christ of
'Latter-day Saints,' to the Citizens of Washington
and to the Public in General,"
Washington, D.C., 9 February 1840
(with Elias Higbee)**

(from *Times and Seasons* 1 [March 1840]: 6870)

FRIENDS AND FELLOW-CITIZENS:

Aware of the anxiety of the public mind in relation to the faith and principles of our society, and of the many erroneous notions which are abroad concerning them, and which are calculated to prejudice the mind before we can obtain a hearing, we cheerfully offer this address, in order to give some information of our real principles, and hope it will be perused in the spirit of candor in which it is written.

The "Latter-Day Saints" believe in the true and living God, and in Jesus Christ, the son of God, who was crucified, according to the Scriptures, and who rose from the dead the third day, and is now seated at the right hand of God as a mediator.

We also believe in the Holy Scriptures of the prophets and apostles, as being profitable for doctrine, reproof, correction, and instruction in righteousness, and that all mysticism or private interpretation of them ought to be done away. The Scriptures should be taught, understood, and practiced in their most plain, simple, easy, and literal sense, according to the common laws and usage of the language in which they stand — according to the legitimate meaning of words and sentences precisely the same as if found in any other book.

Words are but signs of ideas; and if the Deity would communicate ideas to mankind by words, he must of necessity do it according to the laws of the language; otherwise the communication would be unintelligible or indefinite, and therefore unprofitable. — The prophetical and doctrinal writings contained in the Bible are mostly adapted to the capacities of the simple and unlearned — to the common sense of the people. They are designed to be understood and practiced; without which no one can profit by them.

The gospel dispensation revealed and established one Lord, one faith, one baptism, one Holy Spirit; in short one system of religion, one church, or assembly of worshippers united in their doctrine, and built upon the

TRUTH; and all bearing the general name of Saints. God is not the author of jarring and discordant systems. His Kingdom is not divided against itself; and for this reason we have no confidence in the sects, parties, systems, doctrines, creeds, commandments, traditions, precepts, and teaching of modern times, so far as they are at variance with each other, and contrary to the Scriptures of truth. We have, therefore, withdrawn from all these systems of error and delusion, and have endeavored to restore the ancient doctrine and faith which was once delivered to the saints, and to build society upon the truth, in its purity and fullness, hoping thereby to enjoy the peculiar gifts and blessing which were so abundantly bestowed upon the church in ancient times.

In saying this we do not call in question the morality, the sincerity, or the spiritual enjoyment of individuals belonging to any religious system. On the contrary, we feel assured that there are many sincere and zealous persons in every denomination. It is the Principles we reject, not men. It is the System that we wish to see established in purity, that those who are builded upon it may be pure also. It is the fountain that should be pure, and then the stream is easily kept so.

But if any persons prefer their own doctrines to those which we consider to be true, and we cannot by reason and argument convince them of the correctness of ours, we wish them to have the privilege of enjoying their religious rights unmolested. We have no disposition to persecute them.

We hold it as the duty of all men to believe the gospel to repent of their sins, and to be immersed in water in the name of Jesus Christ for remission of sins. And we hold that all who do this in a proper manner, and under proper authority, are legally entitled to the remission of sins, and to the gift of the Holy Ghost, according to the Scriptures. — Now faith and repentance go before baptism as a necessary qualification; and, therefore infant baptism is of no use. All penitent believers should be baptized with the faith and expectation of receiving remission of sins and the gift of the Holy Ghost, as much so as Naaman the Assyrian washed seven times in Jordan with the expectation of being healed of his leprosy; or as much so as the Israelites sounded the trumpets around the walls of Jericho with the expectation of their being thrown down; for the same God who attached a promise to the performance in these cases, has attached a promise to the conditions of the gospel. (See Acts, chapter 2.)

But now, concerning authority in the administrator. When a minister from England comes to our Government to do business as an ambassador, he must be commissioned by his Government, or all his transactions will be null and void, and England would never fulfil any promise which he might make in her name, however sincere our nation might be in believing him sent.

And so it is with the ambassador of Christ. He must be specially sent, or commissioned to minister in his name, or all his baptizing and other ordinances will be null and void, so as never to entitle the candidate to remission of sins and the gift of the Holy Ghost according to promise.

The "Latter-day Saints," after immersion, lay on hands, in the name of Jesus, for the gift of the Holy Ghost according to the ancient pattern. They are then considered saints, or members of the Church of Christ, in full fellowship and communion. They are then taught to observe all things which are required or commanded by Christ and his apostles — such as meeting together often to sing, to pray, to exhort, to testify, to prophesy, to speak with tongues, to interpret, to relate their visions, revelations, and in short, to edify and perfect each other, by a free exercise of all the gifts of God as set in order among the ancient churches. We also teach them to walk in all the ordinances of God blameless: such as the partaking of bread and wine, in remembrance of his broken body and shed blood, on the first day of the week; and also, to send for the elders of the church, when any of them are sick, that they may pray for them and lay their hands on them in the name of Jesus, or anoint them with oil in the name of the Lord, that they may be healed, according to the scriptures. We also teach them to abstain from all immorality: such as injustice, pride, vanity, dishonesty, evil-speaking, falsehood, hatred, envy, avarice, intemperance, adultery, fornication, lasciviousness, and to practise all the virtues; such as love to God and good will to man, brotherly kindness, charity, temperance, and industry. He that has two coats let him impart to him that has none, and he that has food let him do likewise; but he that will not work neither shall he eat. In short, we teach them to do all the good in their power — to visit the widow and the fatherless in their affliction, and to keep themselves unspotted from the world.

As to the fulfillment of prophecy, we believe in the great restoration of Israel, and the rebuilding of Jerusalem, in Palestine, and that, when that time comes, the Saviour will come in the clouds of Heaven, and all the saints with him; that the dead in Christ will rise to meet him: and that he will destroy the wicked by the brightness of his coming, and bring the whole earth under his own dominion and put it into the possession of the saints; when there will be a reign of universal peace for one thousand years; after which comes the resurrection of the wicked and the last judgment.

As to the signs of the times, we believe that the gathering of Israel and the second advent of Messiah, with all the great events connected therewith, are near at hand. That it is time for the saints to gather together and prepare for the same. But we disclaim all fellowship with the predictions of the Rev. Mr. Miller, Rev. Joseph Wolff, and others — such as, that the Lord will come in 1840, 1841, 1843, 1847, and so on. We do not believe that he will come until the Jews gather to Palestine and rebuild their city.

Having given this brief sketch of our faith and principles thus far, the inquiry may arise whether we believe in any other writings or books besides the Bible? To which we reply in the affirmative; for, like all other Christians, we believe in every true book within our knowledge, whether on science, history, or religion. We have implicit confidence in the "Book of Mormon," not, however, as a new Bible to exclude the old, as some have falsely represented. We consider the "Book of Mormon" as a historical and religious record, written in ancient times by a branch of the house of Israel, who peopled America, and from whom the Indians are descended. — The Book of Mormon corroborates and confirms the truth of the Scriptures, by showing that the same principles were revealed and enjoyed in a country and among a people far remote from the scenes where the Jewish bible was written.

Suppose a traveller should find in China, in the East Indies, or in America, or New Holland, an historical record, handed down for thousands of years or deposited in their sacred archives, or among their sepulchral ruins or their monuments of antiquity — and in this record should be found the principles of eternal truth, revealed to that nation, and agreeing with the revelation and principles contained in the Jewish records. Or suppose, for instance, when the ten tribes of Israel are discovered, preparatory to their return to Palestine, a record should be found among them giving their history from the time they were carried captive by Salmanezer, King of Assyria, and this record should be interspersed with prophecies and doctrine, as revealed among them since their captivity. Would it be any thing incredible or injurious in its nature, or any thing against the truths revealed in the Jewish records? Certainly not. So far from this, it would be hailed by every lover of truth as a most interesting and important discovery. Its light would be hailed as a new era in the history of the great events of modern times.

And similar in its nature is the Book of Mormon. It opens the events of ancient America. It pours a flood of light upon the world on subjects before concealed — upon the history of a nation whose remnants have long since dwindled to insignificance in midnight darkness, and whose former greatness was lost in oblivion, or only known by the remains of cities, palaces, temples, aqueducts, monuments, towers, fortifications, unintelligible inscriptions, sepulchres, and bones. The slumber of ages has now been broken. The dark curtain of the past has been rolled up. — The veil of obscurity has been removed as it regards the world called new. The ancient events of America now stand revealed in the broad light of history, as far back, at least, as the first peopling of the continent after the flood. This discovery will yet be hailed among all nations as one of the most glorious events of the latter times, and as one of the principal means of overwhelming the earth with knowledge. But why, then, is it so much opposed and neglected at the present time? Why do prisoners groan in chains and martyrs bleed in its promulgation to the world? Answer. Upon the same principle that a Messiah was crucified, a Stephen stoned, a James slain, a Paul beheaded, a Peter crucified, a John banished, a Rogers burned, a Columbus neglected, ridiculed, and envied, a Newton counted mad, and a Fulton laughed to scorn. In short, it is because they know not what it is.

N.B. If the people wish further information we are now here in Washington, and would freely avail ourselves of the opportunity of giving a course of lectures, if a suitable house and audience can be obtained. — We are willing, also, to supply the public with such books as will give information on our religion, as well as the history of our unparalleled persecution in Missouri.

We reside, at present, at the corner of 9th and D streets.

We are, respectfully.

E. HIGBEE.
P. P. PRATT.

Washington. February 9, 1840.
P.S. Editors through the States would oblige us by publishing the above.

{5}

Plain Facts,
Showing the Falsehood and Folly of the Rev. C. S. Bush,
(a Church Minister of the Parish of Peover,)
Being a Reply to His Tract Against the Latter-day Saints

(Manchester: W. R. Thomas, Printer [1840])

We have a Tract now in our possession purporting to be written by the Rev Mr. Bush, entitled "Plain Facts, showing the falsehood and folly of the Mormonites or Latter-day Saints," &c.

The writer commences by saying, "With plain and honest people, facts are always important things."

He then lays down the following for his first fact. He says, "The Bible is the word of God, *and that there is no other Revelation of him, than that which he has given us in that Book of Life."*

Now, we admit that the Bible contains the word of God: but the statement that there is no other Revelation of him than that which he has given in the Bible is not a *fact*, but a *falsehood* of the most glaring kind; being contrary to the word of God, and to the experience of all Christians, as we shall now proceed to demonstrate.

The Bible quotes more than twelve books, which are not to be found in it—most, if not all of which, were written by prophets or seers, whose inspiration the Bible itself acknowledges. We will here mention a few of these books.

Book of Jasher	*Joshua* c. x, v. 13.
Book of the Acts of Solomon	1 *Kings*, c.xi, v. 41.
Book of Nathan the prophet	1 *Chron.* c.xxix, v. 29.
Book of Gad the seer	1 *Chron.* c.xxix, v. 29.
Book of Nathan the prophet	2 *Chron.* c.ix, v. 29.
Book of the Prophecy of Ahijah	2 *Chron.* c.ix, v. 29.
Book of the Visions of Iddo the seer	2 *Chron.* c.ix, v. 29.
Book of Shemaiah the prophet	2 *Chron.* c.xii, v. 15.
Book of Iddo the seer	2 *Chron.* c.xii, v. 15.
"Written in the story of the prophet Iddo."	2 *Chron.* c. xiii, v. 22.

If necessary, we could bring quotations in the Bible for several other books some in the Old Testament, and some in the writings of the apostles, referring to epistles which are not in the Bible.

74

If so many books are left out of the volume, and yet actually quoted in it; there may have been hundreds of others of which we have not account.

But, besides all these, it is evident that God was Revelator to man from the days of Adam to the days of Moses, who commenced to write the Bible; and surely, the Bible cannot be supposed to contain the thousandth part of the word of the Lord which had been revealed in those early ages.

Indeed, the Bible contains but a very small portion of the word of the Lord which was spoken and revealed to man during the progress of those writings; that is, from Moses to John the Revelator.

Does it contain the words of the prophets who prophesied in the camp of Israel at the time Moses exclaimed, "Would to God the Lord's people were all prophets?" Or, will any one contend that what they prophesied, was not the word of the Lord. Does the Bible contain what the Corinthians, Ephesians, Romans, and others prophesied in the churches, when assembled together from time to time in the enjoyment of the different gifts of the Spirit? Does the Bible contain the word of the Lord which he has manifested in visions, in prophesying, and revelations, from age to age, down to the present day? Does it contain all which God has revealed to other nations remote from Jerusalem, and all that he will reveal on or before the day of judgment? Shall we stand before a DUMB God at the judgment day, who, if he speaks in order to pronounce judgment, will be found a transgressor of his own Book, by speaking after the "Canon of Scripture is complete?"

Does it contain that which God will speak to Israel in the wilderness in the great restitution, when he "pleads with them face to face," in fulfillment of the 20th chapter of Ezekiel?

The Bible holds forth the doctrine of CONTINUAL and UNIVERSAL REVELATION, so far as men would live up to their privileges.

"If ANY MAN lack wisdom, let him ask of God, who giveth to ALL MEN liberally and upbraideth not, and it SHALL BE GIVEN HIM."

Again, the apostle prays that God will give unto the children of men the spirit of WISDOM and REVELATION in the KNOWLEDGE OF GOD.

Again, it is written, that no man knoweth the Son but the Father, and him to whom the Father REVEALS him.

Do away the principle of direct Revelation then, and we do away the religion of the Bible, and have nothing left but atheism.

Do away the principle of direct and continued Revelation, and you have not a witness on earth that Jesus is the Christ.

Do away the principle of continued Revelation, and there is not a man on earth who knows his sins forgiven, or that can get a call to preach the gospel.

Do away the principle of continued revelation, and you worship a DUMB and changeable God, and have no communion with the ANGELS, nor with the HOLY GHOST.

We call upon the hundreds of thousands of Methodists — upon the Society of Friends or Quakers — upon the Christian world at large — nay, — upon the Church of England herself, to speak out upon this subject — to rise up in the dignity and majesty of their holy profession, and bear their testimony against this atheism in a new dress — this religion which shuts heaven, and cuts off all communication between God and his creatures.

So much for the Reverend Gentleman's first pretended "fact," we now come to his second pretended "fact."

He says "There are men come to us, who profess that they have found a revelation, which they say is from God. I will prove by facts that what they say cannot be true, because the widow of the man who wrote the book which they pretend is a revelation from God, has published a letter proving that it was "written by her late husband, &c."

He further says, that "the title-page may be considered as a specimen of the blasphemous jargon of the whole. He then proceeds to quote the title-page in part, but does not point out one thing which is jargon or blasphemy in it. Therefore the reader is left at a loss "that Jesus is the Christ, the Eternal God manifesting himself unto all nations."

He says, "at least thirty pages of the book are copied from the Holy Gospels." With the same propriety he might say that the "Holy Gospels" were copied from each other, because they are nearly alike. The thirty pages to which he alludes contain the gospel and teachings of the Son of God, as revealed to another branch of Israel, in a distant land from Jerusalem. Why should his Gospel not be the same in one nation or country as in another? Does it alter it to reveal it to another people? He puts us in mind of the decision of the Mahometan tyrant in relation to the Alexandrian Library, who ordered the 600,000 manuscript volumes to be burned for this reason, that if they agreed with the "Koran", they were useless, as that was all-sufficient; but if they did not agree with it, they were false any how.

So this gentleman condemns one part of the book for agreeing with the "Gospels," and the other part for some other reason. But after all, can find no ground of condemnation for 600 pages of "closely written matter" except to call it stupid, without reading it, and let it go.

He then mentions, that the book contains the testimony of eleven witnesses, who all testify that they have seen the original copy which has been found; and three of these witnesses testify that they know the truth of it by the ministering of an angel, and by the voice of God.

This evidence he can pass over in silence, while, at the same time, he can take newspaper statements, containing a forged letter with an old woman's name signed to it, and publish it for a POSITIVE FACT, which he supposes will have great weight with the honest.

But lest the people should still be disposed to doubt his statements, he again affirms as follows: "My object is not to mislead by false statements or pretended truths—I WRITE ONLY FACTS." I suppose he thinks that the statement of a Reverend, to something he has read in a newspaper, is quite sufficient—that people will not have the impoliteness to call it in question for a moment. But the days of such credulity have gone by—it requires something more than a forged letter in a newspaper, with an old woman's name signed to it, and the statement of a Reverend, who never pretended to know any thing about it himself, to go down with the people for fact: the people require some evidence.

He complains of one of our ministers, as having denied that the Bible is the "whole truth of God." But who, in the name of common sense, will contend that the Bible is the "whole truth of God?" It is a truth that America exists; but the Bible does not tell it. It is a truth that Washington lived and fought; but that truth is not in the Bible. It is a truth that her Majesty Queen Victoria now reigns in England; but the Bible does not contain it. It is a truth that men have invented steam-boats and rail-roads; but the Bible does not tell it. It is a truth that the Rev. C. S. Bush is in existence, (I suppose) but the Reverend Gentleman himself disputes it; for he says the Bible contains the whole truth of God, and it nowhere mentions the existence of this gentleman, and surely he will not have the impiety to believe in any thing which is not in the Bible, as it contains "the whole truth of God." Surely then he will call in question his own existence.

But to the Reverend gentleman's next "fact." He says, "I have just received from a brother minister the following FACT.—In describing a conversation held with a young woman who has heard them, and whose sister has been deluded by them, he made use of the word "Mormonite."—"O yes" she said, "my sister tells me that is their name; they go by the Book of Mormon, and they say that the Bible is only true in part."

Now the foregoing must be received as FACT; for a Minister heard a "Brother minister" say, that he heard a young woman say, that she heard a young woman say, that she heard some member of our society say, that we held so and so; and whoever knew any thing but FACTS so come from ministers and young women when associated with each other in so holy a cause!!!

This last FACT is so well authenticated that we shall not be so uncourteous to the ladies and clergy as to call it in question.

We therefore proceed to notice his next "fact." He says "There is no revelation from God but that which proceeds from him."

This is a fact which we do not wish to call in question: but we merely quote it as a specimen of the Reverend gentleman's logic, and to give him the credit which would seem to be his just due, for having discovered an axiom so important.

It would be similar use of language to say, there is no news from France except that which proceeds from France.

The gentleman quotes Paul to Timothy, where he says "from a child thou hast known the Holy Scriptures, which are able to make thee wise unto salvation, through faith which is in Christ Jesus."

He then observes: "Here the Holy Scriptures, and not pretended revelations from angels, are spoken of as being able to make men wise unto salvation."

What does he mean by this? Surely he is not ignorant that Paul and others received revelations from angels both before and after this letter to Timothy. Did not John receive a revelation from an angel many years after Paul wrote this Epistle? Surely he did.

I know not why the gentleman quoted this text, unless it was to infer that we must reject all Scripture which was given later than that which Timothy was acquainted with when a child. If this text proves anything against modern revelation, it proves too much; for it speaks expressly of the Old Testament Scriptures, and no other, because no other was in existence when Timothy was a child. Indeed, the New Testament did not yet exist when Paul was writing this text.

Will Mr. Bush give up the New Testament, and say it is not necessary, because the other was able to make one wise unto salvation? Will he reject everything which has been revealed by angels since that text was written? It seems so, from the inference which he has drawn.

But now to his next "fact."

He says, "THE WORD OF GOD'S REVELATION IS CLOSED FOR EVER." He then quotes Rev. xxii. 18, 19, and Proverbs xxx. 5, 6. The latter is, "Add thou not unto his words, lest he reprove thee, and thou be found a liar." In the former text he was for rejecting all the Scriptures, except the Old Testament which Timothy had known from a child; but now he seems inclined to reject all which has been added since the Proverbs were written. This sweeps off most of the prophets. I think by the time he gets through with his logic we shall have but a small Bible indeed; that is, if his conclusions are tenable. What object can he have in quoting this text, except to cut off all which has been added since?

These texts do not prohibit God, or angels, or the Holy Spirit, from

giving revelations to man, in any age of the world. But they only prohibit man from perverting that which God gives, by additions or
diminutions of their own.

Mr. Bush intimates, that the Latter-Day Saints are "open to the excommunication of the Church of Christ," and "open to being denied
CHRISTIAN BURIAL," and "lost for ever;" to which we reply, that we want
no fellowship with a professed Church of Christ, whose charity is so
limited that it denies BURIAL to the dead bodies of those who dissent
from them, or even to the heathen. As to burial, we are not careful with
whom or by whom we are buried; but the great object with us is to
secure part in the first resurrection.

He says, "This must be true," (that we are lost for ever) "if Christ is
the only way, truth, and light, for we point out another way — we appeal to another so called truth, that of Mormon, and seek guidance from
another light than that of the spirit of the Holy One, that of the wicked
lie, Mormon."

In reply to this false accusation, we will quote some of the writings
of Mormon, to show to all men that Mr. Bush has misrepresented
Mormon, as well as those who believe in his writings. The following
are some closing remarks made by Mormon, in his writings to the remnant of Israel, his brethren; and it is such doctrine that this gentleman is
pleased to term "damnable doctrines" and "wicked lies." We quote Book
of Mormon, page 560:

"And now, behold, I would speak somewhat unto the remnant of
this people who are spared, if it so be that God may give unto them my
words, that they may know of the things of their fathers; yea, I speak
unto you, ye remnant of the house of Israel, and these are the words
which I speak, know ye that ye are of the house of Israel. Know ye that
ye must come unto repentance, or ye cannot be saved. Know ye that ye
must lay down your weapons of war, and delight no more in the shed-
ding of blood, and take them not again, save it be that God shall command you. Know ye that ye must come to the knowledge of your fathers, and repent of all your sins and iniquities, and believe in Jesus Christ,
that he is the Son of God, and that he was slain by the Jews, and by the
power of the Father he hath risen again, whereby he hath gained the
victory over the grave; and also in him is the sting of death swallowed
up. And he bringeth to pass the resurrection of the dead, whereby man
must be raised to stand before his judgment seat. And he hath brought
to pass the redemption of the world, whereby he that is found guiltless
before him at the judgment day, hath it given unto him to dwell in
the presence of God in his kingdom, to sing ceaseless praises with the
choirs above, unto the Father, and unto the Son, and unto the Holy
Ghost, which are one God, in a state of happiness which hath no end.

Therefore, repent and be baptized in the name of Jesus, and lay hold upon the gospel of Christ, which shall be set before you, not only in this record, but also in the record which shall come from the Gentiles unto you. For, behold, this is written for the intent that ye may believe that; and if ye believe that, ye will believe this also; and if ye believe this, ye will know concerning your fathers, and also the marvelous works which were wrought by the power of God among them; and ye will also know that ye are a remnant of the seed of Jacob; therefore, ye are numbered among the people of the first covenant; and if it so be that ye believe in Christ, and are baptized, first with water, then with fire and with the Holy Ghost, following the example of our Saviour, according to that which he hath commanded us, it shall be well with you in the day of judgment. Amen."

The foregoing is a sample of the purity of Mormon's doctrine throughout his record; and we challenge Mr. Bush, or the world, to produce from the 619 pages of the Book of Mormon one principle of doctrine which does not breathe the same spirit of purity and holiness. "Damnable doctrines!" "wicked lie!" What loving terms, what charitable expressions for a professed follower of the meek and holy Lamb of God! but they are in accordance with that spirit which would leave a dissenter without a decent BURIAL.

He further says, that, when we baptize a person, we require him to "renounce all other religions on the face of the earth." This we acknowledge to be true. We most freely renounce all other religions but the religion set forth in the page of Mormon's writings which we have quoted, and other writings which are in accordance with it. We want no religion but pure Christianity. He says, "It can easily be proved, too, that they have used and quoted the Book (of Mormon) at their meetings." To this we reply, that we will own it, and save them the trouble of proving it. We do use and quote the Book of Mormon; and, farther than this, we intend to publish it to all nations and languages under heaven; for we know, and hereby testify, that it is an ancient record, written by the commandment of the Lord, and that it is now sent forth by his commandment; and all the powers of earth and hell will never stop its progress till earth is overwhelmed with its light and glory.

He says, they "have declared that parts of the Bible are the WORDS or WORKS of bad men and bad women, an assertion which at once ranks them with the infidel dangers of the inspiration of the Bible." This, too, we acknowledge to have said, and we do still say it; and, if it ranks us with the infidel, we cannot help it. It is what the Bible professes; and while we believe the Bible, we are bound to believe that it contains some of the works and words of bad men and bad women—nay, more, it contains the words of a SERPENT, of DEVILS, and of an ASS; and he that says to the contrary is an infidel, and not a believer in the Bible at all. We will here give a few samples: —

The word of the serpent to Eve.
The word of the ass to Balaam.
The word of the Devil to Christ.
The word of the wicked men and women of Ephesus, crying, "Great is Diana of the Ephesians."
The word of Potipher's wife to Joseph, saying, "Come, lie with me."
The word of Job's wife, "Curse God and die."

We could give a hundred other examples, but we trust these will suffice. We now leave this part of the subject for a candid public to judge which is the infidel — whether it is Mr. Bush, who believes all the above Scriptures to be the word of the Lord, or whether it is the Latter-Day Saints, who believe they are just what they profess to be.

Mr. Bush quotes the words of John, in his second Epistle, 8, 9, 10, and 11. It speaks concerning those who transgress and abide not in the DOCTRINE of Christ, and declares that they have not God. To this we would reply, that we are willing to compare our doctrine with that of the Church of England at any time, and let the world see which comes up to the standard of the doctrine of Christ. The doctrine of Christ was a doctrine of REVELATION and miracles: the doctrine of Mr. Bush is the opposite. He says, we are to receive NO REVELATIONS; but Christ promises us the Holy Spirit of revelation, which would guide us into ALL TRUTH, teach us ALL THINGS, *and show us things to come.*

He quotes Paul to the Galatians, concerning preaching another gospel, and asks the question, "Was the Book of Mormon, its baptism, its folly, preached of Paul?" "Was it of Christ?" He answers "No;" and then proceeds to curse those who preach the principles of Mormon. Well, let him curse. But still we will reply to his questions. We say, then, as to the doctrine or gospel contained in the Book of Mormon, together with its baptism, it is precisely the same as taught by Paul and Christ. This, Mr. Bush himself has acknowledged, and even said it was copied from the "Holy Gospels;" but, for further proof of its being the same gospel, we again refer to the page of the writings of Mormon, which we have already quoted in this pamphlet. But as to the "folly" of the Book of Mormon, Mr. B. has not been so kind as to point out one specimen of its "folly," and we, after several years' acquaintance with it, have not been able to discover any "folly" in it. If there is any in it, perhaps Paul would have preached it; for, if his own testimony is to be credited, he wrote folly to the Corinthians, and requested them to "bear with him a little in his folly."

But if the question be asked, whether Jesus and Paul preached the Book of Mormon, we answer, "No;" for surely we would not expect them to preach a book in Asia which was only had in America, and especially 400 years before it was written, or before the writer lived. Jesus and Paul lived in Palestine 1800 years since, and Mormon lived in America about 1400 years since. But this question makes as much against many of the books of the New Testament as it does against the Book of Mormon.

Paul and Christ did not preach any book except the Old Testament. The gospel did not consist of a book, but rather of a message of glad tidings proclaimed among the people, whereby they might be saved.

I ask, did Paul preach the Revelations of John, which he received on the Isle of Patmos many years after Paul was dead? I answer No. What then? Shall we reject John's book? No. But Mr. Bush's argument would make as much against the Book of Revelations as against the Book of Mormon, for Paul preached neither; and Mr. B. curses those who preach a book which Paul did not preach. Paul did not refer to a book which he had preached, and then curse those who should preach any other; but he referred to certain principles, and wherever these principles are found, whether written or verbal, they are the same gospel which was preached by Paul. Let them be written by Matthew, Mark, Luke, John, Paul, or Peter, in Asia, or let them be written by Nephi, Alma, Mormon, or Moroni, in America, they are still the same unaltered Gospel. Let them be written on parchment, papyrus, tables of stone, paper, or plates of gold, they are still the same unchangeable principles. They will remain the same although the material on which they are written should perish or be dissolved,—the same, even if heaven and earth should pass away. . . .

{6}

An Epistle of Demetrius, Junior, the Silversmith,
To the workman of like occupation,
and all others whom it may concern,
— Greeting: Showing the Best Way to Preserve Our Craft,
and to Put Down the Latter Day Saints

(Manchester: Wm. Shackleton and Sons, Printers [1840?])

Sirs, — Ye are well aware of those men who turn the world upside down having come hither also; viz: the "Latter Day Saints," and that they teach customs which are not lawful for us to receive, being sectarians. And behold they are rapidly increasing, not only in America, but throughout the whole world; so that not only this our craft is in danger, but our great goddess who sits upon the scarlet colored beast with the golden cup in her hand, is like to be spaken against — her magnificence despised and her temples deserted — even her, whom all the world worshipeth.

Now, I will tell you the way these Latter Day Saints continue to lead the people astray from our old, smooth, comfortable ways, in which we and our fathers have walked for so many ages; —

In the first place, being ignorant and unlearned, they know no better than to tell the people to believe the Bible as it reads, and to no longer give heed to the spiritualizings of our learned priests. Even setting aside and despising that glorious name on the forehead of our goddess, — that word "MYSTERY" which stands most conspicuous among the great and venerable names which encircle her on every hand. Thus having burst the veil of mystery, and taking the scriptures as if common sense was to be exercised, they read the commandment which says "Be not yet called Rabbi, for one is your Master, and all ye are brethren." This, in their ignorance leads them to suppose that all the other names, titles, and dignities which are written on the goddess are to be equally despised and avoided such for instance as "Doctor of Divinity," "Very Rev.," "His Grace," "His Holiness," "Right Rev. Father in God," "Lord Bishop," &c.

These great and glorious names, the very foundation of the honor and wealth of our goddess, these Saints consider as so many blasphemies, and that our goddess is therefore full of names of blasphemy. They also read in Paul to the Corinthians, that, "not many wise men after the flesh, not many mighty, nor many noble are called: but, that God hath chosen the simple, base, despised, weak things, to confound the wise, that flesh might not glory in his presence," &c. And that such as were called were to go without taking thought for the morrow, consequently they were not to hire out for a salary, or to have palaces, and pleasure grounds devoted to them by oppressing and taxing the poor. Now these Latter Day Saints are so blind and ignorant, or so deluded that they really think that these Scriptures mean what they say; and consequently they don't believe that our holy bishops, our spiritual lords, our gentlemen non-resident clergy, or indeed any, of any order, who preach with their learning, and preach for hire, are the true shepherds; or that their followers are the true sheep; so they withdraw from the fold and go their own way.

Again, they read the passages which Jesus and his Apostles taught in relation to giving to the poor, &c. "He that hath two coats let him give to him that hath none, and he that has meat let him do likewise." "Go sell that thou hast and give to the poor," &c. — They even go so far as to take these things literally, and think that a bishop or a nobleman cannot be a christian unless he sells his palace, his pleasure grounds, and all his unnecessary things, and gives it to feed the millions of his fellow-country men around him, who are starving while they work hard, or would be glad to work if they had anything to do: and even those who are not noblemen, but who possess moderate fortunes must do likewise. Now who ever heard of such wild delusion? Why, if we should let it alone, and it should prosper, all our christian dignity and greatness would be lost: our idleness and luxury would be dismissed: and his grace the bishop would be on a level with his grace the common laborer. This would utterly turn us, and reduce society to that state which the apostles were trying to do, when my venerable father Demetrius made such a bold stand at Ephesus.

These men also read that passage in the 4th chapter of Ephesians, where it is said "there is one Lord, one faith, one baptism, and one Spirit." This they take literally, and say that there can be but one true system of religion, and but one true church of God, all built upon the same truths, and all united and under the general name of Saints. Here again they come in contact with our systems, and endanger our craft; for what man is there among us, but what knows that our blessed goddess, among the venerable names which cover her, has Catholic, Protestant, Episcopal, Methodist Primitive, Calvinists and hundreds of others: and all these have their different Lords, faiths, baptisms and Spirits, which all contribute to make our craft good, and to decorate the magnificent temples of our goddess.

But this is not all. These men preach up, that people should believe in the gifts and power of God as the ancient churches did; such as the gifts of revelation, visions, dreams, prophesying, interpretations, healings,

&c. Now we might perhaps have borne with their other delusions, if it had not been for these last mentioned. But these are absolutely intolerable, for let the people in, and obtain such blessings and it will show the difference between our systems of craft and the real principles which were once delivered to the saints. Our goddess and her followers are willing that every and any system should exist, which will be content with a form without the power of godliness; for she and her followers know that it was this power which was so dangerous in old times to our ancient craft. Daniel was cast into the lion's den for believing in revelations and angels. Lot was mobbed for entertaining angels. The children of Bethlehem were slain by Herod because a revelation had come that a King of the Jews was born. Paul was imprisoned and martyred for his testimony of having seen a vision and heard a voice. In short my fellow craftsmen, you see that men of our occupation never have been willing to allow any thing to exist on the earth in the shape of gifts and revelations from God. Why! This would reveal the mystery of our iniquity, it would tear off the covering under which we hide our secret workings, would root up our systems to the very foundations, and fill the earth, not with religious opinions, but with an actual knowledge of the TRUTH.

I might say much more, sirs, in relation to these Latter Day Saints, and their foolish delusions; but I trust I have said quite sufficient to convince you all how dangerous they are: and ye yourselves know, how, after the death of the "old deceivers," Paul and Peter and their contemporaries, my venerable fathers of the Demetrius family, together with their numerous friends, contrived to modify the christian religion; which, with the various modifications it has undergone since, have at length brought it into perfect agreement with the world, and the world loves it; the kings glorify themselves and live deliciously with it; the priests and nobles fat themselves as in a day of slaughter; the sons and daughters of the church are adorned with gold and silver and fine linen, and decked with purple, scarlet and silk; they trade in horses and chariots and SLAVES, and SOULS OF MEN. By this means, the merchants of our craft have waxed rich, through the abundance of our delicacies; and all nations have drunken the golden cup which is in the hands of the great goddess. Must all this be despised? must so great riches come to naught? must these saints be suffered to come along and tell the people that all this is not religion, and that the world would hate religion if it was genuine?

My friends, if the founders of the christian system had known how to do as we have done; to modify and decorate the christian religion, what a world of suffering it would have saved them: the world would never have hated them, but would have contributed to the spread of the gospel. But now after many ages have witnessed the christian religion and the world going on hand in hand, in unison with each other, here comes these mischievous men, which the world always hated, and always will hate: and look how it begins to hate them, even while the church is in the bud!

Now all these things are too much for us to bear, let us be up and doing:

But the grand difficulty is, to know what to do! Almost every thing that could be invented, has been already tried, with as little effect as the new ropes were in the binding of Samson—This little, insignificant, infant of a system, (for it is only about 12 years old,) has, from its very birth been belied, slandered, and misrepresented in every way and shape which our honorable fraternity could invent: but all of no use, it still rolled steadily onward, increasing at every step. The people have been told that it was so small that it was not worth notice, but still they could not smother it: they have been told that it was so large that it was in danger of overruning the world—and still the people would go after it.

The learning, the talent, and the ignorance of all sects have been arrayed against it, and still it stands. Ignorance, superstition, and bigotry, have ever raised their bulwarks in vain. It has scaled their highest ramparts, and still it is onward with steady and dauntless march. And last, when all these have failed, the sword and bayonet has been unsheathed, and have pierced the hearts of many of the Latter Day Saints; the deadly rifle has laid them low in the dust: their leaders have been dragged to prison, and bound in chains and dungeons; their houses burned, their property robbed, their women and children driven from their homes by thousands, to seek shelter where they could find it; and then we fondly hoped it was overcome and put down, but alas! we were disappointed still. The chains were rent, the dungeons were burst. The prisoners and others are again abroad in the earth, and their system is spreading with tenfold rapidity.

What, my fellow craftsmen, can we do! I pause for a reply,—Well sirs, I think, upon mature deliberation, the most successful way to preserve our own pure religions, and to prevent this system from spreading, is, for all with one accord to join, in the cry of—great is the godess who sits upon the scarlet coloured beast: great is the mystery of her who holds in her hand the golden cup. This may for a time drown the voice of truth. In the mean time let us keep the tracts and newspapers well filled with lies against the Saints, and above all let us persuade the people to judge them without hearing them or reading their books.

I remain, Sirs, with sentiments of high consideration, your fellow-craftsman.

DEMETRIUS, JUNR.

{7}

A Letter to the Queen of England, Touching the Signs of the Times, and the Political Destiny of the World

(Manchester: Printed and Published by Parley P. Pratt, 1841)

ADDRESS

To Her Gracious Majesty Queen Victoria,
Sovreign of Britain:

It has fallen to the lot of your Majesty not only to live in a most eventful period of the world, but to occupy a station the most conspicuous of any individual of the present age.

It has pleased the Almighty disposer of events who governs and rules among the kingdoms of the earth, to raise your Majesty, while in the morning of life, to a throne of power, at the head of an empire, which, in many respects stands foremost among the nations and kingdoms of the world. It is with feelings of that profound respect which is justly due to so high an office that I offer this address. The importance of the subject and the obligations which I am under to the God whom I serve, and to the people of the age in which I live, are the only apologies which I offer for thus intruding upon the attention of your Majesty.

Know assuredly, that the world in which we live is on the eve of a *revolution*, more wonderful in its begining, more rapid in its progress, more powerful in its operations, more extensive in its effects, more lasting in its influence, and more important in its consequences than any which man has yet witnessed upon the earth: a revolution in which all the inhabitants of the earth are vitally interested, both religiously and politically, temporally and spiritually; one on which the fate of all nations is suspended, and upon which the future destiny of all the affairs of the earth is made to depend. Nay, the angels have desired to look into it, and heaven itself has waited with longing expectation for its consummation.

I will now proceed to show from the scriptures first, what this revolution is, secondly, that the present is the time of its fulfilment.

The first great and universal monarchy after the deluge was the kingdom of Babel, or Babylon. This was founded by Nimrod, on the plains of Euphrates, and continued to strengthen itself until the time of Nebuchadnezzer, whom the Lord raised up to be his servant, to execute his vengeance upon the nations. By a series of the most striking prophetic declarations of Jeremiah the prophet and others, and their no less striking fulfilment, this monarch marched forth, conquering and to conquer, till Tyre, Egypt, and Judea, and all the surrounding nations, were subdued and brought into captivity for seventy years. This was so extensive that Daniel the prophet exclaimed to the king of Babylon, "The God of Heaven hath given thee a kingdom, power, strength, and glory. And wheresoever the children of men dwell, the beasts of the field, and fowls of the heaven hath he given into thine hand, and hath made thee ruler over them all."

This monarch, standing at the head of nations and swaying his sceptre over all the kingdoms of the world, was the favored instrument to whom the Almighty made known his purposes touching the government of the world in all succeeding ages. While resting upon his bed in the deep silence of midnight, when the busy world was lost in slumbers, and wearied nature hushed to silence and repose, an anxious enquiry arose in his breast in regard to the things which should "come to pass hereafter." His mind roamed down through the dark vista of future and distant periods, and would fain have understood and contemplated the events of the "latter days." Thus lost in contemplation, and overwhelmed with deep sleep his mind was suddenly caught from the subject of his meditation, and the visions of heaven were opened to his view. A great image stood before him whose head was of fine gold, his breast and arms of silver, his belly and thighs of brass, his legs of iron, and his feet and toes part of iron and part of clay. He beheld till a stone was cut out of the mountain without hands, which smote the image upon the toes; then was the whole image broken to pieces together, and became like the chaff of the summer threshing-floors, and the wind blew it away; but the stone became a great mountain and filled the whole earth. When the king awoke from this vision, he sent for his wise men, but none of them could unfold unto him his dream and the meaning thereof, till Daniel was forthcoming with this striking declaration: "There is a God in heaven that revealeth secrets." This man of God then proceeded to tell the dream and the interpretation thereof. The head of gold represented Nebuchadnezzer, and the kingdoms over which he reigned, the breast and arms of silver represented the Medes and Persians, who next succeeded in the government of the world; the belly and thighs of brass represented the empire of Alexander and his successors, this being the next in succession; the legs of iron represented the Roman empire, which was the fourth great monarchy of the world; and the feet and toes, part of iron and part of clay, represented the dissolution of the Roman empire and its subdivision into the kingdoms of modern Europe, as they now exist in their divided state, partly Roman and partly Protestant, and not cleaving one to another, even as iron and clay will not adhere or unite in mutual strength.

Of course then, the government of England is one of the toes of this image.

Now, in the days of these kings, [or kingdoms represented by the feet and toes,] the God of heaven should set up a kingdom which should not be left to other people but should break in pieces all these kingdoms and stand for ever, as represented by the little stone.

This is the interpretation which the God of heaven himself gave to Daniel, and which Daniel has given in the scriptures; and England has given the scriptures to the world—thus actually revealing to the world its destiny and her own.

But before we proceed further, we shall go back and take another view of the same subject, as revealed to Daniel on another occasion, and under a different figure. He saw (Dan. vii.) these same four kingdoms, viz.: the Babylonians, Medes and Persians, Greeks, and Romans rise and reign in succession under the figure of four beasts. Out of the fourth beast he saw, under the figure of ten horns, ten kingdoms rise, which are the same that the feet and toes represented, viz.: the kingdoms of modern Europe. "And he beheld till the thrones were cast down, and the Ancient of Days did sit, and judgment was given to the SAINTS, and the time came that the Saints possessed the kingdom." Again he said, "The saints of the Most High shall take the kingdom, and possess the kingdom forever, even for ever and ever." Again, "The kingdom and dominion, and the greatness of the kingdom under the whole heaven, shall be given to the people of the saints of the Most High, whose kingdom is an everlasting kingdom, and all dominions shall serve and obey him." Again, he says, "I saw in the night visions, and behold one like the Son of Man, came with the clouds of heaven, and came to the Ancient of Days, and they brought him near before him. And there was given him dominion and glory, and a kingdom, that all people, and nations and languages should serve him; his dominion is an everlasting dominion, which shall not pass away, and his kingdom that shall not pass away, and his kingdom that which shall not be destroyed." The kingdom so often spoken of in this 7th of Daniel is evidently the same that is represented by the stone which smote the image, as recorded in the 22d chapter.

From this it appears that this new kingdom will be established over the whole earth, to the destruction of all other kingdoms, by nothing less than the personal advent of the Messiah in the clouds of heaven, with power and great glory, but preceded by a personage called the "Ancient of Days."

The 11th chapter of Zechariah confirms this testimony, by predicting that the Lord will stand with his feet on the mount of Olives; that he shall come and all the saints with him, and that in that day there shall be ONE Lord, and his name ONE, and he shall be king over all the earth.

The Revelation of John bears the same testimony, saying, "The kingdoms of this world shall become the kingdoms of our God and his Christ."

There are many other scripture illustrations of the same subject, which would be extremely interesting to your Majesty, and to the world, but these must suffice.

From all these facts so clearly set forth in the scriptures, I feel warranted in saying that, as sure as all these events have succeeded each other from the days of Nebuchadnezzer, king of Babylon, untill the days of Victoria I on the throne of Britain, so sure will that portion be fulfilled which is yet future, and which relates to the casting down of thrones, the termination of the political and religious establishments of the earth, and the setting up of a new and universal kingdom, under the immediate administration of the Messiah and his saints.

Connected with the ushering in of this new era will be the restoration of Judah and Israel from their long dispersion. They will come home to their own land, and rebuild Jerusalem and the cities of Judea, and rear up the temple of their God. This city will be the seat of empire for the eastern world, and all the surrounding nations for the next thousand years at least. See Zechariah 14.

This restoration will take place by a series of miracles, signs, wonders, revelations, judgments &c. which will far exceed the dispensation of Moses, and the deliverance of Israel from Egyptian bondage. Jer. 16, Ez. 20, Isa. 11, Ez. 36 to 39 inclusive. With the revolution will be connected the resurrection of the saints that have slept. See Dan. xii, 2; Job xix, 25, 26, 27; and Rev. xx.

A physical change also awaits the earth at this time. The mountains will be thrown down, the valleys exalted, the rough places will become smooth and the crooked places straight, the barren deserts fruitful and the parched ground well watered, and even the beasts of prey will be wrought upon by the Spirit of God—will lose their thirst for blood, and become perfectly harmless, feeding on vegetable food only.

Isaiah and others have written upon all these things so extensively that it would be needless for me to give the quotations in this place. Connected with this restitution will be judgments and signs in heaven above and earth beneath, which will distress the nations by famine, pestilence, sword, tempests, hail, earthquakes, floods and whirlwinds, and which will finally terminate in a fire, as fatal to all the proud and them that do wickedly as the flood of Noah, and the fire that fell upon Sodom.

Then, as Noah was a survivor of a world destroyed, and himself and family, the sole proprietors of the earth, so will the saints of the Most High possess the earth and its whole dominion, and tread upon the ashes of the wicked. See Isa. xxiv, 1 to 6, Malachi last; Luke xxi, 25 to 30; Joel ii.

Having laid before your Majesty a faint description of that great revolution which awaits the world, I now come to the second part of my subject, viz.:

THE TIME OF ITS FULFILMENT.

The Apostles were in expectation of its immediate fulfilment while Jesus was yet with them until he taught them better. They inquired of him, saying, "Wilt thou *at this time* restore the kingdom to Israel?" But he answered them saying, "It is not given for you to know the *times* and *seasons* which the Father hath put in his own power." As much as to say, that it was not part of *their* mission, and was not to be fulfilled in their day. So, being corrected in this thing, the Apostle Peter afterwards informs us (Acts iii.) that the heavens must receive Jesus Christ until the times of restoration of all things spoken of by the Lord, by the Holy Prophets, and that at the times of restitution God would send him again. Jesus himself speaks of this same time when he says, [Luke xxi.] "Jerusalem shall be trodden down of the Gentiles, until the times of the Gentiles are fulfilled." Paul also comes to the same point of time, [Romans xi.] "Blindness in part is happened to Israel until the fulness of the Gentiles is come in."

These texts all have an allusion to one and the same time, viz.: the revolution of which we have spoken.

The Lord, [Luke xxi.] after speaking of the signs of his coming, says, "When ye see these things begin to come to pass, then know that the kingdom of God is nigh at hand," and then says that the generation who are witnesses of these signs beginning to come to pass will not pass away till all shall be fulfilled, including his second coming and kingdom.

Now the kingdom of God here spoken of cannot possibly allude to the kingdom of God which was set up in the days of the apostles, for that kingdom was already at hand when the Saviour predicted these things, and was set up immediately after his resurrection, and without the signs spoken of in the 21st of Luke having come to pass. Therefore he must have alluded to the kingdom of which Daniel and others spoke, which was to be set up "in the days of these kings," as represented by the feet and toes of the image; and it is well known to your Majesty, and to all Christendom, that these ten kingdoms out of the ruins of the Roman empire did not arise until many hundred years after the days of the apostles.

Let us here enumerate the signs spoken of which are to precede the Messiah's second coming and the setting up of his kingdom. "There shall be signs in the sun, and in the moon, and in the stars, and upon the earth distress of nations, with perplexity — the sea and the waves roaring, men's hearts failing them for fear, and for looking after those things which are coming on the earth: for the powers of heaven shall be shaken, and THEN shall they see the Son of Man coming in the clouds of heaven with power and great glory."

I beg leave barely to remind your Majesty that these signs have for the last ten years been fulfilling in the eyes of all people. I need not here particularize or point out their fulfillment, for passing events are too notorious to be hidden.

I now beg leave to call the attention of your Majesty to an important discovery, which has poured a flood of light upon these subjects, and which has actually revealed, and demonstrated that the present age is the time of their fulfillment. I allude to the discovery of an ancient record among the antiquities of America, a copy of the translation of which was lately presented to your Majesty; and another to his Royal Highness Prince Albert, by Mr. Brigham Young. The discovery of this record and the things connected with it, as they are now ushering in upon the world, are of more importance than any single event which has transpired in modern times. The discovery of America by Columbus 300 years since opened a new era upon the world, and poured a flood of light upon the startling nations. They awoke from the slumber of ages, and gazed with astonishment and wonder. As the first transports of admiration subsided, a spirit of enterprise seized the people, and a new impulse was given to the minds of men, which has resulted in mighty changes in the scientific, commercial and political departments; and which has mainly contributed in forming all the great outlines of modern character.

But it remained for the nineteenth century to open a treasure of knowledge, and to present to the world a discovery more extensive in its information, more glorious in its intelligence, and of greater magnitude in its final bearing upon men and things than all the discoveries of Columbus and his contemporaries. I allude to this ancient American record. By this means the history of the past in relation to half the world, has been opened as far back as the confusion of languages at Babel. A nation whose "bones are dried" and whose ruined temples and monuments have reposed for ages in silent, solemn and awful grandeur, has now spoken from the dust, and revealed to the world their history and with it their prophecies and their testimony of Jesus as the risen Messiah, and the Saviour of the world, not of Asia, only, but America also. From this record, we learn the astonishing fact that the Gospel was revealed among the ancient inhabitants of that continent, and the risen Jesus ministered in person unto them, setting in order all the offices and ordinances of his kingdom, and opening all the great outlines of his doctrine, together with a knowledge of the future down to the restoration of which we have spoken. By this means we are enabled to come to a knowledge of these points of doctrine and prophecy, and to understand clearly that which has been rendered obscure by coming down to us through the dark ages, robbed of its plainness by priestcraft and superstition, and mingled with the traditions of men. By this means we are enabled to understand definitely the signs of the times, and how and when the prophecies are to be fulfilled in relation to the great revolution so clearly set forth in this letter. And by this means we understand the fate of the world and the destiny to which the nations are hastening.

This ancient record was discovered in 1827 in Western New York in the bowels of the earth, where it had been concealed for 1400 years. It was there deposited by a holy prophet whose name was Moroni, in order to preserve it, at a time when a great nation was overthrown. It was translated, and published in English in 1830. Since that time it has been a principal means in the hands of God, of working a greater revolution among men than was ever known in so short a time. It has given rise to the Church of Christ of Latter-Day Saints, which was first organized with six members on the 6th of April, 1830, but which now numbers many thousands, both in America and Europe.

This Church professes to hold the ancient order of the Gospel as revealed both in the Bible and in this American record. They discard infant baptism as an invention of priestcraft, and hold to the baptism of penitent believers for remission of sins and to the gift of the Holy Ghost by the laying on of hands in the name of Jesus; and to the gifts of healing, prophecy, miracles, &c. as Jesus has promised in his word.

The Church of the Saints thus organized upon the ancient faith once delivered to the Saints, must grow and flourish, and spread among all nations, and must increase in faith and power and might and glory, until as a bride adorned for her husband, she is prepared for her coming Lord, and for the marriage supper of the Lamb.

Perhaps a few words of one of the prophets, as contained in this ancient record will serve to shew what is at hand to be fulfilled in plainer terms than any modern style of language can express. From the 57th page of the First Book of Nephi, as contained in this ancient record, I extract the following:

"The Lord will proceed to make bare his arm in the eyes of the nations, in bringing about his covenants and his gospel unto those who are of the house of Israel. Wherefore he will bring them again out of captivity, and they shall be gathered together to the lands of their inheritance — and they shall be brought out of obscurity and out of darkness, and they shall know that the Lord is their Savior and their Redeemer, the mighty One of Israel. And the blood of that great and abominable Church, which is the whore of all the earth shall turn upon their own heads, and they shall be drunk with their own blood. And every nation which shall war against thee O house of Israel, shall be turned one against another, and they shall fall into the pit which they digged to ensnare the people of the Lord; and all that fight against Zion shall be destroyed. And that great whore who hath perverted the ways of the Lord, yea that great and abominable Church, shall tumble to the dust, and great shall be the fall of it. For behold the time cometh speedily, that Satan shall have no more power over the hearts of the children of men; for the day soon cometh that all the proud and they who do wickedly shall be as stubble; and the day cometh that they must be burned. For the time soon cometh that the fulness of the wrath of God shall be poured out upon all the children of men, for he will not suffer that the wicked shall destroy the righteous, therefore he will preserve the righteous by his power, even if it so be that the fulness of his wrath must come, and the righteous preserved even unto the destruction of their enemies by fire. Behold I say unto you that these things must shortly come, yea, even blood, and fire and vapour of smoke, must come, and it must needs be upon the face of this earth; and it cometh unto men according to the flesh, if it so be that they harden their hearts against the Holy One of Israel; for behold the righteous shall not perish; for the time surely must come, that all who fight against Zion shall be cut off. And the Lord will surely prepare a way for his people, unto the fulfilling of the words of Moses, which he spake saying, "A prophet shall the Lord your God raise up unto you, like unto me; him you shall hear in all things whatsoever he shall say unto you." And it shall come to pass that all those who shall not hear that prophet shall be cut off from among the people.

And now I, Nephi, declare unto you that this prophet of whom Moses spake was the Holy one of Israel, wherefore he shall execute judgment in righteousness; and the righteous need not fear, for they are those who shall not be confounded. But it is the kingdom of the Devil which shall be built up among the children of men, which kingdom is established among them which are in the flesh, for the time speedily shall come that all the churches which are built up to get gain, and those which are built up to get power over the flesh, and those which are built up to become popular in the eyes of the world, and those who seek the lusts of the flesh and the things of the world and to do all manner of iniquity, — yea, in fine all those who belong to the kingdom of the Devil are they who need fear and tremble, and quake; they are those who must be brought low in the dust; they are those who must be consumed as stubble. And the time cometh speedily that the righteous must be led up as calves of the stall, and the Holy One of Israel must reign in dominion and might, and power and great glory. And he gathereth his children from the four quarters of the earth and he numbereth his sheep and they know him, and there shall be one fold and one shepherd; and he shall feed his sheep, and in him they shall find pasture."

I have given the above extract from this ancient prophecy, in order that your Majesty and the people of your dominion, may be aware of future events which are nigh, even at the door.

I must close this letter by forewarning the Sovereign and people of England, in the most affectionate manner, to repent and turn to the Lord with full purpose of heart. When I say repent, I mean my message for the lords and nobles, clergy and gentry, as well as Sovreign and people. Let them deal their bread to the hungry — their clothing to the naked; let them be merciful to the poor, the needy, the sick and the afflicted, the widow and the fatherless, — let them set the oppressed free and break every yoke; and dispense with their pride, extravagance, their luxury and excess, for the cries of the poor have ascended up to heaven, and their groans and tears have ascended up before the Lord, and his anger is kindled and he will no longer suffer their afflictions to go unnoticed.

In short, let them bring forth fruits meet for repentance, and come and be baptised in the name of Jesus, for remission of sins, and then shall they receive the Holy Spirit, and become the saints of the Most High, the children of Might; and signs shall follow them that believe; the sick shall be healed in the name of Jesus, devils shall be cast out, the deaf shall hear, and the dumb shall speak, and the poor shall have the gospel preached unto them.

Now, if the rulers, clergy, and people of England hearken to this message they shall have part in this glorious kingdom so clearly set forth in this letter, but if they will not hearken to the words of the prophets and apostles, they will be overthrown with the wicked, and perish from the earth.

The God of Israel hath sent his angel with this message to the children of men; "to them that dwelt upon the earth, and to every nation, and kindred and tongue and people, saying with a loud voice, "fear God, and give glory to him: for the hour of his judgment is come, and worship him that made heaven and earth, and the sea, and the fountains of waters."

With sentiments of profound respect, and with the most anxious desire for the welfare and prosperity of the Sovreign and people of England, I have the honor to subscribe myself,

Your Majesty's Humble Servant
And Loyal Subject,

{8}

"The Fountain of Knowledge"

(from *An Appeal to the Inhabitants of the State of New York,*
Letter to Queen Victoria,
(Reprinted from the Tenth European Edition,)
The Fountain of Knowledge; Immortality of the Body,
and Intelligence and Affection
[Nauvoo: John Taylor, Printer, 1840])

Modern men have been traditionated to believe that a sacred book was the fountain of Divine knowledge; That the heights and depths, and lengths and breadths of heavenly intelligence is contained therein, and that the human mind must be limited and circumscribed thereby, so as never to receive one particle of knowledge except the small amount contained within its pages.

This cannot be correct, as we shall now proceed to demonstrate.

However sacred and true may be the principles contained in a book yet these principles were true before they were written; and each truth was revealed before it was written, consequently known before it was written; therefore it follows that all revealed knowledge was obtained without books and independent of them; — while on the other hand no sacred book could come into existence without the pre-existence of all the principles of revealed knowledge contained therein. It is therefore a self-evident fact, that sacred books are the productions of revealed knowledge, and revealed knowledge is not originally produced from books. Hence a book cannot be the fountain or source of knowledge; but is at best but a stream from the fountain.

Again all books written on perishable materials are liable to destruction; but the fountain of knowledge cannot be destroyed. And should all books be distroyed, all the knowledge contained in them would still exist, and man might derive the very same knowledge from the very same fountain from whence it emenated previous to its being written.

Again, all mankind have not had the use of letters, they have not been qualified to read books. Very many of them have lived in ages and in countries where a copy of the Bible could not be procured. The art of printing is a modern discovery; previous to this improvement every copy must needs be written in manuscript at a vast expense of time and labor, which placed them beyond the reach of the greater portion of community, — not to mention the fact that even among the most enlightened portions of the earth the scriptures were prohibited by law from being possessed and read by the common people. Where then was the source of divine knowledge to which these millions could come, and drink, and live; if not to the God of heaven who revealeth secrets? If the sacred books were the only source of divine knowledge, then salvation must have been very limited indeed.

Again, a sacred book could never be made to contain a millionth part of the knowledge which an intelligent being is capable of receiving and comprehending.

Let us contemplate for a moment the mind's capacity, small indeed at first, but capable of infinite expansion, while a boundless field is extended on all sides, inviting enquiry and meditation.

O man! burst the chains of mortality which bind thee fast; unlock the prison of thy clay tenement which confines thee to this groveling, earthly sphere of action; and robed in immortality, wrapped in the visions of eternity, with organs of sight and thought and speech which cannot be impaired or weakened by time or use; soar with me amid unnumbered worlds which roll in majesty on high. Ascend the heights; descend the depths; explore the lengths and breadths of organized existence. Learn the present facts, the past history and future destiny, of things and beings: of God and his works; of the organizations of angels, of spirits, of men and animals: of worlds and their fullness; of thrones and dominions, principalities and powers. Learn what man was before this life and what he will be in worlds to come. Or seated high on a throne celestial, surrounded with the chaotic mass of unorganized existence; search out the origin of matter and of mind. Trace them through all the windings of their varied order, till purified and exalted all nature seeks a grand sublime repose and enters into rest, to change no more. Enter the sacred archives of the third heavens; hear with John the seven thunders speak, while forked lightnings flash around thy head; and trumps and voices loud proclaim the mysteries which are not lawful for man on earth to utter. And thus with knowledge stored, return to earth, and attempt to write all thou hast seen or heard or known of heaven and earth, of time and eternity, in a book.

You will then realize the truth of the language of the poet.

> Could we with ink the ocean fill,
> Was the whole earth of parchment made,
> And every single stick a quill,
> And every man a scribe by trade,
> To write the love of God above,
> Would drain the ocean dry,
> Nor could the whole upon a scroll
> Be spread from sky to sky.

It is not then to a book, however true or sacred or useful it may be that we would point to as the fountain of knowledge; but rather to the great fountain of light and truth enthroned in the midst of the heavens; the revealer of secrets and the author of all the truths in existence, whether written or not.

Knowledge from this source can only be derived by means of direct revelation.

It is communicated unto man by means of the voice of Jehovah; by the ministry of angels; or by visions; and by dreams, as well as by the spirit of prophecy and revelation.

By these means the ancients received all their knowledge of things past, present, and to come, as well as all their knowledge of principles, doctrines and commandments, by which they pleased God, and by which they obtained promises and a hope of immortality and eternal life.

By this means an Enoch was translated, a Noah saved from the flood; an Abraham honored and feared among the nations; a Jacob delivered; a Joseph exhalted to a throne.

By this means a Moses burst the chains of a tyrant and made a nation free.

By this means a Joshua conquered; and a David excelled all the wise men of the east.

By this means Jesus Christ conquered death and hell and ascended to the throne of his father. By this means his apostles spread his gospel among the nations with such unparalleled success. And in short, by this means a Joseph in modern times has restored the fullness of the gospel; raised the church out of the wilderness; restored to them the faith once delivered to the saints; and caused them to escape the edge of the sword, to break off the fetters of iron, to burst the gloomy vaults of Missouri's dungeons, to put to flight the armies of the aliens, and to confound all the deep laid plots of wicked priests and rulers which have been laid for their destruction.

By this means the Latter Day Saints have risen from obscurity, and after wading through seas of oppression; have obtained their chartered rights; have organized their councils, have commenced to rear their cities, and temples, have marshaled their legions and hurled defiance at the enemies of law and order, and have unfurled far on high the ensign of freedom: while the wisdom of their legislation and the power and purity of their doctrine have attracted the attention and won the admiration of millions at home and abroad, who are rallying to the standard; and thus the nucleus is formed for the universal dominion of freedom, peace and truth; and for the restoration of all things spoken by the prophets.

The gift of revelation is the key of knowledge. Without it we know comparatively nothing, and with it we may know all things, even the deep things of God.

From the foregoing observations some persons may be disposed to take advantage of the prejudice of the present age, by asserting that we are opposed to the scriptures, or that we wish to throw them out of use, and to turn the minds of men from them, or at least from a just estimation of their value: But such is not the case.

The scriptures are sacred and true, and useful in their place. Although they are not the fountain of knowledge, nor do they contain all knowledge, yet they point to the fountain, and are every way calculated to encourage men to come to the fountain and seek to obtain the knowledge and gifts of God. For instance, who can read of a Noah saved from a flood, of an Abraham delivered from famine and war, of a Lot saved from the flames of Sodom, of a Joseph delivered from prison and exalted to a throne, of a Moses emancipating a nation, of a Samuel exalting and dethroning kings, of a David rising from obscurity and contending with the legalized opposition of thrones and dominions, till seated on the throne of nations he reigns triumphantly glorious, and transmits to his son a kingdom, and riches, and wisdom, and glory, and honor, and power, far more excellent than had before been known among men? Who can read of a Daniel arrayed in robes of royal state, to preside over presidents of provinces, to teach senators wisdom, to instruct and reprove kings of the earth, to penetrate with prophetic eye the distant future, and to point out with nice precision the rise and fall of kingdoms, states, and empires! Who can read of Zachariah and Elizabeth, of Joseph and Mary, of Anne and Simeon, of the Shepherds of the plains of Judah, of the wise men of the east, of John the Baptist and Nathaniel, of Jesus Christ and his Apostles, of Paul and the disciples, of Cornelius and Annanias, of the churches of Rome, of Corinth, and of Ephesus, of John on the Isle of Patmos, and the seven churches of Asia, of Jew and Gentile; in short of all the people of God, under all dispensations and circumstances, whether patriarchal, Mosaic or Christian; who can read of all these, instructed, governed, and perfected by holding constant communion with heaven by revelations, by visions, by dreams, and by angels and the spirits of just men made perfect, and not feel a kindling desire in his bosom, to partake of the same blessings, and to hold intercourse with the same powers? Who, in view of all these would not feel a desire to hear the voice of Jehovah, to be wrapped in the visions of eternity; to gaze upon and hold converse with angels and spirits, to be instructed by visions and dreams of the night, and to partake of the testimony of Jesus, the spirit of prophecy?

Who with all these examples before him would not feel encouraged and emboldened to approach a throne of grace, and seek for things so reasonable, so useful, and so delightful?

But me thinks I hear the sighs and groans, and behold the tears of a broken hearted sinner whose bosom heaves with emotions of alternate hope and fear, of doubt and desire, while faith on the one hand invites him onward, and the strong bands of deep rooted tradition on the other holds him back, and the precepts of men whisper in his ears, that revelation has ceased for ever, that visions, angels, dreams, and the gift of prophecy are not for us; that we must be contented with the history of what others have enjoyed without expecting to enjoy the same ourselves.

To such I would say, be not deceived, God is the same yesterday to day and forever. His arm is not shortened that it cannot save; his ears are not heavy that he cannot hear; neither is he dumb that he cannot speak. His angels are ministering spirits to the heirs of salvation; and his spirit, is the same spirit of prophecy and revelation that it was in days of old.

The scriptures command you to covet earnestly the best gifts; but more especially the *spirit of prophecy*. Paul prays that you may be enriched with the spirit of *wisdom* and *revelation* in the *knowledge* of God. James says, "If *any man* lack wisdom let him ask of God who giveth to *all men* liberally and upbraideth not, and it *shall be given him*." Again, Jesus Christ declairs, that no man knows either him or his father, except it be revealed to him. He also declares that "to *know* God and *Jesus Christ* whom he hath sent, is life eternal." Consequently all who enjoy eternal life must *know* God *by revelation to themselves*.

"Come ye weary heavy laden," ye humble seekers after truth, take courage from all these glorious examples and precious promises: lay hold of the blessings which are calculated to exalt the mind, to enlarge the heart, and to enlighten the understanding, and thus prepare and qualify poor worms of the dust to shine with the wise as the brightness of the firmament and as the stars forever and ever.

The scriptures are given for the very purpose of inviting and encouraging men to come unto the great fountain of light and truth where they may enjoy all the blessings which are recorded in them, as having been enjoyed by the Ancients. And those who are contented to enjoy the history of blessings instead of the blessings themselves, may be compared to a man on a desolate island who has nothing to eat or to drink. But while he is famishing, and ready to perish with hunger and thirst he pulls a book from his pocket which contains the history of a feast of things once enjoyed by his forefathers. He reads with rapture of delight of the delicious meets, the rich viands, the sweet fruits and sparkling wines which were spread upon the plentious board, and of the joys of those who feasted freely there. But these recollections only serve to whet his apetite, and to increase his cravings after food. In the anguish of hopeless despair, he exclaims: O that I were at my father's house, O that I too might partake of the feast. At this moment a messenger appears before him in the attitude of an instructor, and kindly offers to relieve him. With a sudden ray of hope springing in his bosom and with an emploring look of confidence he enquires; what must I do to be saved from hunger and thirst and to feast as did my fathers? O friend, save or I perish.

But judge his feelings of disappointment and anguish when he is gravely told by his instructor that he does not need food as his fathers did. That it was only given to them because they had no sacred record, no history of the past to feast their souls upon, but now the cannon of feasting is complete, the record is full, he need not eat as they did, nor drink as they did; but to read the history of their feasting and to believe it and rejoice in it would answer the same purpose, and that it was wicked and even presumptious to desire or ask any food other than that which the reading of their record afforded him. In short, that they had the feast and he had the history of it, which amounted to the same thing; and he must therefore be content.

With these instructions he strives to restrain his apetite, he condemns himself a hundred times for feeling hungry and a thirst; the keener his desires for food and drink, the closer he pursues his study of the history of the feasting. He reads it over and over again, he commits it to memory, he presses it with fervor to his heart, he kisses it with reverence, he lays it for a pillow when he sleeps, and awakes but to read a new. But still finds no relief; in spite of himself his soul hungers and thirsts for food, such as his parents enjoyed and he pines out a wretched existence. But reading still the history of the past he discovers at last that he had overlooked an important sentence; a sentence which informs him that he must partake of the food for himself as they did for themselves or starve to death; and at the same time a messenger arrives with food, and wine in plenty, and kindly invites him to eat and drink; nay, says he, my instructor told me that this history was all the food I need, that it was enough for me to read and believe that my fathers ate that it was all the same as to eat myself. But says the kind instructor, that man was a deceiver, he has imposed upon you. Does not common sense teach you; does not experience teach you, and does not the history itself teach you that you must feast as well as they, or perish forever. The poor starving man is at last brought to his senses and is prevailed on to eat and drink and live. His spirits are then renewed, his soul is satisfied, and he looks with astonishment and wonder upon his former absurdity and that of his teacher and is surprised to think that such foolish ideas should have ever entered the human mind.

So is the man, who, led by the vain traditions and precepts of men is made to believe that the gifts of revelation, vision, the ministry of angels, and prophecy, and all the keys of knowledge which the ancients did enjoy, are not now needed, or to be enjoyed; but that the Bible which contains the history of them is all that is necessary.

O ye hungry, famishing souls who have thus been deceived, rouse from your slumbers, break off the shackles of your minds, burst through the thick darkness and gloom of ages with which you are surrounded, and emerge forth into the light and liberty of the gospel, that you may enjoy those great and glorious privileges which have been hid from ages and generations; but which are again made manifest in these last days, for the restoration of all things spoken by the prophets.

{9}

"Immortality and Eternal Life of the Material Body"

(from *An Appeal to the Inhabitants of the State of New York,*
Letter to Queen Victoria,
(Reprinted from the Tenth European Edition,)
The Fountain of Knowledge; Immortality of the Body,
and Intelligence and Affection
[Nauvoo: John Taylor, Printer, 1840])

Many philosophers and divines have written largely on the immortality of the *soul*, while the *body* and its material connections have been almost entirely neglected or lost sight of, as a mere temporary structure, having no interest in, or connection with the life to come.

An opinion prevails that the material worlds, were formed from nothing; they serve a momentary purpose, connected only with our present state of existence, and are then to be annihilated, — that the life to come is a life purely spiritual, having no connection with or dependence on any thing material.

Hence the idea of a "God without body or parts" — men without flesh and bones — and a heaven beyond the bounds of time and space — a world without buildings, or materials out of which to form them, or foundations on which to place them. Indeed, a world without food, clothing or any other substance, or property of which the mind can possibly conceive. And hence too, the idea, that all materialists must necessarily be infidels.

The object of the following treatice is to demonstrate both from revelation and reason, that these are errors of the grosest kind — mere relics of mysticism and superstition, riveted upon the mind by ignorance and tradition — in fact, that all persons except materialists must be infidels, so far at least as a belief in the scriptures is concerned. That man's body is as eternal as his soul, or his spirit.

That it is essential to his perfect organization, and that both are destined to an eternal union in the life to come. That the earth and our material bodies are the subjects of redeeming love, and are included as principle objects in the purchased possession.

In short, to set forth a system of eternal life and immortality which will include the heavens and the earth, and the inhabitants thereof, with all material substance. An eternal life of realities, of bodies and spirits immortal, of flesh and bones incorruptable, of inheritances of everlasting, of mansions eternal, of food and clothing, and gold and silver, and precious stones, and cities, villages and gardens celestial; of relationship, and affections, and endearments, and associations, and loves, and conversations, and intellectual enjoyments of every kind; in connection with riches, and honor and thrones and dominions, and principalities and powers, which God hath laid up for them that love him. A life and immortality which will be of such thrilling interest to all who understand it that kings would relinquish their thrones and cast away their crowns to possess it.

In order to convey some idea of the subject in hand by a simple illustration, suppose for instance a medicine had been invented, which would prove an effectual remedy for DEATH, with all its train of disorders, pains and sorrows; and by which the human system might be secured from the effects of time and age, and be renewed in all the freshness, bloom and beauty of eternal youth. What price would be too dear, or what sacrifice too great in order to obtain such a medicine. Honor, wealth, pain, ease, every thing man could posses in this vain world would be counted as dross, and would be at once relinquished as the merest trifle, in order to obtain so inestimable a blessing, as an eternal deliverance from disease and death. And this even with a view of only a natural or temporal existence in this imperfect world. Philosophers and statesmen, heroes and conquerors, philanthropists and benefactors, kings and commoners, have each in turn, in the midst of their vast plans, projects, and pursuits, looked upon the monster death as the king of terrors, who stands in their way, like Bunion's Apolion, to cut short their journey in pursuit of fame or wealth, of honor or renown. And who, like a terrible tyrant, mingles his poison in every cup of bliss and weakens all their aspirations.

But could we gain a victory over this monster with all his train of diseases, and live forever in this life of mingled bliss and sorrow: such an order of the things though vastly precious and desirable to short sighted mortals, must fall infinitely short, in comparisons of that state of perfection to which worlds are destined to arrive, in the wisdom and order of their great creator.

Perhaps by this time the reader will be ready to lay this book aside with contempt and to suppose that such a system is too good to be true; and that no satisfactory proof can be presented to the mind, of a life and destiny so different from the conceptions of men in general; but to such I would say, be patient, read a little farther, and a little farther still, and you shall be fully satisfied that a material renovation and eternal life is not only supported by revelation and reason, but that it is the only system of salvation revealed to man, and the only order of things promised, expressed, or hoped for by Jesus Christ and his prophets and apostles.

Man, unenlightened in regard to the past and future, may be compared to a passenger on a vessel floating swiftly down the current of an unknown river; surrounded with a dark mist which obscures from view every object in the distance. He sees the surface of the river immediately around him, and gliding swiftly onward, while its source and termination are both equally wrapped in mystery, and to him unknown.

So is man on the stream of time. At the first dawn of reason and reflection, he finds himself afloat on a current which bears him swiftly onward; while he knows not from whence he is, nor whither he goes. A mist too deep and dark for mortal eye to penetrate, shuts in his vision on every hand; while an unexplored eternity expands before, behind, and all around him.

Revelation and reason, like the sun of the morning rising in its strength, dispel the mists of darkness which surround him; till at length heaven's broad, eternal day expands before him, and eternity opens to his vision. He may then gaze with rapture of delight, and feast on knowledge which is boundless as the ocean from which it eminates.

There are two important facts connected with material existence, which appear self evident to every reflecting mind; and which are no where contradicted by any discoveries made by the aid of either revelation, science or reason, they are as follows:

1st. Matter cannot be originated form nonentity.

2d. Matter cannot be annihilated.

Hence it follows that the original elements of matter are eternal.

I am aware that it has been often asserted that in six days God made all things out of "*nothing*," but such an idea is no where found in the scriptures. It has originated in the mysticisms of modern times, and been kept alive by ignorance and folly.

The Hebrew word *baurau*, translated *he* (God) *created*, does not signify that he originated matter from nothing; but, implies that he formed, built, made or organized it. For instance, we say of a mechanic, that he created a building, a watch, or a steam engine; that is, he made it out of existing matterials.

As a proof that we have applied the term "*create*" correctly, we would here offer several examples, where the Almighty created beings out of materials, and not out of nothing. For instance, he made fish and fowl out of the water: he also created cattle, beasts, and creeping things out of the ground; and he created man also out of the ground, and woman out of a rib.

So, when we read that God made the heavens and the earth, we understand that he made them out of eternal elements, by organizing, combining, seperating and arranging them in such manner as to form earth, air, water, fire, etc. each in their respective place, proportion and order.

The earth and other planetary systems thus formed from original chaos would still, while without inhabitants or productions, be considered empty and desolate. Hence the Hebrew words *to hoo vaubohoo* are introduced in the original text, to express this idea; and should be translated, *empty and desolate*: the sentence would then read, *the earth was empty and desolate,* instead of, "*the earth was without form and void.*" The latter sentence is a contradiction to itself, as well as to common sense. Nothing can exist and still be without *form* and *void.*

The great architect of the heavens and of the earth, having organized and arranged a world finds it still empty and desolate. He then proceeds to the organization of animal and vegetable life, all of which he formed from existing elements, and not from nothing.

Now if it were in his power to form them out of nothing, why make use of earth in order to form man, and beasts, and plants, and flowers? and why subject Adam to a deep sleep and the loss of a rib, as a material out of which to make a woman, when it was just as easy to have formed her out of nothing?!!! As scripture no where gives us to understand that things were made from nothing, let us turn to reason and philosophy.

These would teach us that something cannot be made out of nothing; because this would contradict a manifest law of truth.

The laws of *truth* are omnipotent and unalterable—no power in heaven or on earth can break them in the least degree. Among these laws we find that two and two make just four—that five from eight leave three, and that nothing added to nothing is nothing still. And ten thousand nothings multiplied together cannot increase the amount.

If it still be argued that something can be made from nothing, we would enquire how many solid feet of nonentity it would require to make one solid foot of material substance? The very idea is the climax of absurdity.

Therefore we argue that it is a self evident fact, clearly manifested to every reflecting mind, that the elements of matter are eternal. That the earth was formed out of the eternal elements, and man's body out of the earth. These facts are not only proven from scripture, reason and philosophy, but are also demonstrated or confirmed by daily experience. The work of creation has been proceeding in every age up to the present time upon the same unchangable principles. That is, all material organization in our world is produced from the earth, or from its own elements, as we daily witness; while there is not a single instance of a thing, or being, produced from nothing, so far as has come within the sphere of man's observation.

Modern discoveries in the science of geology have had a tendency to illustrate and confirm these important facts; and to explode the systems of mysticism, which while they throw a vail over the whole subject, as if too sacred for investigation, would fain make the world believe, that a God without body or parts, whose centre is every where and his circumferance no where; originated all things from nothing, some six thousand years since, while at the same time formations are found in the bowels of the earth which indicate an existence of perhaps hundreds of thousands of years.

These narrow minded sectarians whose motto is that *"ignorance is the mother of devotion,"* not only shun all investigation on these subjects and teach others so to do; but they would fain compel all scientific men to be infidels whether they are willing or not. That is, they would compel them to disbelieve in the revealed word of God, or else on the other hand deny plain facts which they know perfectly to be true. On the other hand, many well informed men fall into unbelief of the scriptures, simply for want of knowledge to distinguish between that which is really revealed and the mysticisms, absurdities and nonsense which ignorance, bigotry and superstition have thrown over it.

Suppose for instance, discoveries should yet be made which would demonstrate that some of the formations of our earth had existed for millions of years. This would prove that sectarianism is false in its statement, that God made all things out of nothing some six thousand years ago; but it would not prove anything against the idea that he organized the earth at that time out of the ruins of a former world; or out of elements which had existed from all eternity. Therefore, for ought that appears in the history of creation, the scriptures might still be true.

Again, the first idea which we receive from Moses in regard to the existence of the earth, is, that it was overwhelmed in, or mingled with the elements of water. Whether this state represents the ruins of some former world destroyed by a flood, or whether it was the begining of an original organization, he does not inform us. But suffice to say, God's spirit moved upon the surface of the waters, and he gathered or assuaged them so far, that some part of the globe became dry land. This, together with the flood of Noah, abundantly accounts for the shells and other marine formations, found in the interior of the earth, in the tops of the high mountains and in the interior of the vast continents; proving that all parts of the earth had at some remote period been for a long time overwhelmed in water.

Having arrived by careful investigation to ONE IMPORTANT FACT, and that is, that the elements of matter are eternal; that they are co-existent with the life time of the Almighty; we now proceed to the investigation of the other proposition, viz: that no material substance can be annihilated. As we have shown the absurdity of a material substance being produced from nonentity, we must now show the utter impossibility of its ceasing to exist. One error is often productive of a thousand more, while the discovery of one truth often turns the key to innumerable other truths. One of the foundation errors of modern times is the belief in a Deity without body or part, whose centre is every where, and circumference no where. This leads to the idea that we in order to become like him, must become immaterial beings, and cease to be connected with material things. Consequently, the material world is by such, considered as a work of yesterday, originating from nothing, to serve a momentary purpose, like the temporary frame-work beneath a stone arch, and destined to be torn down and cease to exist the moment the key-stones are placed in the spiritual structure. Such persons would go on from one error to another, deceiving and being deceived, till in their imaginations and hopes, (in the language of Milton,) "the great globe itself would desolve, and disappear like the baseless fabric of a vision," and all the material orbs which shine with resplendent glory in the firmament of heaven would cease to be: and a God without body or parts, high seated on a top-less throne, far beyond all space, and surrounded with myriads of beings like himself; (that is, without body or parts,) would be all in all.

What then could exist, I answer nothing. Ten thousand such Gods, and thrones, and places, and beings, all taken together, would be of less consequence than the smallest part of an atom. In fact they could neither be substance nor shadow. I here confess that a God without body or parts as described in the Church of England Confession of Faith, in the Presbyterian Articles, and in the Methodist Discipline: and as worshipped by a large portion of christendom, is not with me an object of veneration, fear, or love. It is not in his power to hate or love, or to do good or evil to any being whatever. But when this same God is said to have "his center every where and his circumference no where, it forms in the rational mind a monster so inconceivably absurd, that I am almost tempted to indulge in irony and compare it to the Paddy's definition of the term nothing, "*a footless stocking without a leg.*" Pardon me, ye worshippers of this singular God, I ought to respect your feelings and rights sufficiently to refrain from any expression that would wound your feelings in the least.

But to return to the main thread of our subject, viz: the impossibility of the annihilation of matter, we would enquire in the first place what the scriptures reveal on the subject.

The Psalmist declares that the heavens and the earth shall be folded up as a vesture and that they shall be changed.

Isaiah and other prophets testify that they will be burned; and pass away and there will be a new heavens and a new earth.

The Apostles adopt the same language on this subject with this addition, that the *"elements shall melt with fervant heat."* And finally the Lord declares by the mouth of John, saying; "Behold I make *all things new."* Now every one the least acquainted with terms, must know that none of these expressions convey the least idea of annihilation; but on the contrary they clearly reveal the destiny of the material world, viz: that the elements are to be melted, changed, purified, and renewed; EVEN ALL THINGS. And it is further said, that the new heavens and the new earth shall endure forever.

Therefore the scriptures decide in the most definite terms that nothing will be annihilated; but that *all things* will be made new.

The science of chemistry serves to illustrate the subject in the most clear and lucid manner. For instance, by burning or melting any substance, not one particle is annihilated, they are only separated, decomposed, analized, and changed, and could the whole operation be reversed they would be restored to their former state without the loss of a single particle.

If then, we find ourselves composed of, and associated with material substance, which is eternal in its elementary principles, and inseparable connected with all organized existence in all worlds, past, present, and to come, we must feel the same interest in, and the same solicitation for the salvation, exaltation, and perfection of our bodies that we do for our souls or spirits.

But a terrible and apparently insurmountable barrier presents itself at the very outset of the subject of the salvation of the body. It is this. Our experience proves, that our material bodies are subject to *dissolution, decay* or *death.* If there is no remedy for this; if there is no conqueror, no deliverer from this awful monster: no restoration from under his dominion, then farewell to all our hopes, as to the salvation of the material body. For, notwithstanding its elementary principles are eternal, yet its present organization, its shape, form, and proportions, consequently its association with our spirits must have an end.

The great inquiry at length arises, which is perhaps of more importance to the welfare and happiness of our being than any other point now under consideration. Is death, or dissolution inseparably connected with a material organization? is it an elementary principle, an attribute of all material existence? that is, are all material formations of such a nature that they must, according to the laws of their existence, wax old, decay and die? To this inquiry we answer in the negative.

The whole material world, in its first formation was good: the maker himself being judge. There is no intimation of any principle of death, pain, sorrow, dissolution or decay, as connected with any part of all his works, while existing in their original purity; neither have we any reason to believe that they were constructed as to be incapable of enduring forever.

In this world of original life and purity, we discover at once the purpose, the object and uses of every part of our material system. The earth, as a necessary foundation, or dwelling place of animal existence, teaming with every variety of production, calculated for their increase and comfort. The material body, with all its organs of power, with all its parts so constructed as that each performs a part which is indispensably necessary for the comfort and convenience of the whole. For instance, the eyes to see, the ears to hear, the mouth to taste, the hands to handle, the feet to walk, the tongue to speak, etc., each of which principles directly contribute to the happiness of our being. To dispense with either of these parts would be to diminish a portion of our enjoyment without which we could not arrive at perfection. Such then, is the nature and purpose of our material being, considered in its original pure and uncorrupted state.

How then shall we account for the introduction of pain, sickness, disease, sorrow, and death into a world so happy, and so good?

The scriptures inform us that Adam and Eve transgressed the law of their creator, and that the penalty is DEATH. Here it is said by Paul, *"that sin entered into our world and death by sin."* *"That death is the wages of sin."* Also, that, *"by one man came death."* Again, *"the sting of death is sin; and the strength of sin is the law."*

Here then, is the *root* of the *evil*. Hence lies the whole mistake. Instead of death being necessarily connected with our original nature, he has intruded himself into our midst, as an enemy to happiness. Once he had no place, power or dominion in our world; nor could he enter there till *sin*, that vile traitor prepared his way, and opened to him the gates. He soon entered in triumph, with his numerous train of associates: dethroned old father Adam, our lawful sovereign, and put our garrison to the sword.

He then usurped the dominion of the earth, placed his numerous ministers in power around his royal person: and thus commenced the reign of *terror*, which has caused "all creation to groan in pain together until now: waiting for the redemption of the body.

So long, and so little interrupted has been his reign, that many of his subjects have concluded it is his right. They therefore resign their bodies together with the earth and its fullness to his everlasting dominion; and as they suppose to eternal dissolution and destruction: being quite contented in the hope, (like Socrates,) of escaping with nothing but their spirits, to some immaterial world.

Having shown that the elements of matter are eternal: that they did not originate from nonentity and cannot be annihilated: that they have their uses, which are essential to our happiness, and that death is not connected with our original nature; and consequently makes no necessary part of our material organization; but is a usurper, a tyrant, to whom we have been subject; *"not willingly but by reason of him who hath subjected the same in hope."* We must now inquire after the great plan of deliverance and restoration.

"As in Adam all die, even so in Christ shall all be made alive." "As by one man came death, by one man comes also, the resurrection of the dead." Christ came to destroy him who had the power of death, that is the devil; and to deliver those who, through fear of death were all their lifetime subject to bondage." So says the great apostle.

From the above texts, and from what follows we shall be able to demonstrate that one of the principle objects of our blessed Redeemer in coming into our world, was the redemption of our material bodies, and the restoration of the whole phisical world from the dominion of sin, death, and the curse.

If we can give one example of a material organization; of flesh and bones, actually rescued from the dominion of death and the grave, and made immortal, and capable of eternal existence, then the immortality of the body is clearly established: and the same example will form a precedent, from which (reasoning from analogy,) we may draw a safe conclusion as to the redemption of all others, especially if we have direct and positive promises to that effect.

SUCH WAS JESUS CHRIST, THE CRUSIFIED AND RISEN SAVIOR. It was not enough that he should *die* for the sins of the world; but he must also *rise from the dead.* Christ Jesus and him crusified, would never have been preached by Peter, Paul or any one else, as glad tidings of salvation if he had not risen from the dead. A gloomy solemn silence brooded over all nature, and the once eloquent tongues of the apostles themselves were staid with grief, and their lips sealed with sadness, and the death gloom of despair hung upon their brows, and settled with deep desponding melancholy upon their hearts. Till on a sudden they *"were begotten again unto a lively hope by the resurrection of their master from the dead."* When they first saw him they (like the mystics of modern times,) supposed it was only a spirit, they seemed to have no idea of a physical or material salvation, or existence beyond the grave. But, like Socrates, Plato, Confucius, and other heathen philosophers they thought of nothing more than a spiritual existence.

But judge their surprise and joy, and wonder, when he exclaimed: *"Handle me and see; for a spirit hath not FLESH AND BONES as ye see me have."*

Here was an end of misticism; here was a material salvation; here was flesh and bones, immortal, and celestial, prepared for eternal bloom in the mansions of glory; and this demonstrated by the sense of seeing, feeling, and hearing.

What say ye, my readers, who is the infidel? Is it the materialist who believes in the eternal existence of matter in union with mind? Or is it he who, like the heathen, only fancies to himself an immortality in some fairy world of spirits, some heaven without substance? Or in the language of a modern christian poet:

"Where is heaven? beyond all space,
The distance mind can never trace."

But to return from our short but fanciful flight to a world which only exists in the imagination of sectarians, heathen philosophers, and poets, to our world of realities and tangibility. The apostles not only handled him, and examined his wounds, but ate and drank, and walked, and conversed with him, and found him every way adapted and qualified for an active and useful life; and for an enlarged sphere of action, as a king, lawgiver, priest, mediator, judge, and conqueror, and preacher of the gospel. Hitherto his labors had been confined to Judea, and to his own kindred and people in that small province which gave him birth. But now he might with propriety exclaim, in the language of Montgomery:

"Heaven's broad day hath o'er me broken,
Far above earth's span of sky.
Am I dead? Nay, by this token
Know that I have ceased to die."

Unfettered from the bonds of mortality and death, and clothed with organs, strong and lasting as the immortal mind; and no longer governed by the laws of this limited sphere of action, he could soar away to distant continents and islands, beyond the towering waves and boisterous storms of ocean; and there in other tribes and tongues, make known the glad tidings of immortality and eternal life.

Or winging his way to the abodes of spirits in prison he could there preach deliverance to the captive and the opening of the prison to them that are bound, and thus bind up the broken hearted, and comfort all that mourn. Or taking leave of earth with all its cares and sorrows, and of the dark regions of the unhappy dead; once dark but now illuminated with a ray of hope, he could wing his way to the mansions of his father, and sit down on his throne, as the joy and comfort of better worlds; till the times of restoration should call him again to earth, to reign on the throne of his father Jacob; and to take the universal government of the purchased possession, as a king over all the earth.

His disciples, being by tangible evidence now delivered from mysticism, and made to realise in the most lively manner, a real and substantial salvation from sin, death, hell, and the grave, were filled with joy, as intense as was their sorrow; and were now prepared, when the appointed time should arrive, to be the bearers of glad tidings indeed, to a dark and benighted world; a world who through fear of death had been all their life-time subject to bondage. They not only preached Jesus Christ and him crucified: but they testified of his resurrection, and that he would change our vile bodies and fashion them like unto his glorious body.

This was a message precisely adapted to the wants of the people; it fitted their case, and it still fits ours. What is it my friends which makes us unhappy? Why do we mourn? and why is our souls sorrowful? In short, why does all creation groan in pain together? The answer is: — DEATH, DISEASE, SICKNESS, PAIN, and DEATH. These, together with our sins, weigh us down in gloom and sorrow till me thinks a visitor from a world of eternal life would hardly be able to look upon our world and contemplate the scene for a moment. In view of these things an aged poet exclaimed:

> "I've seen yon weary
> winter's sun,
> Twice forty times return;
> And every time has added proof
> That man was made to mourn."

What kind of salvation then do we need? I reply, we need salvation from death and the grave, as well as from our sins. And we have now shown clearly that this is the salvation provided and brought to light by the gospel; a salvation not only of our spirits, but of our body and parts, of our flesh and bones, of our hands, and feet and head, with every organ, limb and joint. What kind of salvation does the earth need, in order to fit it for the abode of immortal man? I answer, it needs a redemption from the withering curse of sin and restoration to its paradistical state. The inquiry now arises whether this salvation will be universal as it relates to the redemption of the body; to which I answer in the affirmative, as proved by the texts before quoted. This gives rise to another inquiry, viz: whether all who rise from the dead will be equally happy? to which I answer NO. After the resurrection of the body, men are to be judged according to their works; and will enjoy that which they are prepared to enjoy. For instance, our works determine the time of our rising, as well as the enjoyments which we shall possess. We read, Rev. 20, that there will be a first resurrection, enjoyed by the blessed and holy; while the rest of the dead will not rise till a thousand years afterwards.

Again, we read that among the servants of God one man is made ruler over ten cities; another over five; another over none; notwithstanding they all rise from the dead.

So we see, the great object of our life should be to secure a part in the first resurrection, and also to secure all the glory and dominion and power and might and possession and happiness which it is possible for us to secure, by faith, and obedience to the commandments of the risen Jesus.

In the resurrection, and the life to come, men that are prepared will actually possess a material inheritance on the earth. They will possess houses, and cities, and villages, and gold and silver, and precious stones, and food, and rayment, and they will eat, drink, converse, think, walk, taste, smell and enjoy. They will also sing and preach, and teach, and learn, and investigate; and play on musical instruments, and enjoy all the pure delights of affection, love, and domestic felicity. While each, like the risen Jesus can take his friend by the hand and say: "Handle me and see; for a spirit hath not flesh and bones, as ye see me have."

We shall now proceed to examine the writings of the prophets and apostles on this subject, in order to show that a material existence in the flesh, upon the earth, in their glorified and risen bodies. was the doctrine uniformly taught and embraced by holy men of old; and that they all lived and died, in hope of no other, than a material immortality and eternal life.

To begin at the fountain head, let me say that God, the father of our Lord Jesus Christ, is every where in the scripture revealed as a being possessing a bodily organization in all its parts. He is said to have head, eyes, ears, mouth, nose, nostrils, face, arms, hands, fingers, backparts, feet and all other parts. It is also said that man was made in his likeness and image. Jesus Christ is also represented to be the express image of his person.

From all these facts we learn that God the father has a real and substantial existence in human form and proportions, like Jesus Christ, and like man. Men's precepts would carry the idea that it was the *"moral image"* only and not the physical likeness of Diety that man was formed to represent. But as we find no such term in the scriptures as *"moral image;"* and as we presume God has no immoral image or likeness, having but one image or likeness, and that is his features shape or form, which is said to be like Jesus, and like man, therefore we can only judge of his existence by the pattern which represents him. But it is said that *"God is a spirit."* This is often quoted to prove that he does not exist in a personal or bodily form. But I would inquire of such, what a spirit is? Is there such a being as an individual intelligence in personal form, without flesh and bones, and without the grosser properties of matter which are tangible to our senses, or touch? We freely admit there is. For such are we, while our bodies are in the grave. But who shall say that an individual spirit of this kind, is not an organized personage of a proper shape, form, and proportions; and who shall say they are not composed of matter, although of a more subtle and refined nature than we are prepared fully to comprehend, while moving in our present sphere? The fact is, mortal man knows but a very little in regard to the more refined properties of matter as it approaches the confines of spirituality and approximates towards its highest state of refinement, in order to form those links which connect it with mind, or with intelligence. Suffice it to say, that reason and experience teaches that every individual intelligence, must have a deffinite centre and circumference, definite form and shape, and must therefore occupy a certain point in space. And therefore to say that an individual intelligence really exists, *"whose centre is every where and his circumference no where*; or even to assert that an individual intelligence can personally occupy two distinct places at the same time is worse than nonsense; it is folly in the extreme.

It is clearly manifest that Jesus Christ himself cannot occupy more than one place at a time, in person. And we believe it is admitted on all hands, that he partakes of all the fullness of the God-head, and has the same power as his father; and is glorified with the same glory. Indeed, in his prayer to the father, he admits that they are *one*, and prays that his disciples may be *one* with them AS THEY ARE ONE. Now, if the father's centre is every where and his circumference no where, then Jesus Christ is the same; and if the father and son are thus, then all his disciples must in turn have their centre every where and their circumference no where, in order to be one, as they are one. Again, if the father is without body or parts, then the son must also be without body or parts in order to be like him: and if the father and son are thus, then his disciples must be without body or parts, in order that the prayer may be answered, which was, that the father and son and his disciples might be ONE in the same sense of the word. What a world of mystery has been thrown over the subject of the oneness of the father and the son, when the simple truth is this: they are one in the same sense of the word; that all the children of God are required to be one: that is, one by perfect agreement. *"God is a spirit,"* so is Jesus Christ a spirit, and so are we spirits. But then some spirits are associated and connected with bodies of flesh and bones, and some are not. But all intelligent beings have a personal identity, and embodiment; whether it be of flesh or bones, or of some substance more refined. The only difficulty remaining to be solved, is this, how or in what sense can an organized intelligent being be every where present. To this inquiry we reply: not in person, but in influence or representation. In this latter sense of the word at least, it may be said that Queen Victoria is present in China, in India, and many other places at the same time. That is, she has representatives there. So is it with God. He has from all eternity to all eternity a priesthood of the order of his son which is after the power of an endless life, without beginning of days or end of years. This delegated authority acts in his name, and by his power when and wherever it is commissioned. It does the work that he would do if present on the same occasion, a reception or rejection of any person holding this power and authority is emphatically rejecting or receiving him that sent them. Hence Christ said to those whom he sent: whoso receiveth you receiveth me; and whoso receiveth me receiveth him that sent me.

But besides this representative presence, there is another sense in which God may be every where present, not in person; but by a proceeding principle which emanates from him to fill the immensity of space; which principle is light. This proceeding principle is in all things, and is the law by which they live and move and have a being.

But to return to the examination of the prophets and apostles, on the subject of man's material existence and inheritance in the life to come. As Job is one of the most ancient writers let us commence with his testimony. Job, what say ye? did you look for a material existence on the earth after the resurrection, or otherwise? Ans. "I know that my redeemer liveth, and that he shall stand at the latter day upon the *earth*: and though after my skin worms distroy this body, yet in my flesh shall I see God." Job 19, 25, 26.

Let the Psalmist next speak: Come David, speak out, and tell us what you know on this subject. "The righteous shall inherit the land, and dwell therein forever." Psalm 37, 29.

Solomon, are you of the same mind of your father? if so speak. "The upright shall dwell in the land, and the perfect shall remain in it." Prov. 2d. 21st.

Isaiah, your turn comes next, what do you testify? "Thy people also shall be all righteous; they shall inherit the land forever." Isa. 60, 21.

"For as the new heavens, and the new earth which I will make shall remain before me saith the Lord, so shall your seed and your name remain." "And it shall come to pass that from one new moon to another, and from one sabbath to another, shall *all flesh* come to worship before me saith the Lord." Isaiah 64, 22, 23.

Ezekiel, as you are a witness in this case, please relate to us whether any thing was revealed to you in regard to the resurrection of the material body, and its final residence on the earth.

"So I prophesied as I was commanded, and as I prophesied there was a noise, and, behold a shaking and the *bones* came together, *bone* to his *bone*.

"And when I beheld, lo, the *sinews* and the *flesh* came up upon them, and the *skin* covered them above.

"And the *breath* came into them, and they *lived*, and stood upon their *feet*, an exceeding great army."

"Thus saith the Lord God, behold, O my people, I will *open* your *graves*, and cause you to *come up out of your graves*, and bring you into the *land* of *Israel*. And ye shall know that I am the Lord, when I have opened your graves, O my people, and brought you up out of your graves, and shall put my spirit in you, and you shall live; and I shall *place* you in your *own land*: then shall ye know that I the Lord have spoken it, and performed it, saith the Lord."

"And they *shall dwell* in the *land* that *I have given* unto *Jacob* my servant, *wherein your fathers have dwelt;* and they shall dwell therein, even they and their children and their children's children forever: and my servant David shall be their prince forever."

"Moreover, I will make a covenant of peace with them; It shall be an *everlasting covenant* with them; and I will place them, and multiply them, and will set my *sanctuary* in the midst of them *forevermore."* Ezekiel 37.

We will now dismiss this witness who has spoken to the point; and call upon Daniel.

"And many of them that *sleep* in the *dust* of the *earth shall awake.* Daniel 12th. 2d.

"And the kingdom and dominion, and the greatness of the kingdom UNDER THE WHOLE HEAVEN shall be given to the people of the saints of the Most High." Dan. 7, 27.

Very well Daniel. Now here comes little Hosea to give his voice among the rest. Hear him.

"I will ransom them from the power of the grave; I will redeem them from death. O death, I will be thy plague; O grave, I will be thy destruction." Hosea 13, 14.

Let us now hear Zechariah.

"And his (the Lord's) feet shall stand in that day upon the mount of Olives which is before Jerusalem on the east." "And the Lord my God shall come, and all the saints with thee." "And the Lord shall be king over all the earth; in that day shall there be one Lord, and his name one."

"All the land shall be turned as a plain, from Geba to Rimmon, south of Jerusalem: and it shall be lifted up, and inhabited in her place from Benjamin's gate, unto the place of the first gate, unto the corner gate, and from the tower of Hananeel unto the king's wine-presses. And men shall dwell in it, and there shall be no more utter destruction; but Jerusalem shall be safely inhabited."

"And it shall be that whoso will not come up of all the families of the land unto Jerusalem to worship the king, the lord of hosts, even upon them shall be no rain." Zek. 14.

Having selected a few out of many of the most important witnesses on this subject, from the Old Testament, we will now proceed to an examination of New Testament witnesses: beginning with Jesus Christ.

"Blessed are the meek; for they shall inherit THE EARTH." "Thou shalt call his name Jesus." "He shall be great, and shall be called the son of the Highest; and the Lord God shall give unto him the throne of his father David; and he shall reign over the house of Jacob forever; and of his kingdom there shall be no end." Luke 1st. 31, 32.

"Now this I say, brethren, that flesh and blood cannot inherit the kingdom of God; neither doth corruption inherit incorruption." 1st. Cor. 15th, 42, 50.

So numerous are the testimonies of the Apostles in regard to the reserection of the material body, that we do not deem it expedient to quote them at large, but will submit the case to the judgement of our reader, with a single remark on one passage.

"*Flesh* and *blood*" says the Apostle, "cannot inherit the kingdom of God." Now if he had said that *flesh* and *bones* could not inherit the kingdom of God, then he would have excluded a risen Saviour therefrom, together with all those who are to rise from the dead in his image, and in the fashion of his glorious body.

The fact should be carefully borne in mind, that while the prophets and apostles every where speak of flesh and bones, and sometimes even of skin and sinews in connection with the resurrection, they no where speak of a restoration of the *blood* to the physical system, but always substituted the word spirit. Hence we conclude that the immortal body in its new organization is quickened by a fluid called spirit, which emanates from God, and is so pure that it renovates the system, and fills it with eternal life, and vigour.

While the natural body and the spiritual body are alike composed of flesh and bones etc., the one is quickened by the blood, and the other by spirit only. And this seems to constitute the principle difference between them.

Having now examined the highest authorities on the earth, as far back as ancient Job, and down through all former dispensations; and having proved that they all agree in the expectation of a material resurrection and an everlasting possession on the earth:

We will now soar to the heavens, and for a moment listen to the songs of beings who have bid farewell to this vale of tears, and who dwell in the immediate presence of God and the Lamb; and see whether they have altered their mind on this subject since their exit from time into eternity.

"And they sung a new song saying:

> "Thou art worthy to take the book,
> And to open the seals thereof:
> For thou wast slain, and hast redeemed us,"
> To God by thy blood, out of every kindred,
> And tongue, and people and nation;
> And hast made us unto our God,
> Kings and priests: *and we shall reign on the earth*
> Rev. 5, 9, 10.

Thus our readers will perceive that heaven and earth and the inhabitants thereof, as many as are truly enlightened by the spirit of God, all join in bearing witness to the salvation, exaltation, glory and immortality of the physical system of man; and of his *eternal inheritance on the earth*.

Perhaps some soul, just awaking, by the perusal of these pages, from the long night of darkness and error which like a gloomy cloud has brooded over the nations, and begining to come to his more perfect senses, will enquire; is earth indeed our everlasting home? Where then is heaven? To which inquiry we reply, that earth, and the other material creations which spangle the firmament with a flood of glory, are all heavenly kingdoms, together with the inhabitants thereof: so far as they are glorified. Heaven then, composed of an innumerable association of glorified worlds, and happy immortal beings, beaming with an effulgence of light, intelligence and love, of which our earth, small and insignificant as it is, must form some humble part.

Immortal man, made a king and a priest unto God; and associated with a system of systems so grand, so glorious; so extensive and sublime, will by no means be confined, or limited in his sphere of action to this small planet; but will wing his way, like a risen Saviour, from world to world with all the ease of communication, that we now visit different neigborhoods and places on our earth; and thus exploring, conversing, searching, and forming an acquaintance with God and his works: He will be able to receive and impart that finish of education and knowledge which only buds in time; but blooms and ripens in eternity. While the continued and ceaseless exertions of creative goodness will, by the acquisition of new creations, form a sufficient field for the exercise of his priestly and kingly powers: And thus fulfill the prediction on the head of Jesus, as recorded by the prophet Isaiah, "OF THE INCREASE OF HIS KINGDOM AND GOVERNMENT THERE SHALL BE NO END."

"Intelligence and Affection"

(from *An Appeal to the Inhabitants of the State of New York,*
Letter to Queen Victoria,
(Reprinted from the Tenth European Edition,)
The Fountain of Knowledge; Immortality of the Body,
and Intelligence and Affection
[Nauvoo: John Taylor, Printer, 1840])

These, like material things, have their origin in eternal, uncreated elements; and like them, must endure forever. They are the foundations of enjoyment, the main-springs of glory and exaltation, and the fountains from which emanate a thousand streams of life, and joy, and gladness; diffused through all worlds, and extending to all extent.

They are the principle roots from which shoot forth innumerable branches, which bud in time, and blossom and ripen in eternity; producing a perfume more delicious than the balmy sweets of Arabia, and fruits more precious than the apples of Eden.

The human mind in infancy, like the body, is small and weak indeed. It neither possesses intelligence nor affection to any great degree; for the latter is the production of the former; — grows with its growth, and strengthens with its strength; and cannot exist independent and separate therefrom.

This infant mind commences to expand, and continues to enlarge itself just in proportion to the truths that are presented for its food, and the time and opportunity it has to digest and comprehend them. If unassociated with other intelligences, it expands but very little, — all its powers remain in a great measure inactive and dormant.

For instance, let an infant be cut off from all communication with other intelligences, let it grow to manhood entirely alone, and it still knows little more than in infancy.

One child may be raised to manhood possessing only the limited knowledge of a Hotentot, while another is made to comprehend the sublime truths of a Newton.

The human mind then, is capable of a constant and gradual expansion to an unlimited extent. In fact, its receptive powers are infinite.

Once set free from the chains of incorrect tradition; and unfettered from the limited creeds and superstition of men, and associated with beings of unlimited intelligence, it may go freely on from truth to truth; enlarge itself like the rays of the morning; circumscribe the earth, and soar to the heavens; comprehend the mysteries of the past, and remove the veil from the future; till the wide expanse of eternity, with all its treasures of wisdom, is brought within the range of its comprehension.

It is true, that, in this life the progress of the mind in intelligence, is not only gradual, but obstructed in various ways. It has to contend, not only with its own prejudices and the errors of an opposing world, but with innumerable weaknesses, temptations, cares, and troubles, with which it is continually beset.

And finally, its organs are weakened by disease, or worn with age, till it sinks into a backward tendency—loses a portion of that which it has been able to comprehend, and partakes of a kind of secondary childhood.

From this fact, some are ready to conclude, that the mind, like the body, has its limits; its point of maturity, beyond which it can never expand; and that arriving at this climax of maturity, like a full grown plant, it is incapable of a further advance. But this is a mistake. It is not the mind itself that is thus limited and confined within a circle so narrow, but it is the circumstances in which it is placed. That is its bodily organs, once strong and vigorous, are now weakened by disease, or worn with age. Hence, the mind, while connected with them, and dependent on them, is compelled to partake of their weaknesses. And like a strong travellor with a weak companion, or a strong workman with a slender tool, it can only operate as they are able to bear.

What then is the means by which this formidable obstacle can be overcome, and the mind be enabled with renewed vigor, to continue its onward progress in the reception of intelligence?

We will best answer this question by a parable.

A certain child had continued the use of food until its teeth were worn, loosened, and decayed to that degree that they were no longer able to perform their accustomed office. On this account, its food was swallowed in such a manner as not to digest properly.

This soon caused a general weakness and disorder of the system. Some unthinking persons seeing this, came to the conclusion that the child had come to maturity—that it no longer needed its accustomed nourishment, but must gradually sink and die. But in process of time; nature provided its own remedy. The old teeth were shed, and a new set more strong and durable took their place. The system being thus restored in every part to a full, vigorous and healthy action, was enabled to make rapid progress towards perfection, and to receive and digest food far more strong and hard of digestion than before.

So with the organs of the mind. This temporary body, frail and mortal, is to the mind what the children's teeth are to the system. Like them it answers a momentary purpose, and like them its organs become

122

decayed and weakened by age and use; so that many truths which present themselves to the mind, cannot be properly digested while dependent on such weak organs.

But let this feeble and decayed body share the fate of the child's first set of teeth—let it be plucked by death, and the mind set free. Nay, rather let it be renewed in all the freshness and vigor of eternal life; with organs fresh and strong and durable as the powers of eternal intellect.

And the mind, thus provided with organs, fully adapted to its most ardent powers of action, will find itself no longer constrained to linger on the confines of its former limits, where impatient of restraint, it had struggled in vain for freedom. But like a prisoner, suddenly freed from the iron shackles and gloomy dungeons of a terrible tyrant, it will move nimbly onward with a joyous consciousness of its own liberty. It will renew with redoubled vigor its intellectual feast, and enlarge its field of operations amid the boundless sources of intelligence, till earth, with all its treasures of wisdom and knowledge, becomes too small, and the neighboring worlds too narrow to satisfy a capacity so enlarged. It will then, on wings of faith, and by the power of the spirit waft itself far beyond our visible heavens, and "far above earth's span of sky" and explore other suns, and other systems; and hold communion with other intelligences more remote than our weak minds can possibly conceive.

In these researches and discoveries, the mind will be able by degrees to circumscribe the heavens, and to comprehend the heights and depths, and lengths and breadths of the mysteries of eternal truth, and like its maker, comprehend *all things; even the deep things of God.*

While the mind is thus expanding and increasing in intelligence, the affections will expand and increase in proportion, both in this life and in the life to come.

God is light, God is truth, God is love.

The reason why he loves, is because he is light and truth. Or in other words, he loves because he knows; and in proportion to the extent of his knowledge, or intelligence, so is the extent of his love; and so it is with the human mind.

In infancy, our love is as narrow as our intellectual capacity. But as our intelligence increases, so our affection grows, till from knowing and loving our mother, we begin to know and love the circle of our immediate kindred and family. We soon begin to know and love our fathers, our brothers, our sisters, and finally our uncles, aunts and cousins, and our neighbors; and so on, continuing to enlarge our knowledge and consequently our love, till it circumscribes our nation, and finally all mankind. But still, it is far from being perfect. As we advance in the knowledge of all our social connections, duties, dependences, relationships, and obligations, our affections still increase; and as we raise our thoughts to worlds on high, and begin to know something of our Heavenly Father, of our Redeemer, and of angels and spirits who inhabit other and better worlds, and of our relationships to them, we begin to love them. And the more we know of them the more we love them. Thus, love or affection is dependent on knowledge, or intelligence, and can only be increased by an increase of knowledge.

These two principles are the foundations, the fountains of all real happiness.

Some persons have supposed that our natural affections were the results of a fallen and corrupt nature, and that they are "*carnal, sensual, and devilish*," and therefore ought to be resisted, subdued, or overcome as so many evils which prevent our perfection, or progress in the spiritual life. In short, that they should be greatly subdued in this world, and in the world to come entirely done away. And even our intelligence also. Such persons frequently inquire whither they shall recognise their kindred or friends in the life to come? They also caution themselves and others, lest they should love their child, their companion, their brother, sister, or mother too well; for, say they, if you love them too well, it will offend your God and he will take them from you.

Such persons have mistaken the source and fountain of happiness altogether. They have not one correct idea of the nature of the enjoyments, or happiness of heaven, or earth; of this life or any other. If intelligence and affection are to decrease to such a low ebb that we shall neither recognise or love our kindred and friends, then a stone, a block of wood, or a picture on the wall is as capable of the enjoyments of heaven as we are.

So far from this being the case, our natural affections are planted in us by the Spirit of God, for a wise purpose; and they are the very mainsprings of life and happiness — they are the cement of all virtuous and heavenly society — they are the essence of charity, or love; and therefore never fail, but endure forever.

There is not a more pure and holy principle in existence than the affection which glows in the bosom of a virtuous man for his companion; for his parents, brothers, sisters, and children.

If there be one scene in heaven or on earth, capable of calling forth the most refined sensibilities of our nature, it is the expressions of love which kindle into rapture, and which flow out in the soul of a woman towards her infant.

So pure, so chaste, so tender and benevolent, so simple, so ardent and sincere, and so disinterested is this principle, that it could only have been kindled by the inspiration of a spirit direct from the fountain of eternal, everlasting love.

These pure affections are inspired in our bosoms, and interwoven with our nature by an all wise and benevolent being, who rejoices in the happiness and welfare of his creatures. All his revelations to man, touching this subject, are calculated to approve, encourage, and strengthen these emotions, and to increase and perfect them; that man, enlightened and taught of God, may be more free, more social, cheerful, happy, kind, familiar, and lovely than he was before; that he may fill all the relationships of life, and act in every sphere of usefulness with a greater energy, and with a readier mind, and a more willing heart.

All the monkish austerity, all the sadness and reserve, all the unsocial feelings and doings of priests, and monks, and nuns; all the long-facedness, unsocial sadness, groanings, sighs, and mortifications of sectaries, whether of ancient convents, where men and women retire from all the busy scenes and pleasures of life, to live a life of celibacy, self-denial and devotion; or whether in the more modern and fashionable circles of the camp meetings, or the *"mourners bench."*

All these, I say, are expressly and entirely opposed to the spirit, and objects of true religion; they are so many relics of superstition, ignorance, and hypocrisy, and are expressly forbidden, and condemned by our Lord and Saviour.

In all these things, man has mistaken the source of happiness; has been dissatisfied with the elements and attributes of his nature, and has tried, and sought, and prayed, in vain to make himself into a different being from what the Lord has wisely designed he should be.

The fact is, God made man, male and female; he planted in their bosoms those affections which are calculated to promote their happiness and union.

That by that union they might fulfil the first and great commandment; viz: "To multiply and replenish the earth, and subdue it."

From this union of affection, springs all the other relationships, social joys and affections, diffused through every branch of human existence.

And were it not for this, earth would be a desert wild, an uncultivated wilderness.

Man was designed for a social being; he was made to cultivate, beautify, possess, enjoy and govern the earth; and to fill it with myriads of happy, free and social intelligences.

Woman was made for him as a help and a comfort. All the faculties of his nature, are precisely adapted to his several duties and enjoyments. He owes a duty to his wife, to his parents, to his children, to his brothers and sisters, and kindred, and finally to his neighbors, his nation, and to all mankind. He also owes a duty to the earth, and to his God. These several spheres of action are termed in modern times; political, civil, moral, social, domestic, foreign, religious, etc., etc. But they may all be summed up in one term, viz: religious.

Pure religion, includes all these duties, they are all religious duties; and the man who fulfils his religious duties and obligation; acts well his part in every department of life; he is a good citizen, a good ruler, a good general, a good neighbor, a good father, a good husband, a good child, and a good member of society; according as his lot may be cast, or according to the trust committed to him. And he receives and imparts a portion of happiness on every sphere in which he moves.

The man who, through a mistaken zeal, or through the influence of ignorant teachings or incorrect traditions, so far mistakes the object and purpose of his being, as to withdraw from all these; to shut himself from the world, and to seek to overcome and subdue the natural affections with which God has endowed him, is not a religious man at all. On the contrary, he is opposing the will and commandments of God, and neglecting the duties of religion.

How often do we hear of persons, and even whole societies who hold that a religious man or community should have nothing to do with politics, government, and office. Such persons judge of the depth of a man's religion by his indifference to, or retirement from the arduous duties of family, church, or state.

How different is this notion from the facts of the case, if we may judge either from common sense, or from precepts and examples set before us by God's people.

Witness, Adam, Noah, Abraham, Joseph, Moses, Joshua, Samuel, David, Solomon, Elijah, Daniel, Mordica, Esther, and thousands of others of God's prophets and wise men, all medling with civil religious, and political government, and with temporal duties, and financial interests! and who so well qualified as they for to forecast devices, and manage affairs for the good and salvation of man? Think of Jesus himself who came into the world for the very purpose of being a king, and who is yet waiting for the glorious time when he will descend to earth again, and reign over all the kingdoms of the world. Think of Paul, who declares that the saints shall judge the world, and judge angels, how much more than the smaller matters?

Man, know thy self, — study thine own nature, — learn thy powers of body, — thy capacity of mind. Learn thine origin, thy purpose and thy destiny. Study the true source of thine own happiness, and the happiness of all beings with which thou art associated. Learn to act in unison with thy true character, nature and attributes; and thus improve and cultivate the resources within and around thee. This will render you truly happy, and be an acceptable service to your God. And being faithful over a few things, you may hope to be made ruler over many things

What then is sinful? I answer, our unnatural passions and affections, or in other words the abuse, the perversion, the unlawful indulgence of that which is otherwise good. Sodom was not destroyed for their natural affection; but for the want of it. They had perverted all their affections, and had given place to that which was unnatural, and contrary to nature. Thus they had lost those holy and pure principles of virtue and love which were calculated to preserve and exalt mankind; and were overwhelmed in all manner of corruption; and also hatred towards those who were good.

So it was with the nations of Canaan who were doomed to destruction by the Israelites. And so it was with the Greeks, Romans, and other Gentiles in the days of Paul. Hence his testimony against their wicked works, and his warnings to the churches to beware of these carnal sinful, corrupt and impure works of the flesh; all of which were more or less interwoven with their natures by reason of long and frequent indulgences therein. Now it was not because men's natural affections were sinful that all these sins existed; but it was because, wicked customs, contrary to nature, had become so prevalent as to become a kind of second nature.

So it is in the present age; men who do not govern their affections so as to keep them within their proper and lawful channel; but who indulge in every vice, and in unlawful use of that which was originally good, so far pervert it that it becomes to them a minister of evil; and therefore they are led into the other extreme; and begin to accuse their nature, or him that formed them, of evil; and they seek to change their nature; and call upon God to make them into a different being from what he made them at first. In short they seek to divest themselves of a portion of the very attributes of their nature instead of seeking to govern, to improve, and to cultivate and direct their powers of mind and their affections, so as to cause them to contribute to their happiness. All these are the results of incorrect traditions, teachings and practices.

Know then Oh man, that aided and directed by the light of heaven the sources of thy happiness are within and around thee. Instead of seeking unto God for a mysterious change to be wrought, or for your affections and attributes to be taken away and subdued, seek unto him for aid, and wisdom to govern, direct and cultivate them in a manner which will tend to your happiness and exaltation, both in this world and in that which is to come. Yea, pray to him that every affection, attribute, power and energy of your body and mind may be cultivated, increased, enlarged, perfected and exercised for his glory and for the glory and happiness of yourself, and of all those whose good fortune it may be to be associated with you.

As we said in the beginning of this subject, we say again; that our intellect and our affection, only buds in time, and ripens in eternity.

There we shall know and love our kindred and our friends: and there we shall be capable of exercising all those pure emotions of friendship and love, which fill our hearts with such inexpressible delight in this world. And not only so, but our love will be far more strong and perfect in many respects. First, because we shall know and realize more. Secondly, because our organs of thought will be more strong and durable. Thirdly, because we shall be free from those mean, selfish, groveling, envious and disagreeable influences which disturb, and hinder the free exercise of our affections in this world. And lastly, because we shall be associated with a more extensive and numerous society, of those who are filled with the same freedom of spirit and affection that we are; and therefore are objects truly worthy of our love. While those of a contrary nature will be banished to their own place, and not suffered to mingle in the society, or mar the peace of those who have gotten the victory.

Having discovered and set forth in plainness the origin, purpose, and destiny of man's physical organization and the powers, attributes, energies, affections and capabilities of his intellect, till we find him standing erect in God-like majesty, with organs of strength beyond the reach of death: and powers of thought, capable of spaning the heavens, and comprehending all things: We must now inquire into the nature of his employment in that eternal world of joy and bliss.

On this subject as on most others, where investigation has been considered a sin, men have greatly erred.

They have supposed that this short life was the only active one; and that the world to come was a life of repose, or of inactive and eternal rest; where all our powers of body and mind would remain dormant, or only be engaged in shouts, songs and acclamations. To prove this we offer here quotations like the following:

"There is no work, nor device, nor knowledge in the grave whither thou goest." *"As the tree falleth so it lieth."* *"As death leaves us, so judgment will find us."*

To the first of these we would reply that the spirit never goes to the grave; and the body does not stay in it long. And beyond it, in the regions of eternal life there is abundance of work, knowledge and device. To the second, we would say, that the tree lieth as it falleth until it is removed, and used for some other purpose. And to the third, we reply, that it is a sectarian proverb, instead of a scripture; and by the by a false one too. For death leaves us in the grave, with body and spirit separated; and judgment finds us risen from the grave, and spirit and body united.

Thus organized a new, we are prepared to enter upon a life of business and usefulness, in a sphere vastly enlarged and extended.

Possessing a priesthood after the order of Melchesideck; or, after the order of the son of God; which is after the power of an endless life, without beginning of days or ending of years, a priesthood which includes a scepter and kingly office; we are more fully than ever qualified to teach, to judge, to rule and govern; and to go and come on foreign missions. The field of our labors may then extend for aught we know to the most distant worlds — to climes where mortal eye never penetrated. Or we may visit the dark and gloomy regions of the spirits in prison, and there, like a risen Jesus, preach the gospel to those who are dead; *"that they may be judged according to men in the flesh, but live according to God in the spirit."*

Or we may be called upon, with the other sons of God to shout for joy, at the organization of new systems of worlds, and new orders of being; over which we may reign as kings, or to whom we may minister as priests.

These ideas may be considered by some as mere flights of fancy no where supported by positive evidence. But we contend that the very nature of our existence and of our priesthood is such as to warrant the conclusion to which we have arrived. But if proof were wanting, we have only to refer, as a precedent, to the active life and ministry of a risen Jesus; and to his administration as king of kings and lord of lords: as well as to the promises made by him to those whom he had sent. It appears that Jesus Christ after rising from the dead, immediately entered upon a most active ministry; in which he taught, expounded, opened the scriptures, commanded, commissioned, prophesied and blessed. By this means he laid the foundation for his kingdom to be established not only among the Jews and Gentiles; but also among the Nephites and the lost tribes of Israel. He also visited the spirits of the dead and preached the gospel unto them, as is recorded in one of the Epistles of Peter. Not only so, but he assended to realms of exalted glory, where seated on a throne, he still is active both as a king and priest. And, if we look into the future, we shall find that he has yet a great work to do upon the earth, not only as a judge, king and priest; but as an executor, warrior, and a military commander. For he will tread them in his anger and trample them in his fury, and stain his raiment with their blood; while all the armies in heaven follow him in martial splendor, mounted on white horses, and all arrayed in a uniform of spotless white. This same Jesus confered on his apostles an everlasting priesthood, after his own order: as it is written: *"As the father hath sent me, even so I send you."* "And the works that I do shall you do also."

He also promised to be with *them* always even unto the end of the world; and therefore is yet with them in their labors and ministry, whether as men or angels. Those who suppose a man's office or priesthood to end with this life have been in the habit of applying that promise, as if it only ment them and their successors; but he said no such thing. But rather that he would be with *them* always unto the end of the world. If they had successors, it was then time enough for similar promises to be made to them, when they in turn should enter upon their holy and sacred office of the apostleship and priesthood.

These apostles not only hold the perpetual office of the apostleship and priesthood: but also partake of kingly power. Hence it is written *"they shall sit on twelve thrones judging the twelve tribes of Israel."* And this too, when the son of man shall come in his glory. Then will be fulfilled that which was recorded by John, saying: *"thou hast made us unto our God kings and priests; and we shall reign on the earth."* In view of an eternal kingdom, and of an immortal reign and ministry, they might well rejoice when arraigned before the dreadful tribunals of earthly tyrants, knowing as they did that they should reign in turn, and that their persecutors would be in turn arraigned before a judgment bar.

From all these and a thousand other promises made to prophets and apostles, we feel safe in the conclusion, that a field wide as eternity and boundless as the ocean of God's benevolence, extends before the servants of God. A field where, ambition knows no check, and zeal no limits; and where the most ardent aspirations may be more than realized. A field where crowns of glory, thrones of power and dominions of immortality are the rewards of dilligence. And where man — once a weak and helpless worm of dust may sit enthroned in majesty on high, and occupy an exalted station among the councils of the sons of God.

A Dialogue Between Joe. Smith & the Devil!

(New York? Prophet Office? 1845)

[Enter Devil with a bundle of handbills, which he is in the act of posting.]

WANTED IMMEDIATELY,

All the liars, swindlers, thieves, robbers, incendiaries, cheats, adulterers, harlots, blackguards, drunkards, gamblers, bogus makers, idlers, busy bodies, pickpockets, vagabonds, filthy persons, hireling clergy, and their followers, and all other infidels and rebellious, disorderly persons, for a crusade against Joe Smith and the Mormons. Be quick, be quick, I say, or our cause will be ruined, and our kingdom overthrown, by that d— —d fool of an imposter and his associates, for even now all earth and hell is in a stew.

[Joe Smith happens to be passing, and hails his Majesty.]

Good morning, Mr. Devil. How now, you seem to be much engaged; what news have you got there?

DEVIL [slipping his bills into his pocket with a low bow] — O! good morning, Mr. Smith; hope you are well, sir. Why — I — was just out — out on a little business in my line; or finally, to be candid, sir, I was contriving a fair and honorable warfare against you and your impositions, wherein piety is outraged, and religion greatly hindered in its useful course. For, to be bold sir, [and I despise anything underhanded,] I must tell you to your face that you have made me more trouble than all the ministers, or people of my whole dominion, have for ages past.

SMITH. Trouble! What trouble have I caused your Majesty? I certainly have endeavored to treat you, and all other persons, in a friendly manner, even my worst enemies; and I always aim to fulfil the Mormon creed, and that is, to my mind, my own business exclusively. Why should this trouble you Mr. Devil?

DEVIL. Ah! your own business, indeed. I know not what you may consider your business, it is so very complicated; but I know what you have done, and what you are aiming to do. You have disturbed the quiet of Christendom, overthrown churches and societies, you have dared to call in question the truth and usefulness of old and established creeds, which have stood the test of ages; and have even caused tens of thousands to come out in open rebellion, not only against wholesome creeds, established forms and doctrines, well approved and orthodox, but against some of the most pious, learned, exemplary, and honorable clergy, whom both myself and all the world, love, honor and esteem, and this is not all. But you are causing many persons to think who never thought before, and you would fain put the whole world a thinking, and then where will true religion and piety be? Alas! they will have no place among men, for if men keep such a terrible thinking and reasoning as they begin to do, since you commenced your business, as you call it, they never will continue to uphold the good old way in which they have jogged along in peace for so many ages; and thus, Mr. Smith, you will overthrow my kingdom, and leave me not a foot of ground on earth, and this is the very thing you aim at. But I, sir, have the boldness to oppose you by all the lawful means which I have in my power.

SMITH. Really, Mr. Devil, your Majesty has of late become very pious; I think some of your Christian brethren have greatly misrepresented you. It is generally reported by them that you are opposed to religion. But—

DEVIL. It is false; there is not a more religious and pious being in the world than myself, nor a being more liberal minded. I am decidedly in favor of all creeds, systems, and forms of Christianity, of whatever name or nature, so long as they leave out that abominable doctrine which caused me so much trouble in former times, and which, after slumbering for ages, you have again revived; I mean the doctrine of direct communion with God, by new revelation. This is hateful, it is impious, it is directly opposed to all the divisions and branches of the Christian Church. I never could bear it. And for this very cause, I helped to bring to condign punishment all the prophets and the apostles of old, for while they were suffered to live with this gift of revelation, they were always exposing and slandering me, and all other good pious men in exposing our deeds and purposes, which they called wicked, but which we consider as the height of zeal and piety; and when we killed them for these crimes of dreaming, prophesying, and vision-seeing, they raised the cry of persecution, and so with you miserable and deluded Mormons.

SMITH. Then, your most Christian Majesty is in favor of all other religions but this one, are you?

DEVIL. Certainly. I am fond of praying, singing, church building, bell ringing, going to meeting, preaching, and withal, I have quite a missionary zeal. I like also long faces, long prayers, long robes, and learned sermons; nothing suits me better than to see people who have been for a whole week oppressing their neighbour, grinding the face of the poor, walking in pride and folly, and serving me with all their heart. I say nothing suits me better, Mr. Smith, than to see these people go to meeting on Sunday, with a long religious face on, and to see them pay a portion of their ill-gotten gains for the support of a priest, while he and his hearers pray with doleful groans and awful faces, saying, "Lord, we have left undone the things we ought to have done, and done the things we ought not;" and then, when service is ended, see them turn again to their wickedness, and pursue it greedily all the week, and the next Sabbath repeat the same things. Now, be candid Mr. Smith; do you not see that these, and all others, who have a form and deny the power, are my good christian children, and that their religion is a help to my cause?

SMITH. Certainly, your reasoning is clear and obvious as to these hypocrites, but you would not be pleased with people getting converted either at camp meeting, or somewhere else, and then putting their trust in that conversion, and in free grace to save them — would you not be opposed to this?

DEVIL. Why should I have any objection to that kind of religion, Mr. Smith? I care not how much they get converted, nor how much they cry Lord, Lord, nor how much they trust to free grace to save them, so long as they do not do the works that their God has commanded them; I am sure of them at last, for you know all men are to be judged according to their deeds. What does their good Bible say? Does it not say, "not every one that saith Lord, Lord, shall enter into my kingdom, but he that doeth the will of my father which is in heaven." No, no, Mr. Smith, I am not an enemy to religion, and especially to the modern forms of christianity; so long as they deny the power, they are a help to my cause. See how much discord, division, hatred, envy, strife, lying, contention, blindness, and even error and bloodshed, has been produced as the effect of these very systems. By these means I gain millions to my dominion, while at the same time we enjoy the credit of being pious christians; but you, Mr. Smith, you are my enemy, my open and avowed enemy, you have even dared in a sacrilegious manner, to tear the veil from all these fine systems, and to commence an open attack upon my kingdom, and this even when I had almost all christendom, together with the clergy, and gentlemen of the press, in my favor. How dare you venture thus to commence a revolution without reserve, and without aid or succor, and in the midst of innumerable hosts of my subjects?

SMITH. Why, sir, in the first place, I knew that I had the truth on my side, and that your systems and forms of christianity were so manifestly corrupt, that one had only to lift the veil from your fooleries on one side, and to present plain and reasonable truth on the other, and the eyes of the people could at once distinguish the difference so clearly that, except they chose darkness rather than light, they would leave your ranks and come over to truth. For instance, what is easier than to show from the history of the past, that a religion of direct revelation was the only system ever instituted by the Lord, and the only one calculated to benefit mankind? — What is easier than to show that this system saved the church from flood, famine, flames, war, division, bondage, doubt, and darkness, many times, and that it is the legitimate way and manner of God's government of his own peculiar people in all ages and dispensations.

DEVIL. To be candid with you, Mr. Smith, I must own that what you have now said, neither myself nor my most able ministers have been able to gainsay by any argument or fact. But then you must recollect that tradition and custom, together with fashion and popular clamor, have in all ages had more effect than plain fact and sound reason. Hence you see we are yet safe, so long as we continue the cry from press and pulpit, and in Sunday schools, and all these things are done away and no longer needed. In this way, though God may speak, they will not hear; angels may minister, and they will not believe; visions may reveal, and they will not be enlightened; prophets may lift their voice, and their warnings pass unheeded; so you see we still have them as safe as we had the people in olden time. God can communicate no message to them which will be examined or heard with any degree of credence or candor. So for all the good they get from God, all communication being cut off, they might as well be without a God. Thus you see I have full influence and control of the multitude by a means far more effectual than argument or reason, and I even teach them that it is a sin to reason, think, or investigate, as it would disturb the even tenor of their pious breathings and devout groans and responses. Smith, you must be extremely ignorant of human nature, as well as of the history of the past, to presume that reason and truth would have much effect with the multitude. Why, sir, look how effectually we warded off the truth at Ephesus, when Paul attempted to address them in the theatre. Strange, that with all these examples before you, you should venture to raise the hue and cry which has so often been defeated, and this with no better weapons on your side than reason and truth. Indeed, you may thank my christian spirit of forbearance that you have escaped so far without a gridiron; but take care for the future, I may not always be so mild.

SMITH. But why is your majesty so highly excited against me and my plans of operation, seeing that you consider that you have the multitude perfectly safe; and why so enraged and so fearful of the consequences of my course, and the effect of my weapons, while at the same time you profess to despise them as weak and powerless. Alas, it is too true that you have the multitude safe to all appearance at present, and that truth can seldom reach them: why not then be content and leave me to pursue my calling in peace? I can hardly hope to win to the cause of truth any but the few who think, and these have ever been troublesome to your cause.

DEVIL. True, but then you are, in spite of all my efforts, and that of my fellows, daily thinning our ranks by adding to the number of those who think, and such a thinking is kept up that we are often exposed in some of our most prominent plans, and are placed in any awkward predicament, and who knows what defeat, disgrace, and dishonor may befall the pious cause, if you are suffered to continue your rebellious course.

SMITH. But, Mr. Devil, why, with all these other advantages on your side, do you resort to such mean, weak, and silly fabrications as the Spaulding Story. You profess to be a gentleman, a christian and a clergyman, and you ought for your own sake, and for the sake of your cause to keep up outward appearances, of honor and fairness. And now, Mr. Devil, tell the truths for once: you know perfectly well that your Spaulding Story, in which you represent me as an impostor, in connection with Sidney Rigdon, and that we were engaged in palming Solomon Spalding's romance upon the world as the Book of Mormon, is a lie, a base fabrication, without a shadow of truth, and you know that I found the Original Records of the Nephites, and translated and published the Book of Mormon from them, without ever having heard of the existence of Spaulding, or his romance, or of Sidney Rigdon either. Now, Mr. Devil, this was a mean, disgraceful, and underhand trick in you, and one of which even you have reason to be ashamed.

DEVIL. Well, Mr. Smith, to be candid, I acknowledge what you say is true, and that it was not the most honorable course to the world. But it was you who commenced the war, by publishing that terrible book which we readily recognized as a complete expose of all our false and corrupt christianity, not even keeping back the fact that we had continued during the dark ages, to rob the Scriptures of their plainness, and we feel the utmost alarm and excitement, and without much reflection, in the height of passion, we called a hasty council of Clergy and Editors, and other rascals, in Painesville, Ohio, and, thinking that almost any means was lawful in war, we invented the Spaulding Story, and fathered it upon the poor printer Howe, of Painsville, although Doctor Hulburt [thanks to my aid] was its real author. But mark, Mr. Smith, mark one thing, we had not a face so hard; nor a conscience so abandoned, as to publish this Spaulding Story at the first as a positive fact; we only published it as a conjecture, a mere probability, and this you know, we had a right to do; without once thinking of the amount of evil it would eventually accomplish. But, sir, it was some of my unfortunate clergymen who, more reckless, hardened, and unprincipled, than myself, have ventured to add to each edition of this story, till at last, without my aid or consent, they have set it down for a positive fact, that Solomon

Spaulding, Sidney Rigdon, and yourself, have made up the Book of Mormon out of a romance. Now, Mr. Smith, I am glad of this interview with you, as it gives me the opportunity of clearing up my character. I acknowledge with shame that I was guilty of a mean act in helping to hatch up and publish the Spaulding Story as a probability, and I associated with rascals far beneath my dignity, either as a sovereign prince, or religious minister, or even as an old, honorable, and experienced Devil, and for this I beg your pardon. But, really, I must deny the charge of having assisted in making the additions which have appeared in the later editions of that story, in which my former probabilities and mean conjectures are set down for positive facts. No, Mr. Smith, I had no hand in a trick so low and mean; I despise it, as the work of priests and editors alone, without my aid or suggestion, and I do not believe that even the meanest young devils in our dominion would have stooped to such an act.

SMITH. Well, I must give your majesty some credit for once at least, if what you say is true, but, how can you justify your conduct in dishonoring yourself so far as to stoop to the level of the hireling clergy, and their followers, in still making use of this humbug story [which you affect to despise,] in order to still blind the eyes of the people in regard to the origin of the Book of Mormon.

DEVIL. O! Mr. Smith, it does take so readily among the pious of all sects, that it seems a pity to spoil the fun, and I cannot resist the temptation of carrying out the joke now it is so well rooted in their minds. And you can't think how we devils shake our sides with laughter when we get up in the gallery in some fine church, put on our long face, and assist in singing, and in the devout responses; this done, the Spaulding Story is gravely told from the pulpit, while the pious old clergyman wears a face as long as that of Balaam's beast. All is swallowed down for solid truth by the gaping multitude, while we hang our heads behind the screen, and laugh and wink at each other in silence, as any thing overhead would disturb their worship; and as bad as I am I never wish to disturb those popular modes of worship, which decency requires us to respect. So you see, Mr. Smith, we have our fun to ourselves, at your expense; but, after all, we do not mean any hurt by it, although I must acknowledge, upon the whole, it serves our purpose.

SMITH. Well we will drop the subject, as I want to inquire about some other stories which have had an extensive circulation by means of your editors and priests. For instance, there is the story of my attempting to walk on the water and getting drowned the numerous stories of my attempting to raise the dead as a mere trick of imposition, and getting detected in it; and the stories of my attempting to appear as an angel, and getting caught and exposed in the same; and besides this, you have me killed by some means every little while. Now, you old hypocrite, you know that none of these things ever happened, or any circumstance out of which to make them; and that so far from this I deny the principle of a man's working miracles, either real or pretended, as a proof of his mission, and contend that miracles, if wrought at all, were wrought for benevolent purposes, and without being designed to convince the unbeliever. Why, then, do you resort to such silly stories in your opposition to me, seeing that you have many other advantages? Not that I would complain of such weak opposition, as if it were calculated to hinder my progress, but rather to mention it as something well calculated to injure your own cause, by betraying your weakness and folly.

DEVIL [laughing] — Ha, ha, ha, eh, e, O! Mr. Smith; I just put out these stories for a joke, in order to have my own fun, and without the most distant idea, that any being on earth would be so silly as to give any credence to them; but judge my surprise and joy, when I found priests, editors, and people, so depraved in their judgment and tastes, so in love with lies, and so ready to catch at every thing against their common enemy, as they call you, that these jocose stories of ours, actually look in their credulous cranium for grave truths, and were passed about by them, and sought after and swallowed by the multitude as greedily as a young robin swallows a worm when it is dropped into its mouth, which is stretched at full width, while its eyes are closed. So you see, Mr. Smith, that without meaning any particular harm to you, I have my fun, and am besides so unexpectedly fortunate as to reap great advantages from circumstances where I had neither expected nor calculated. So I hope you will at least bear my folly, nor set down aught in malice, where no malice was intended. — You know we devils are poor miserable creatures at best, and were it not for our fun, and our gambling, and our religious exercises, we would have nothing to kill time.

SMITH. Well, well. I see plainly you will have to creep out some how or other, rather than bear the disgrace and stigma which your conduct would seem to deserve. But forgetting the past, let me inquire what course you intend to pursue in future, and whether this warfare between you and me, will still be prosecuted? And if so, what course do you intend to pursue hereafter? You know my course. I have long since taken the field at the head of a mere handful of brave patriots, who are true as the pole stars, and firm as the rock of Gibraltar. They laugh at and despise your silly stories, and with nothing but a few plain simple weapons of truth and reason, aided by revelation, we boldly make war upon your whole dominion, and will never quit the field, dead or alive, till we win the battle, and deprive you of every foot of ground you possess. This is our purpose; and although your enemy, I am bold and generous enough to declare it. So you see I am not taking any unwary advantage, notwithstanding all your pious tricks upon me and the public.

DEVIL. Mr. Smith, I am too much of the gentleman not to admire your generous frankness and your boldness, and too much of a christian not to appreciate your honesty; but as you commenced this war, and I only acted at the first on the defensive, with the pure motive of defending my kingdom. I think this ought in some degree at least to excuse the means I have made use of. And that you may have no reason to complain in future, I will now fully open to you the plan of my future campaign. Here [pulling out a bundle of hand bills] is what I was doing this morning, when by chance we met; and by the reading of which you will see my course. Heretofore I have endeavored to throw contempt upon your course, hopes to smother it and, to keep it under, as something beneath the notice of us well informed christians. For this cause I have generally caused it to be represented, that you was a very ignorant silly man, and that your followers were made up of the unthinking and vulgar, and not worthy of notice. But the fact is, you have made such rapid strides, and have poured forth such a torrent of intelligence, and gathered such a host of talented and thinking men around you, that I can no longer conceal these facts under a bushel of burning lies, and therefore I now change my purpose and my manner of attack. I shall endeavor to magnify you and your success from this time forward, and to make you appear as much larger than the reality, as you have heretofore fallen short. If my former course has excited contempt, and caused you to be despised, and thus kept you out of notice, my future course will be to excite jealousy, fear, and alarm, till all the world is ready to arise and crush you, as if you were a legion of Sampsons, commanded by Bonaparte. This, I think, will be a more successful in putting you down, than the ignoble course I have heretofore taken — so prepare for the worst.

SMITH. I care as little for your magnifying powers, as I have heretofore done for your contempt; in fact, I will endeavor to go ahead to that degree, that what you will say in regard to my great influence and power, though intended by you for a falsehood, shall prove to be true, and by so doing I shall be prepared to receive those whom you may excite against me, and to give them so warm a reception, that they will never discover your intended falsehood, but will find all your representations of my greatness to be a reality; so do your worst, I defy you.

DEVIL. Well, time will determine whether the earth is to be governed by a prophet and under the way of truth, or whether myself, and my christian friends will still prevail. But remember Smith, remember, I beseech you for your own good beware what you are doing. I have the Priests and Editors with a few exceptions, under my control, together with wealth, popularity and honor. Count well the cost before you again plunge into this warfare. Good bye, Mr. Smith, I must away to raise my recruits and prepare for a campaign.

SMITH. Good bye to your Majesty.

(They both touch hats and turn away.)

DEVIL. (Recollecting himself and suddenly turning back,) O! say, Mr. Smith, one word more if you please, [in a low and confidential tone, with his mouth close to his ear,] after all, what is the use of parting as enemies; the fact is, you go in for the wheat and I for the tares. Both must be harvested; are we not fellow laborers? I can make no use of the wheat, nor you of the tares, even if we had them; we each claim our own, I for the burning, and you for the barn. Come, then, give the poor old Devil his due, and let's be friends.

SMITH. Agreed; I neither want yours nor you mine; a man free from prejudices, will give the devil his due. Come, here is the right hand of fellowship, you to the tares, and I to the wheat, [they shake hands cordially.]

DEVIL. Well, Mr. Smith, we have talked a long while, and are agreed at last; you are a noble and generous fellow; and would not bring a railing accusation against even a poor old Devil, nor cheat him of one cent. Come, it is a warm day, and I feel as though it is my treat. Let us go down to mammy Brewer's Cellar and take something to drink.

SMITH — Agreed, Mr. Devil, you appear very generous now.

[They enter the cellar together.]

DEVIL. Good morning, Mrs. Brewer; I make you aquainted with my good friend, Mr. Smith, the prophet. [The landlady smiling a little and looking a little surprised,] why, Mr. Devil, is that you; sit down, you're tired; but you don't say this is Mr. Smith, your greatest enemy? I am quite surprised. What will you have, gentlemen, for if you can drink together, I think all the world ought to be friends.

DEVIL. As we are both temperance men, and ministers, I think perhaps a glass of spruce beer a-piece will be all right — what say you Mr. Smith?

SMITH. As you please, your Majesty.

[They now take the beer.]

DEVIL. [Holding up his glass.] Come, Mr. Smith, your good health. I propose we offer a toast.

SMITH. Well, proceed.

DEVIL. Here's to my good friend Joe Smith may all sorts of ill luck befall him, and may he never be suffered to enter my kingdom, either in time or eternity, for he would almost make me forget that I am a devil, and make a gentleman of me, while he gently overthrows my government, at the same time that he wins my friendship.

139

SMITH. Here's to his Satanic Majesty; may he be driven from the earth, and be forced to put to sea in a stone canoe with an iron paddle, and may the canoe sink, and a shark swallow the canoe and its royal freight, and an alligator swallow the shark, and may the alligator be bound in the north west corner of hell, the door be locked, key lost, and a blind man hunting for it.

(Exit Devil, Prophet, and all.)

{12}

"One Hundred Years Hence. 1945"

(from *The Nauvoo Neighbor*, 10 September 1845)

God, through his servants the prophets, has given all men a clue to the future. In view of this, we were cogitating upon our bed, the other night, what would be the state of the world a hundred years hence. In quick succession the events and periods which have filled up nearly six thousand years, passed before our mind's eyes, together with the accompanying "thus saith the Lord," I will destroy the earth with a flood, after one hundred and twenty years. There shall be seven years of plenty, and seven years of famine in Egypt. Israel shall be held captive in Babylon till the land enjoys her Sabbath's seventy years, and then came Daniel's numbers, and the exact time when the Savior should be born, his crucifixion, and second coming.

While thus looking over the "has beens," we fell into a deep sleep, and the angel of our presence came to the bedside and gently said, "arise." Now it mattereth not whether we were in the body or out of it; asleep or awake; on earth or in heaven; or upon the water, or in the air; the sum of the matter is like this: Our guide, for such we shall call the angel or being that conveyed us, soon brought us in sight of a beautiful city.

As we were nearing the place, a "pillar of fire," seemingly over the most splendid building, lit the city and country for a great distance around, and as we came by, the TEMPLE OF THE LORD IN ZION, in letters of a pure language, and sparkling like diamonds, disclosed where we were. Our guide went round the city in order to give us a chance to "count the towers;" and, as it was nearly sunrise, he conducted us into one, that we might have a fair chance to view the glory of Zion by 'daylight.' We seemed to be swallowed up in sublimity! The "pillar of fire" as the sun rose majestically mellowing into a "white cloud," as a shade for the city from heat. The dwellings so brilliant by night, had the appearance of "precious stones," and the streets glittered like gold, and we marvelled. Marvel not, said our guide, this is the fulfilment of the words of Isaiah:

"For brass I will bring gold, and for iron I will bring silver, and for wood brass, and for stones iron: I will also make thine officers peace and thine exactors righteousness."

Now the eyes of our understanding began to be quickened, and we learned, that we were one hundred years ahead of "common life," and we gloried. The "veil" that hides our view from the glory of the upper deep had been taken away, and all things appeared to us as to the Lord. The great earthquake, mentioned by John, and other prophets before him, had levelled the mountains over the whole earth; — the "sea" had rolled back as it was in the beginning; the crooked was made straight, and the rough places plain. The earth yielded her "increase," and the knowledge of God exalted man to the society of resurrected beings.

The melody and prayers of the morning in Zion, showed that the "Lord was there:" and truly so; for, after breakfast the chariot of Jesus Christ was made ready for a pleasure ride; and the 'chariots' of his 'hundred and forty four thousand' glittered in the retinue of 'earth's greatest and best' so gloriously, that the 'show' exhibited the splendour of *Gods*, whose Father's name they bore on the front of their crowns.

Our curiosity excited us to inquire, what day they celebrated? To which the guide replied: "This is the *Feast-day* of the Lord to JOSEPH AND HYRUM SMITH, for being martyred for the truth, held yearly on the 7th day of the fourth month, throughout all the tribes of Israel."

Flesh and blood cannot comprehend the greatness of the scene; the worthy of the earth, with Adam at their head; the martyrs of the different dispensations, with Abel at their head; and honorable men from other worlds composed an assemblage of majesty, dignity, and 'divinty,' so much above the 'little pageantry' of man in his self-made greatness, that we almost forgot that mortals ever enjoyed anything more than misery, in all the pomp and circumstance of *man's power over man!* This was a feast-day for truth! This was the reward of integrity! — This was the triumph of "kings and priests," unto God, and was a holiday of eternity! Who could be happier than he that was among the holy throng? No one, and away we rode out of Zion among her stakes.

At the first city out, we found the same spirit — ALL WERE ONE. While there the following news, by post, came from the east. It was read from one of the papers just published that morning:

"In digging for the foundation of our new Temple in the 124th city of Joseph, near where it is supposed the City of New York once stood, a large square stone was taken from the ruins of some building which, by a seam in it indicated more than mere stone. The seam being opened, disclosed a *lead box* about six by eight inches square. This box was soon found to contain several daily papers of its time, together with some coin of the old Government of the United States. It will be recollected that all the inhabitants of this city which were spared from calamity, were 'slung out when the earth was turned upside down,' some forty or fifty years ago, for their wickedness."

The account of 'fires' in one of these papers was truly lamentable, destroying, as the paper said, more than *twenty-five millions worth of property*, in about three months. Each contained a large number of 'murders,' 'suicides,' 'riots,' 'robberies,' and hints of 'war expected,' with columns of divisions among the sectarian churches about *slavery*, Onderdonking, and the 'right way.' The 'Archer of Paradise' remarked as these horrors of 'old times' were being read, that *'all that* was transacted in the last days of Babylon, before Satan was bound.'

Joseph Smith said, "Lord, we will put those papers and coin in the repository of relics and curiosities of satan's kingdom of the old world;"—which was agreed to, by all, after exhibiting the coin. The silver coin contained the words 'United States of America,' and 'half dollar,' round the image of an eagle on one side, and a woman sitting upon the word 'LIBERTY,' and holding up a night cap, between thirteen stars, over '1845,' on the other.

The only idea that could be gathered from all this was, that the government had fallen from the *splendor* of an eagle to the pleasure of women, and was holding up the night cap, as a token that the only liberty enjoyed then, was star-light *liberty*, because their deeds were evil.

Another coin had the 'appearance' of gold, with 'five doll' upon it, but upon close examination it was found to be nothing but 'fine brass.'

While this was going on the Lord said, 'beware of the leven of old; — Let us enjoy our day.'

In a moment, this 'band of brethren' were off, and what could equal the view? No veil, no voice; the heavens were in their glory, and the angels were ascending and descending. The earth was in its beauty; the wolves and sheep; the calves and lions; the behemoth and the buffalo; the child and the serpent, enjoyed life without fear, and all men were one.

As we were passing to another city amid all this perfection of the reign of Jesus before his ancients gloriously, we discovered the fragment of a hewn stone, of a lightish blue color, with an abbreviated word 'Mo.' and the figures '1838' upon it. To which the 'Lion of the Lord' exclaimed: — *'The wicked are turned into hell*, and forgotten, but the righteous reign with God in glory,' and it seemed as if the echo came from a redeemed world, *'glory.'*

At about two, after five hours ride among the cities and stakes of Zion, we returned to the capitol to partake of the feast of the martyrs.

The preparation was perfect. A table through the grove of Zion for more than three hundred thousand saints, where *Jesus Christ*, sat at the head of the fathers and mothers, sons and daughters in Israel, was a sight, which the world, even Babylon, in its best days, never witnessed. Says Jesus, as every eye turned upon him,

"Our Father, and thine,
Bless me and mine: Amen."

After the 'feast' (the sentiments, words of wisdom and other touching matters were to be published in 'Zo-ma-rah,' or 'Pure News,' and are omitted) we stepped into the 'news room' and the first article in the 'Pure News,' which attracted our attention, was, the minutes of the General Conference held in Zion on the 14 day of the first month, A.D. 1945, when it was motioned by Joseph Smith, and seconded by John the Revelator, That *fortyeight* new cities be laid out and builded, this year in accordance with the prophets which have said, 'who can number Israel who can count the dust of Jacob? Let him fill the earth with cities.' Carried unanimously.

Twelve of these cities to be laid out beyond eighteen degrees north, for the tribes of Reuben, Judah and Levi. Twelve, on the east, at the same distance, for the tribes of Joseph, Benjamin, and Dan. Twelve on the south, at the same distance, for the tribes of Simeon, Issacher, and Zebulon — and twelve on the west, at the same distance, for the tribes of Gad, Asher, and Napthali."

The paper contained a notice for the half yearly Conference, as follows:

"The general half yearly Conference will be held at Jerusalem on the 14th day of the seventh month, alternately with the yearly conference in Zion.

It is proposed that the 'high way cast up' between the two cities of our God, be decorated with fruit and shade trees between the cities and villages, (which are only eighty furlongs apart,) for the accommodation of 'wayfaring men of Israel.' Gabriel has brought from Paradise, some seeds of fruit and grain, which were originally in the Garden of Eden, and will greatly add to the comfort and convenience of man."

While we were engaged in reading, a strain of music from some of the 'sweet singers of Israel,' come so mellowly over our sensations for a moment, that we hardly knew whether the angels or saints of the millenium, were chanting a vesper to their Savior. We were so delighted with the performance, as we saw the 'musical chariot' pass, filled with young men and maidens, all in *white robes*, that we only remember the following verses: —

> "Death and Satan being banish'd;
> "And the 'viel' for ever vanish'd;
> "All the earth's again replenish'd,
>   "And in beauty appears:
> "So we'll sing hallelujah's;
> "While we worship our Savior,
> "And fill the world with cities
> "Through the *'great thousand years.'*"

Our eye next caught a map showing the earth as it was, *and is.* We were delighted with the earth as it is. Four rivers headed a little south of Zion, for Zion, is situated in 'the sides of the north.' The first river is called 'Passon,' and runs west. The second is called 'Gion,' and runs south. Third is called 'Haudakal,' and runs north; and the fourth is called 'The Fraters,' and runs east. These four rivers divide the earth into *'four quarters'* as was in the days of Adam, and with their tributaries give an uninterrupted water communication over the face of the world, for in the begining the earth was not called 'finished' till it was *'very good,'* for every thing.

By the paper we were reading, we learned that rain was expected in the beginning of the seventh month, according to the Law of the Lord; for the promise is, "it shall rain moderately in the first and seventh month, that the ploughman may overtake the reaper."

Contemplating the greatness of the earth in its glory, with Jesus Christ for her king, president and lawgiver, with such wise councillors as, Adam, Noah, Abraham, Moses, Elijah, Peter, and Joseph, we were imperceptibly led to exclaim: "Great is the wisdom, great is the glory, and great is the power of man with his maker!" — When of a sudden our guide came in and said "you must drink wine with the Lord in his kingdom and then return." This we did, and many things which we saw are not lawful to utter, and can only be known as we learned them, by the assistance of a guardian angel.

When we were ready to return, our guide observed, "may be you would like to look through the *Urim and Thummim of God,* upon the abominations of the world in the day of its sin." "Yes," was our reply, and he handed us the "holy instrument." One look, and the soul sickened. Eye hath not seen, ear hath not heard, neither hath it entered into the heart of man, what folly, corruptions, and abominations are wrought among men to gratify the lust of the flesh, the lust of the eye, and the cunning of the devil. But they shall come. We returned, and awoke, perfectly enamored with the beauty and glory of Zion *to be* — as well as the splendor and harmony of the "feast of the martyrs," determining in our minds, at some future day to give a sketch of the TEMPLE wherein Jesus sat and reigned with the righteous, when there was "not a Canaanite in the land," nor anything to hurt or destroy in all the Holy Mountain — when the earth should be full of the knowledge of God as the waters cover the sea. In short, the heavenly reality of *one hundred years hence.*

An Apostle of the Church of Jesus Christ of Latter-day Saints,
was in the Island of Great Britain, for the Gospel's Sake;
And being in the Spirit on the 21st of November, A.D. 1846,
addressed the following words of comfort
to his dearly-beloved Wife and family,
dwelling in tents, in the camp of Israel,
at Council Bluffs, Missouri Territory, North America;
where they and twenty thousand others were banished
by the civilized Christians of the United States,
for the word of God, and the testimony of Jesus

(Printed by Br. J. B. Fanklin [London, 1851?])

MY DEAREST WIFE,
    Thy kindly soul and all
Thine acts of love to him, thy chosen head
Are treasured deep in memory's archives.
    And when amid the busy throng of towns
I pass unheeded, — Or wander lonely
In some country lane, or gravelled highway
Lined with hawthorn hedge, — Or turn aside
From the busy walks of men in meadows green, —
Or wander 'mid the solitary grove
At twilight hour, where silence reigns, and the
Fading tints of autumn tell of time's flight,
And the low murmur of the whispering breeze
Steals o'er the senses like a funeral dirge, —
Or flying swift o'er country hedge and ditch
In flaming chariot, while hills and vales,
And towns, and villas, farms, plains, and woods
Are swiftly whirled behind, — Or musing in
The midnight hour in lonely solitude
Upon my bed: 'Tis then I think of thee. —
    Sweet thoughts steal gently o'er the memory;
And my spirit wanders o'er the wide sea
And far away o'er Alleghany's heights,
And down the broad Ohio, from its source
To where it mingles its limpid waters
With the dark waves of Missouri's current:

And onward still, with lightning speed it flies,
Till towns and cities all are left behind;
And the last trace of Gentile dwelling fades
From view, and disappears in the far east.

At length the long-sought vision bursts to view
And stays my spirit in its onward flight.
Towering bluffs — deep indented vales — wide spread
Prairies — boundless plains and beauteous groves
Expand to view; all clad in green, and deck'd
In summer's richest livery of flowers
Or with the grey tints of fading autumn
Crown'd — Emblem of nature's dissolution.

There, one eternal silence seems to reign,
And slumb'ring nature rests in solitude.

There peace prevails — the sabbath rules the year;
And, in its own primeval innocence,
Uncursed by man's polluted touch, the earth
Seems resting in sacred, sublime repose.

No Gentile tyrant sways his sceptre there —
No pris'ners groan in solitary cells.

There freedom dwells: no superstitious creed
Enslaves the mind of man — no christian mobs
To drive him from his home, or shed his blood.

O sacred solitude, divinely blest —
Zion's retreat — where dwell the great and good.

There, with delight my spirit lingers still,
And would prolong the heavenly vision.

I love thee, for thyself, O land of Zion!
The beauty of thy landscape, — thy flowers, —
Thy boundless immensity of green fields,
Mingling with the wide expanse of heaven's
Blue arch; — thy star-bespangled firmament
Have charms for me.

The mellow moon light
Gently stealing o'er thy sacred forests; —
The fading tints of twilight painted on
Your evening sky; — the soft and plaintive voice
Of the autumnal cricket, as he sings
The funeral knell of expiring insects,
Or sounds a requiem to the closing year: —

All these steal o'er my senses with delight,
And wake the memory to scenes afar:

They whisper to the lonely exile,

And tell of youth, and friends, and native clime.
 Yet not for these charms alone I love thee:
Nor yet for peace, or freedom sweet, or rest,
Or sacred sabbath of sublime repose.
 All these, though dear to me, are worthless toys,
Mere baubles, — compared to that precious *gem*
Which yet remains to beautify my verse,
And swell the music of my joyous theme.
 There dwell my family, — my bosom friends, —
The precious lambs of my Redeemer, — my
Best of heaven's gifts to man, — my germs of
Life and immortality, — my hope of heaven, —
My principality on earth began, —
My kingdom in embryo, big with thrones
Of endless power and wide dominion.
 Ye kindred spirits from world's celestial!
Offsprings of Diety; — Sons and daughters
Of Eternity; — Ye nobles of heaven
Whose dwellings were of old among the Gods
In everlasting mansions, and who stood
In the councils of the High and lofty
One, ere chaos sprang to order, or the
Foundations of the everlasting hills
Were laid: Why came ye to this world of woe?
Why this disguise? — This painful sojourn in
A land of death? —
 Why wander far from heaven's eternal fold,
And from the bosom of your Father there?
Had *He* no love? No fond affection for
His own, that you are banished thus, and left
As exiles wandering in some dreary waste?
And if thus fallen, and forsaken quite,
Like evil spirits thrust from heaven, to
Return no more; — why that latent spark of
Heaven's pure love still glowing in your breast?
Why does your bosom swell with hope and joy,
And fire celestial kindle in your eye?
 O heavenly gift! The key of knowledge
Restored to man, the mystery unfolds
Of God's elect — their final destiny.
 You are here because your father loved you;
Because in heaven ye kept your first estate,
And remained when angels did rebel,

And Lucifer drew a third of heaven's host
From God; and with them sunk in dark despair.
　　You are here for further proof and trial; —
For a second estate; which if ye keep
As ye did the first, will purify your souls,
And fit you for a heaven celestial.
　　You came to the earth to be born of flesh,
To fashion and perfect your earthly house, —
To *live*, to *love*, to suffer and to die, —
To *rise*, and *reign*, in immortality.
　　To form your kindred ties with kindred souls,
To blend your sympathies, by mutual acts
Of kindly charity: —
　　To love and serve
Each other in ten thousand nameless ways:
And thus give exercise to mutual love,
And qualify yourselves for union endless
In that world of bliss.
O ye beings of noble birth! ye lambs
Of celestial origin, to Zion bound!
I know ye now; and knowing, can but love.
　　O my Father in heav'n! Thine they were,
And Thou gavest them to me — Precious gifts!
Endear'd by long acquaintance in the heavens,
By the soul's best affections on the earth,
By mutual love and sympathy of soul,
By all the kindred ties which twine around
The heart in sacred, inexpressible
Delight. — Made nigh by a Saviour's blood —
Seal'd by the Holy Ghost, and secur'd
By the spirit and pow'r of Elijah, —
By which the hearts of the fathers are turn'd
To the children: Enliven'd by the hope
Of endless union in that world of life
Where all is pure: —
　　Thrones, principalities,
Powers, majesty, might and dominion,
As a mutual reward! Who can but love?
　　O precious kindred! my loveliest, best!
Are motives wanting still to prompt my love,
And kindle my soul's affection to its
Highest, purest flame, sweet memory dwells
On all the past, — Your sufferings with me;

Your sacrifices for the Gospel's sake.
    For *me* and truth you gladly left your home,
Your native clime, your father, mother, friends,
And kindred dear, and wandered far away
O'er mountain, seas, and continents. The wide
Expanse of ocean—its waves and tempests
Could not quench your love, or cool your courage:—
    Towering mountains rose before you; rivers
Intervened to check you on your journey:
    Wide lakes, gloomy forests, and desert plains
Forbid your further progress, but in vain.
    Truth was the prize you sought; and love impell'd
You onward. These overcome, a host
Of fiends assailed you next, with lying tongues
To flatter, frown, to pity or deceive;
To coax, or drive you from your chosen course.
    When slander, rage, and lies, and pity fail'd,
Then came the deadly strife!—The fire comsum'd;
The sword devour'd;—Widows and orphans mourn'd:
Hell's artillery bellow'd; Martyrs bled;
The world exulted:—Devils hugely grinn'd;—
Heaven wept; saints pray'd; Justice stood aghast:—
Mercy, retiring, dropp'd a tear of blood:—
Angels startling, half drew their glittering swords;
And the Gods, in solemn council decreed
A just VENGEANCE.
    Amid these awful scenes ye firmly stood
For truth, and him you loved; And leaving house
And home again behind, in poverty
Ye fled; and pitch'd your humble tent, amid
The storms of winter: And wandered o'er the
Wide, unsheltered plain, ye braved the tempest
Many a weary month without a murmur:—
    Without a *murmur!* Nay more—Ye smiling
Stood, amid the awful storms, and hail'd the
Tempest welcome. The solitary wilds
Reverb'rated with freedom's joyful songs.
While there you fondly prest your infant to
Your bosom,—smil'd on your Lord,—receiv'd his
Smile in turn, and realized your freedom.
Supremely blest with heaven's approving smile,
With peace and friendship, liberty and love:
And with the daily presence of your Lord,—

Whose best affection sweeten'd every care:
Ye still were happy in your low estate.
Nor sighed for more.
      One only sacrifice remained for us
To make, to further our depth of love
For God and truth: — 'Twas all that heaven could ask.
      Will you, my lambs, be left *alone*, to spend
Another winter in this dreary wild,
While him *you love* shall wander far away
Beyond the sea: — for truth and Zion's sake?
      Your pulse beat quick; your bosom heav'd a sigh:
Your heart swell'd with emotion; a big tear
Gush'd forth, and stole in silence down your cheek:
While your spirit said — *"If I must, I will!"*
      The Recording Angel smil'd; — Heaven approv'd,
And said — *"It is enough:"* record the same,
And with it Our decree: — They are Elect!
Eternal life is theirs: They shall be ONE,
WHILE ENDLESS AGES ROLL!

{14}

Proclamation! To the People of the Coasts and Islands of the Pacific; of Every Nation, Kindred and Tongue

(Published for the author, by C. W. Wandell, Minister of the Gospel [Sydney, 1851])

CHAPTER I.

A NEW DISPENSATION

AN APOSTLE OF JESUS CHRIST, to the people of the coasts and islands of the Pacific, of every nation, kindred, and tongue—Greeting:—

It has pleased the Lord Jesus Christ, the Messiah, who died on a Roman Cross at Jerusalem, one thousand eight hundred and fifty years since, and who arose from the dead on the third day; and, after giving commandments to his apostles, ascended into the heavens, henceforth to reign till his enemies are made his footstool; to send forth his angels in this present age of the world, to reveal a NEW DISPENSATION.

Thus restoring to the earth the fulness and purity of the gospel, the apostleship, and the church of the Saints, with all its miraculous gifts and blessings.

Which gospel, thus restored, with its apostleship and powers, must be preached to every nation, kindred, tongue, and people under the whole heavens, with the signs following them that believe: and then shall the Lord Jesus Christ, the great Messiah and King, descend from the heavens in his glorified, immortal body, and reign with his Saints, and over all the kingdoms of the earth, one thousand years.

Having obtained a portion of this ministry, and being appointed and set apart by my brethren of the apostleship, to take the presidency and especial charge of a Mission to the countries mentioned herein—which includes nearly one-half of the globe—I have, in pursuance of these responsibilities, commenced my mission by sending forth this proclamation; first, in English; and to be translated and published by especial messengers, in due time, in every language and tongue included within the bounds of the Mission.

First of all, (having declared my object, purpose, destination, and commission) I hereby invite, and most earnestly plead with all men to repent, to turn away from their sins, and to believe on the Lord Jesus Christ, and come with humble hearts and contrite spirits, and be baptized, (immersed) in the name of Jesus Christ, for the remission of sins; and they shall receive the gift of the Holy Ghost by the laying on of the

152

hands, in the name of Jesus, of the apostles and elders, who are sent forth by the church of the Saints.

Which Holy Spirit shall bear witness of the truth of this message, and of the remission of the sins of all them who obey the same with full purpose of heart; and shall fill their minds with joy and gladness, and with light and intelligence; and shall also open to their understanding many things which are to come.

While some shall be blessed with visions, with the ministry of angels, with the spirit of prophecy and revelation:

And others, with the gift to heal the sick or to be healed by anointing with oil in the name of the Lord, accompanied with prayer, or the laying on of hands in the name of Jesus.

The deaf shall hear, the dumb speak, the lame walk, and the eyes of the blind see, inasmuch as they have faith sufficient to receive the same. And not many years hence, as faith, knowledge, union, and power increases, the dead shall be raised in some instances; the violence of fire be quenched; the prisons rent, if necessary; and the very elements controlled by the servants of God, in the name of Jesus.

All these gifts are included in the new dispensation, and are to be bestowed upon man in due time, as faith shall increase.

The church being yet in its infancy, its members have not yet attained to all these gifts; but they have progressed with astonishing rapidity, and are in many instances, enjoying many of these gifts in various countries.

I am aware that the astounding declarations contained in this proclamation, of necessity come in contact with the traditions of this and former ages; and also with the various priesthoods, organizations, and ordinances of the world called Christian, as well as with the various religions of the Pagan, Mahomedan, and Jew; but with all kindly feelings and respect for my fellow man, I cannot avoid this contact. I am the friend of man, and the friend of truth.

I, therefore, feel myself bound to bear witness of the truth as it is, and was, and is to come.

The Christian minister will inquire, "What need of a new dispensation, where the old has been perpetuated by an apostolical succession?"

To which I reply, "That I know of no succession of the kind; I acknowledge none; but, for the satisfaction of others, I will point out the way to determine the negative or affirmative of that all-important question."

Search the sacred writings of the apostles of old for any other order of apostles, ministers, ordinances, gifts, or powers, as constituting the true church, or connected with it, than the order set forth in the foregoing pages, and you will search in vain. The New Testament system was a system of inspiration, apostolical powers, miracles, healings, revelations, prophesyings, visions, angels, and all the gifts recorded in that book.

It was a system of ordinances—such as baptism for remission of sins, by immersion in water in the name of Jesus Christ; the laying on of hands for the gift of the Holy Spirit; the laying on of hands for healing the sick; also anointing with oil for the same purpose; also the administration of bread and wine, in remembrance of the death of Jesus Christ, and the blood of atonement.

Such was the New Testament system. Peter himself had no right to alter it, neither had Paul: in so doing, they would have forfeited their apostolic powers and their Christian standing; and would have been accursed, as it is written by Paul, "THOUGH WE, OR AN ANGEL FROM HEAVEN, PREACH ANY OTHER GOSPEL, LET HIM BE ACCURSED."

This being an undeniable fact, which no man can successfully controvert or deny; the question of apostolical or church succession resolves itself thus:—

Has the foregoing order of things been handed down in purity and power to this day? its apostleship, its powers of vision, revelation, prophecy, miracles, gifts, ordinances, and powers unaltered, unimpaired, unperverted?

If so, we have apostles, church, &c., NOW; without a new dispensation, or a new commission.

If not so, then there is no apostleship, no church, no Christian ministry and gifts on the earth, except commissioned by a new dispensation.

In the latter case, I would inquire, by what standard shall the Millennium, the age of peace, and universal truth, and knowledge be ushered in?

By what standard *shall the knowledge of the Lord cover the earth as the waters cover the sea?*

By what standard *shall there be one Lord, and his name one, and he be the king of all the earth*, as saith the prophets?

To what standard shall the Jews and the other tribes of Israel be restored, when the fulness of times is come in? *when their times are fulfilled*; when the full time arrives for the *restoration of the things spoken of by all the holy prophets since the world began?*

In which, of all the branches of the so-called Christian church, shall the power and miracles of God be manifested, when he shall make bare his arm in the eyes of all the nations, in the restoration of all the tribes of Israel and Judah?

Will his power and wisdom be displayed to restore them to a broken covenant? to doctrines corrupted? to ordinances perverted? to a Church divided, and destitute of the miraculous powers and gifts?

In short, to Christendom, who has ruled all nations with a rod of iron, and made the nations and their rulers drunken with the wine of their abominations?

No, I BOLDLY ANSWER NO!

What then? shall the words of the prophets fall to the ground unfulfilled?

NO, NEVER!

Hence the unavoidable necessity of a NEW DISPENSATION, *a new Apostolic commission.*

Such commission is now restored; such dispensation is now committed, and is held by the church of the Latter Day Saints, their apostles and elders.

Such the cause in which martyrs have bled, and a whole people been disfranchised, robbed, plundered, dispersed, slandered in every possible way, and driven to the mountains and deserts of the American interior.

Honest, pious, and well meaning Christians (for such there are in every sect under heaven) we hereby solemnly warn you, and intreat you, in the name of the Lord, to come out of every sect, and from all the Christian "*Babels;*" yea "*come out of her my people,*" as saith the ancient Apostle, "*for her sins have reached unto heaven, and God hath remembered her iniquities.*"

Come out, then, and unite with the church of the Saints, and henceforth devote your faith, your prayers, your strength, and your means to the work of God.

This same invitation is meant for all sincere, well-meaning, and devoted clergymen, whether Roman or Protestant, as well as the other members.

The sincere, zealous, and devoted missionaries and their supporters, who bear the *Bible* to foreign lands; and who toil amid fields of ice, or burning sands; amid deserts, mountains, or in the solitude of the wilderness; or in the lone and distant isles, surrounded by the infinite expanse of air and ocean, because of their love for Jesus and their fellow man.

To you we bring tidings of great joy!
The latter day glory has dawned upon the world!
The prayers of the faithful of all ages are heard!
The heavens have been again opened!
Angels have descended, bearing a dispensation to man!
The Holy Ghost has been again shed forth!
The fulness of the Gospel is revealed!

The sick are healed!

Demons are cast out!

The Kingdom of God has come!

The standard of truth and freedom is reared!

And to those who are in darkness a light has dawned!

And ere long, darkness, ignorance, and oppression shall cease from the earth!

Open your hearts, then, and receive and learn the way of God more perfectly; return fully to the system of that Bible which you publish, and to that God whom you serve.

And to those who are only Christians by nation, by birth, or by profession, and not by conduct; I would say by the commandment of the Lord, and also by way of invitation, turn from all your iniquities and abominations, your lyings, deceivings, whoredoms, blasphemies, drunkenness, gambling, idleness, extravagance, pride, and folly.

Also from your murders, theft, and robbery, and from all sin. Cease to take the name of God, the Father of Jesus Christ, in vain. Pledge yourselves by a covenant and a fixed purpose to serve the Lord, and come and be baptized in his name, and you shall receive remission of sins and the gift of the Holy Ghost. And then, if you endure to the end in keeping the commandments of Jesus Christ, you shall be saved in the celestial kingdom of God. You shall also have part in the first resurrection, which will come in a few years, and shall reign, in the flesh, on the earth with the King, the great Messiah, one thousand years.

CHAPTER II

ADDRESS TO PAGANS.

To those who are not Christian, but who worship the various Gods of India, China, Japan, or the Islands of the Pacific or Indian Oceans, we say — turn away from them; they are no Gods; they have no power. Open your ears and your hearts, and hear the apostles and elders of the church of the Saints. Learn of the true God, and of his Son Jesus Christ, who was dead and is alive, and shall live for evermore; and who is your King, and will soon come down from the more glorious planet where he dwells, and reign as the King of all nations; and your eyes shall see him, your acclamations hail him welcome, while he is crowned Lord of all.

Open your houses and your hearts, and receive and feed the elders who come among you; give them means and aid them in their travels; and verily your sick shall be healed, the evil demons which trouble you shall be cast out, and you shall have good dreams and visions of the Lord, and angels shall minister to some of you, and your hearts shall swell with love and gladness; and you will feel to forsake your sins and be baptized by the elders; and in so doing, they shall lay their hands upon you, bearing witness in your hearts of the truth, and enlightening your minds in the same.

CHAPTER III

ADDRESS TO THE JEWS.

To the Jews we would say — turn from your sins and seek the God of your fathers. Search the prophets, for lo your Messiah cometh speedily, and all the Saints with him. Yea he will descend upon the Mount of Olives near your ancient city, disperse your enemies, defend Jerusalem, and establish his kingdom over your nation and city, and over all the earth.

But what will be your astonishment, when gazing at him and falling at the feet of HIM as your great deliverer, you discover the wounds in his feet, in his hands, and in his side, and inquire, *"What are these wounds in your hands and in your feet?"*

And he will exclaim, "These are the wounds with which I was wounded in the house of my friends. I am Jesus of Nazareth whom your fathers crucified. I am the Son of God your deliverer and your eternal King." O who can describe the mingled feelings of joy and gladness, and gratitude, and shame, and remorse, and repentance, and amazement, and wonder which will then fill your bosoms. How you will repent and flock to the water, and be baptized in his name for the remission of your sins. With what power the Holy Ghost will fall upon you, when the apostles shall lay their hands upon your heads in the name of that Jesus who will stand in your presence. The big tears of joy will gush forth and stream upon the ground, while many of you will fall upon his neck, or kiss his feet, and bathe them in your tears.

Blessed is he that has seen him and believed; but more blessed are they who have not seen him and yet believed.

If any of you can so far overcome your prejudices and traditions, as to admit the probability, or even possibility, that Jesus of Nazareth is the Messiah, and that when your Messiah comes to fulfil your national redemption, and to establish his kingdom over all the earth, it will not be the first time that he has appeared among men, or even to your own nation; why, then, search diligently on the subject, and earnestly pray to Jehovah that you may understand the truth of a subject of such thrilling and vital importance.

After you have carefully reviewed your own prophets, search the New Testament with the same careful and prayerful attention, and then

157

obtain a copy of the Book of Mormon, and search that with the same degree of candour and earnestness, and I think your minds will expand, and you will be constrained to say, that Jesus of Nazareth is the Christ.

If so, then come to the standard of the New Dispensation—to the apostles and elders of the Church of Jesus Christ of Latter Day Saints; for you will readily see that there is no other system now extant, which even resembles, or will compare at all with the system established by him and his former apostles. Yea, come to them, repenting and turning from your sins, and go down into the waters of baptism, in the name of Jesus Christ, the Messiah. Receive the laying on of hands for the gift of the Holy Ghost. You will then know the truth, and be prepared for less surprise and a more glorious triumph on the Mount of Olives, in the day of your returning King.

I have now shown you the door of admission into the kingdom of God, into which you would do well to enter; and after entering therein, it will be required of you to keep the commandments of Jesus, and to look earnestly and daily for the fulfilment of the prophets which speak of the restoration of Israel and Judah, the downfall of Gentile rule, and the prevalence of that kingdom which shall be universal and have no end.

You would also in the meantime do well to contribute liberally of your means to the elders and missionaries of the church, for they are your brethren; they verily believe the Prophets, and they look, and pray, and labor earnestly for their fulfilment.

CHAPTER IV

ADDRESS TO THE RED MAN.

To the Red Men of America I will next address a few lines. You are a branch of the house of Israel. You are descended from the Jews, or, rather, more generally, from the tribe of *Joseph*, which Joseph was a great prophet and ruler in Egypt.

Your fathers left Jerusalem in the days of Jeremiah the prophet— being led by a prophet whose name was Lehi.

After leaving Jerusalem, they wandered in the wilderness of Arabia, and along the shores of the Red Sea, for eight years, living on fruits and wild game.

Arriving at the sea coast they built a ship, put on board the necessary provisions and the seeds brought with them from Jerusalem, and setting sail they crossed the great ocean, and landed on the western coast of America, within the bounds of what is now called "Chili."

In process of time they peopled the entire continents of North and South America.

They were taught by prophets from age to age. They were also favored with a personal visit from the Messiah, the Lord Jesus Christ, after he had risen from the dead. His own mouth taught them the Gospel, and his own hand ordained twelve apostles of their own nation, and endowed them with the same powers as the other twelve at Jerusalem. His own teaching opened to them the events of unborn time, and more particularly the future events pertaining to the American continent. His gospel and prophetic instructions were written by his commandment, and by the inspiration of his own Spirit.

In after ages your fathers sinned against all this light and knowledge, and lost the gospel privileges.

Their apostles were destroyed, or taken away and hid from the world. The working of miracles ceased because of iniquity. Civil government was broken up. Terrible and desolating wars ensued, which finally resulted in the darkness, ignorance, the divisions and sub-divisions in which the white man from Europe found you, upwards of three hundred years ago.

Mormon was one of your fathers. He lived about one thousand four hundred years ago, in North America. He wrote an abridgment of your history, prophecies, and gospel, from the records of your more ancient prophets and apostles; engraved the same on plates of gold, which records, at his death, descended to his son Moroni.

This Moroni, is the last of the ancient prophets of America. He completed the records of Mormon on the plates, and made a sacred deposit of the same in a hill called Cumorah, which hill is now included within the limits of New York, United States.

This deposit was made about the year four hundred and twenty of the Christian era.

The plates, thus deposited, were taken from their place of deposit, in the year one thousand eight hundred and twenty-seven of the same era, by Joseph Smith, and were by him translated and published to the world, in English, in the year one thousand eight hundred and thirty; the records and their contents having been revealed to him by an angel of God.

Many others saw and handled the plates and the engravings thereon, and have solemnly given their names to the world in testimony of the same, which testimony is published in full in said book.

There were also three other men, who in open day saw the vision; saw the angel of the Lord descend from heaven; heard his voice bear record of the plates and of their correct translation, and were commanded by him to bear testimony to the world. Their testimony is also published in full in said book.

Red men of the forest; Peruvians, Mexicans, Guatimalians, descendants of every tribe and tongue of this mysterious race, your history, your gospel, your destiny is revealed. It will soon be made known to you and to all nations — to every kindred, tongue, and people. It has come forth as a standard — a sign of the times of restoration of all things spoken of by all the holy prophets since the world began.

Turn then from your drunkenness, idolatry, murders, wars, and bloodshed — yea, turn from bowing down to images, the work of men's hands, which have no power to do either harm or good; turn from adultery, fornication, filth, and all manner of abominations; and seek the Lord and Saviour Jesus Christ, who was once dead and is alive, and, behold, he lives for evermore. Seek peace with each other, and with all mankind. And when the elders of the church of the Saints come among you, receive them, feed, lodge, and assist them; and hearken to their voice, for they bring glad tidings of great joy. Put away your sins and be baptized, (buried in the water) in the name of Jesus Christ, for the remission of the same, and receive the laying on of the hands of the apostles and elders of this church, for the gift of the Holy Ghost. And you will be filled with joy and gladness, with light and knowledge. You will know and bear witness of the truth. Some of you will be able to speak by the gift of the Holy Ghost, in great power. And by signs, and by visions, and by dreams, and by divers healings and miracles, will God confirm his word among you; for, behold, he purposes your restoration as a righteous branch of Israel.

The Book of Mormon, the record of your fathers, will soon be published among you in English, in Spanish, and in every written language in use among your various tribes and tongues. Messengers will also be sent among you to read, recite, and interpret the contents of said book, as far as necessary, to those who cannot read — so that to say the least you may have the gospel of your forefathers, and some knowledge of their history and prophecies.

CHAPTER V

GENERAL ADDRESS RESUMED. — ANCIENT RECORDS OF
THE WESTERN HEMISPHERE.

Having addressed myself in turn to pious Christians and Christian sinners, Pagans, Jews, and the Red Men of America, I will now return, and again address the whole of the people within the bounds of my mission.

The Book of Mormon is destined to be published as fast as possible to every nation, and in every language and tongue.

Its contents more deeply interest the world, and every intelligent, accountable being therein, than that of any other book (save the Jewish Scriptures) which is now extant in the world.

Its history penetrates the otherwise dark oblivion of the past, (as regards America) through the remote ages of antiquity; follows up the stream of the generations of man, till arriving at the great fountain head — the distributor of nations, tribes, and tongues — the TOWER OF BABEL, where it ceases, or is lost in, and sweetly blended with, that great Adamatic river whose source is in Paradise, the cradle of man — whose springs issue from beneath the throne of the Eternal city — and whose secret fountains comprise the infinite expanse, the boundless ocean of intellect, fact, and historic truth, as recorded in the archives of eternity.

Its prophetic vision separating from its history at that definite point, which by its authors might be called the *present*, opens the events of un-born time, and gives a view of things to come with all the clearness of history.

The Ten Tribes of Israel, the Jews, the white nations of Europe, the red tribes of America — even the *proud states of the American Union* — may each see themselves and their actions in the prophetic telescope of that book.

Their destiny is there written: and much of it from the mouth of him who spake, and Jerusalem was deluged in blood — wrapped in the flames of desolation and death — and trodden down for eighteen centuries. Who prophesied, and that holy structure, the temple of God, the pride and confidence of a nation, was *thrown down and "not one stone left upon another."* Who uttered his voice and a nation withdrew before him, ceased to be, and its fragments made wanderers among the nations, till *"the times of the Gentiles shall be fulfilled."*

The fate of nations; the restoration of Judah and Israel; the downfall of corrupt churches and religious institutions; the end of Gentile super-stition and misrule; the universal prevalence of peace, and truth, and light, and knowledge; the awful wars and troubles which precede those happy times; the glorious coming of Jesus Christ as king over all the earth; the resurrection of the saints to reign on the earth, are all pre-dicted in that book: the time and means of their fulfilment pointed out with clearness, showing the present age more big with wonders, than all the ages of Adam's race which have gone before it.

Its doctrines are developed in such plainness and simplicity, and with such clearness and precision, that no man can mistake them. They are there as they flowed from the mouth of a risen Redeemer, in the liquid eloquence of love, mingled with immortal tears of joy and compassion, and as written by men whose tears of overflowing affection and gratitude bathed his immortal feet.

All men are invited and instructed by the doctrines to turn from their sins and live; to believe on his name; to go down into the waters of baptism, in his name, and arise to newness of life, receiving the gift of the Holy Ghost, enjoying the gifts of the same, and keeping his commandments to the end of their lives. On these conditions they are promised eternal life and exaltation in his presence, where is fulness of joy.

Such is the BOOK OF MORMON, that book of books—that Ensign to the nations, which in twenty-one years has, by the aid of apostolic powers and the gift of the Holy Ghost, diffused its light over half the globe.

I am aware of the prejudice of *"Christians"* in favor of the Bible, and against all other books claiming to be of divine origin; but I also know perfectly, and bear record that their prejudice is founded in ignorance, and is without any real or reasonable foundation. Such traditions and such prejudices grow out of the same *narrow* views which, in the days of Columbus, would not let the geographical knowledge of man expand, or his aspirations or thoughts to reach beyond the boundaries of the old world, lest the very thought should be blasphemy—lest a world should be discovered where the Jewish apostles had not been, and thus render their commission to preach the gospel to every creature, an inconsistency.

I would ask such narrow minds the following questions:—

Are there more countries than one?

Are there more nations than one?

Did the Great Father of all, create those several countries?

Did he people them with intelligent beings, candidates for immortality and eternal life?

Did he love those beings without respect to nation or country?

Did his Son Jesus Christ shed his blood for all?

Did he partake of death, and mourning and sorrow?

Did all stand in need of the knowledge and comfort brought to light by his resurrection, and triumph over death, hell, and the grave?

Is it reasonable, right, and consistent, that all nations should have the good news of so glorious an event, and be comforted and taught?

Was Jesus Christ in his resurrected body, capable of overstepping the physical barriers of ocean and desert, and of paying a personal visit to the other hemisphere?

Were his angels capable of overcoming the wave and winds, and of bearing the glad tidings to the remotest lands?

Did they mean it when they said to the shepherds of Judea, *"We bring glad tidings of great joy which shall be to all people?"*

I think a candid man will answer all these questions in the affirmative.

If so, I would still inquire whether a risen Saviour and his angels, in visiting the Western hemisphere, had a right to command the people there to write the facts of their ministry, and to record their doctrines? Whether his Spirit had a right to inspire and indite those writings? And after being so written, they would constitute a book; a holy scripture; a volume or volumes of the word of God?

I would further inquire, whether the risen Jesus and his angels, have not the right and the power to reveal such records to the world; when, where, and by whom it seemeth them good?

If so, when should we look for them to come to the knowledge of the world, if not in the dawn of the restoration of all things which God hath spoken by the mouths of all his holy prophets since the world began?

I beseech you, dear reader, whoever you are, to ponder well these questions, and they will swell and enlarge your heart.

I now solemnly predict, in the name of the Lord God of Israel, that in a few years, the world shall bring together and compare ancient records, as sacred and as true as the words of Jesus Christ—as holy as the Bible. Records which unfold the gospel of the Son of God, revealed, at least, to three distinct nations of the earth, by his own ministry in his glorified body.

I will also name these records: as follows:—

Records of the Jews, (the Bible) written in Asia.

Records of the remnant of Joseph, the Nephites, (Book of Mormon) written in America.

Records of the Ten Lost Tribes of Israel: country not yet revealed.

These three national records will be familiarly known among the nations, in a few years: will be demonstrated as to their truth; and each of them will contain an account of the ministry of Jesus Christ to their respective countries, as he did really appear to them after his resurrection. The words which he spake, the doctrine he taught, the gospel and ordinances as he set forth and commanded, will be written in each record.

In Judea, he chose and ordained twelve apostles, viz., Simon Peter, Andrew, James, John, Philip, Bartholemew, Matthew, Thomas, James, Simon Zelotes, and Judas Iscariot.

In America, he chose and ordained twelve apostles, viz., Nephi, Timothy, Jonas, Mathoni, Mathonihah, Kumen, Kumenonhi, Jeremiah, Shemnon, Jonas, Zedekiah and Isaiah.

In the country of the Ten Tribes, he, of course, chose other twelve, whose names will appear in due time.

Besides these records of his personal ministry, there were many of other countries and nations, (which held no communication with the nations where these administrations were had, and these quorums chosen) which received a knowledge of his death and resurrection, and the gift of the Holy Ghost. They have, also, written an account of the same.

Now, all these records which are saved, and which contain the word of God, will come to light and be revealed. There is nothing hid which shall not be made known; neither is there anything secret which shall not be revealed and come abroad, in connection with the *"times of the restoration of all things, which God hath spoken by the mouths of all his holy prophets since the world began."*

"The Jews shall have the words of the Nephites; and the Nephites shall have the words of the Jews. And the Nephites and the Jews shall have the words of the lost tribes of Israel; and the lost tribes of Israel shall have the words of the Nephites and the Jews." And thus the word of God shall be brought together and embodied. And the Nations who have written it, shall be brought together and embodied also. And the things of all the Nations shall be revealed; and the earth be overwhelmed with the knowledge of the Past, the Present and the Future; and darkness, bigotry, superstition, and falsehoods of every description, shall flee away as the fleeting shadow of a cloud, from off all the earth.

The inquiry will be, What are the evidences upon which rests the truth of the Book of Mormon? To which I answer: Search the book and learn for yourselves. You will find,

First — The testimony of the witnesses.

Second — The consistency, harmony, and evident truthfulness of its history and prophecies.

Third — The simplicity and purity of its doctrines.

And last, and best of all — The gift of the Holy Spirit of truth, which bears witness to the heart of every honest, prayerful man, who desires to know and do the truth.

Truth is light.

Light is spirit.

Light cleaveth unto light.

Truth embraceth truth.

Intelligence comprehendeth intelligence.

Spirit recognizeth spirit.

Like embraceth like in all spiritual things.

These are some of the laws of nature in the spiritual world, and are as true, and as capable of demonstration, as any physical law of the universe.

Two balls of quicksilver placed in contact, immediately recognize and embrace each other. Two blazes of fire, placed in near contact, will immediately spring toward each other and blend in one. Two drops of water placed upon a table will remain in a round or globular form, until they are enlarged so as to expand their circles; when, as they mutually touch each other, they will instantly mingle and become one globular form. So it is in spiritual things. There is in every man a portion of the spirit of truth; a germ of light: a spiritual test or touchstone, which, if strictly observed, studied, and followed by its possessor, will witness to him; and will, as it were, leap forward with a warm glow of joy and sympathy, to every truthful spirit with which it comes in contact: while by a shudder of disgust, it will recognize a false spirit, a lie. Call this spiritual magnetism, or what you please; it is so, and is a law of nature.

Herein consists the mystery of the agency of man.

This is the reason why a man is under condemnation for rejecting any spiritual truth; or, for embracing any spiritual error.

A man's deeds are evil. His monitor is unheeded; his good angel, and the good spirit within, is grieved: and, after many admonitions which are not heeded, they retire, and leave him in the dark. He loves his own. He cleaves to a lie—he rejects the truth—darkness still increases: the world, the flesh, and the evil demons allure him onward, till death closes the scene, and ushers his spirit from the rudimental state of man, into the next sphere. When his evil demons and companions in darkness surround him, and dwell with him. Each contributes his portion of the darkness; till cloud mingled with cloud, envelopes the whole in black despair, obscures the vision, forbids the eye to behold, the tongue to utter, or the pen to describe.

On the other hand, a man's deeds are good; as saith the Scriptures— "He that doeth truth cometh to the light, that his deeds may be made manifest that they are wrought in God."

He obeys this monitor within him. He welcomes to his bosom every true and holy principle within his reach—he puts it into practice, and seeks for more: his mind expands: the field of intelligence opens around, above, beneath him: wide and more widely extends the vision: the past, the present, the future, opens to his view. Earth, with its tribes; heaven, with its planets and intelligences; the heaven of heavens, with its brilliant circles of suns, and their myriads of angels and sons of God, basking in sun-beams of pure intelligence; and streams of light and love. Each adding to, and mingling in the light of the other, till the whole enlightens the vast universe, both spiritual and physical; and the vision loses itself in its very immensity, on the confines of its own infinitude.

Let a person look back on his past life, carefully review and examine the days of his innocent childhood, his first approaches to temptation, immorality, or crime. Does he not remember to have felt a disagreeable burning in his bosom; a disgust, a trembling of nerve and muscles, a hesitation; in short a something disapproving of the act he was about to commit? And, if he still persisted, did not this burning and uneasy feeling increase almost to a fever.

Well, reader, this was your monitor. The Spirit of God within you. Had you heeded it, it would have kept you from every temptation and crime.

On the other hand, do you not remember, many times in the course of your life; of a fire, a warm glow of joy; a pleasing burning or sensation of pure light and pleasure, in your bosom, approving of a good act, or prompting you to do the same? In short, a feeling of pure good will, kind sympathy, and boundless love to all good intelligences, and to man? A purifying of heart and sentiment, as if you could wish to do good continually, and never sin?

That was the promptings of the spark of divinity within you. It was the teachings, inspirations, and whisperings of that light, which lighteth every man that cometh into the world. It is sweeter than honey; more harmonious than music; more pure than the drops of dew on the roses of Paradise; more tender than the apple of thine eye; and more valuable than the gold of Australia. Blessed are they who cultivate and nourish it in their bosoms, and carry it out in their lives; for it is an emanation from the fountain of eternal life: and those who follow up from whence it came, will arrive at that fountain, as surely as a sunbeam leads upward to the centre of light.

CHAPTER VI.
ON LAWS AND GOVERNMENTS.

Having borne my testimony, as a faithful and true witness, of the gospel, and of things past, present, and to come; I will now give some information on the subject of the laws and governments of men; and the duties we owe to them, and the duties we sustain to them, as members of the Church of Jesus Christ in all the world.

Every government of man is permitted by the Lord, and is needful, until he reigns whose right it is to reign; and until he subdues all enemies under his feet.

We are not sent forth to revolutionize the world in a political sense; but to warn the world of approaching events, instruct the ignorant, and call sinners to repentance.

The laws of every land will be your law, in a civil and political sense of the word.

We are in duty bound to obey magistrates, judges, rulers, governors and kings, who hath the legitimate rule in the various countries where we live, or where we travel or sojourn.

If the spirit of modern European and American institutions, pertaining to liberty of conscience; and a free interchange of intercourse, thought, and speech, marches onward from conquest to conquest; and thus opens the way for all nations to diffuse their light and interchange their knowledge; then let us rejoice in the same, and improve the opportunity to declare the testimony of Jesus, and publish the gospel of salvation, the good news of eternal life; wherever the foot of man has made an imprint; wherever sorrow and tears, and mourning and death, have cast their shadows of despair.

If the still advancing improvements in steam navigation, of railroad conveyance, and electric communication, follow universally in the wake of freedom's triumphs and conquests; then O ye saints of the Most High! ye elders and apostles of Israel

> Let fly your thoughts on the lightning car,
> With the speed of light to the realms afar.
> Mount, mount the car with the horse of fire,
> Outstript the wind! he will never tire.
> Let the wild-bird scream as he lags behind,
> And the hurricane a champion find.
> Search the darkest spot where mortals dwell,
> With a voice of thunder the tidings tell.
> Proclaim the dawn of a brighter day,
> When the King of Kings will his sceptre sway.
> Bid pain, and anguish, and sorrow cease,
> And open the way for the Prince of Peace.
> He will conquer death—bid sorrow flee,
> And give to the nations a jubilee.

As you travel from one nation to another, you will find their laws, religions, ordinances, ceremonies, institutions, domestic arrangements, marriages, &c., &c., widely clashing, and at variance with each other, and with the laws of God.

But, remember that yours is a universal commission, of peace on earth and good will to man.

Yours is a proclamation of universal reformation and repentance. You are sent forth as the ambassadors of the King, the Lord Jesus Christ; to command all persons who have arrived to the years of accountability, to repent and be baptized in his name, for the remission of sins. You are sent forth to administer the gift of the Holy Ghost, by the laying on of hands in the same holy name.

You are sent forth to bear witness of the truth of this dispensation, and of a crucified and risen Saviour. You are sent forth to prophecy, and warn the world of things to come.

You are sent forth to lay your hands on the little children of the members of the church, and bless them, and confirm upon them their Christian names, as members and heirs of the covenant of promise.

You are sent forth to baptize the nations, and thus prepare the way for the coming of the Son of God. You are sent forth to lay your hands on the sick the lame, the blind, the deaf, the afflicted of every description, who believe in your testimony, and have faith to be healed. Yea, verily, to lay your hands on them and anoint them in the name of Jesus Christ, the Son of God.

You are sent forth to command demons, devils, and unclean and foul spirits of every kind, in the name of Jesus Christ, to depart from the tabernacles of persons afflicted by them.

You are sent forth to preach deliverance to the captive, to bind up the broken hearted, and to comfort all who mourn; to proclaim the acceptable year of the Lord, and the day of vengeance of our God.

You are not sent forth to intermeddle with the civil, political, or domestic institutions, established by law, and rendered sacred by antiquity, or long established usage; except in so far, as those institutions come in contact with liberty of conscience; and the commandments of Jesus Christ. When the latter is the case, you must obey God rather than man, and take the consequences, or flee to another place.

{15}

"Mormonism!" "Plurality of Wives!"
An Especial Chapter, for the Especial Edification
of certain inquisitive News Editors, Etc.

(San Francisco, 13 July 1852)

A certain Editor in this town, (San Francisco,) in reviewing our late Spanish and English Proclamation, complains sorely of our neglect of our own countrymen, the Americans, in our religious instructions. He also enquires, with all the seeming anxiety of a penitent man at the anxious seat, as to his excellency Gov. Young's family matters, and whether "Mormonism" allows a man more wives than one!!!

We inform him, that *"Mormonism"* is not in a corner, nor its light under a bushel, in the United States. Its books and ministry have long been within the reach of every reader in the English language. If the Americans wish information let them read the Bible, the Book of Mormon, and our other works, and seek the truth at the hand of God, and at the hand of our Apostles and Elders. And let them repent of their priestcraft, errors and folly, and humble themselves as in the dust, and learn to speak and publish the truth.

In regard to Gov. Young's family matters, we never had the curiosity to inform ourselves, although we have been a near neighbor of his for many years. This much we do know, — that his morality is above all suspicion in the circles where he is known, and we presume the number of his family does not exceed the late estimates, which have been the rounds of the American Press. At any rate his family are respectable and virtuous; and as patterns of faith and piety, and good works, they are honored in every department of society. Marriage, in nearly all countries is regulated by civil legislation, and is therefore beyond the jurisdiction of our Apostleship, or ministry. Some governments allow to each man *one* wife, some *two*, some *four*, and others as many as they can obtain and support.

Every person who reads the Bible must know that the commission is to preach the Gospel to every creature in all the world, and to baptize all who believe, and repent. The Lord, in giving this commission, made no exceptions to the exclusion of any particular family organization growing out of the varied civil institutions.

It is also known, or ought to be, that this commission, without variation has been renewed to the Latter Day Saints, and that every baptized penitent, is a member of the church in good standing, while he observes the laws of God and his country Whether these laws legalize to him *one* wife or *"sixteen."*

Our instructions to all nations are that they believe in Jesus Christ, and repent and be baptised. And then serve God and obey the laws and civil institutions under which they live, or a country whose institutions are more congenial to their faith.

But, in all cases to be sure and love, sustain, honor, and cherish every soul of the family which the laws of God or man has given them, and to abstain forever from all unlawful intercourse between the sexes. For all unlawful intercourse of this kind is adultery, or fornication, and by the law of God is punishable with *death.*

Is it possible there is *still* in *"Christendom,"* (after so many years of Mormon progress,) a *man*, or even an EDITOR so ignorant as to suppose that the eternal principles of the Priesthood, Ordinances and Kingdom of God, sent forth as a *Standard of Universal Restoration* for the *Tribes of Israel*, and for *all nations*, would narrow itself down to the petty prejudices, local superstitions, and narrow views of that small minority of mankind known as *"Christendom!"*

And thus exclude Abraham, Isaac, and Jacob, and the kings, patriarchs, and prophets of old from the kingdom of God, and three quarters of the present generation of mankind from all participation in the Gospel ordinances, merely because their *family is so large*!!!

Nay, more! The narrow, ignorant legislation of some Churches and States, would imprison, for years the Patriarch Jacob, turn his four wives, twelve sons and a daughter into the street, without father or husband, dishonored and rendered illegitimate; and then, if possible, demolish the very gates of New Jerusalem; because the names of the sons of Jacob, by Rachel, Leah, Bilhah, and Zilpah were found engraven on the gates.

This done and the family of Israel broken up, all the good citizens, law makers, judges, and lawyers who had thus shown their indignation against *"vice"* and their zeal for *"virtue"* might by the laws of the same State, seduce and ruin as many females as they pleased, by merely paying a fine, and a certain amount of damages!

Or, in other words: so much disease, shame, dishonor, ruin, death and damnation, of our fair daughters for so much money. So much gold for so much blood! — murder! No — Editors! — ;this is not *"Mormonism!"*

Should the United States, or any other nation ever rise from the degradation into which a false *"Christianity"* has plunged them: should they ever ascend to the level of the heathen nations of ancient Egypt or Babylon, and like a Pharaoh, Nebuchadnezzer, or a Cyrus, engage a Prophet or an Apostle to teach them; a Joseph or a Daniel to give them wisdom and revelation in the knowledge of God, and in the science of government, — then "Mormonism" will teach their Senators wisdom and their Judges justice; and the latter day Apostles and Prophets restore to them the laws of God. As it is written by Isaiah, Chap 2d, verses 2d, 3d, 4th and 5th.

"And it shall come to pass in the last days, that the mountain of the Lord's house shall be established in the top of the mountains, and shall be exalted above the hills, and all nations shall flow unto it.

And many people shall say, come ye, and let us go unto the mountain of the Lord, to the house of the God of Jacob; and he will teach us of his ways, and we will walk in his paths, for out of Zion shall go forth the law, and the word of the Lord from Jerusalem.

And he shall judge among the nations, and shall rebuke many people, and they shall beat their swords into ploughshares, and their spears into pruning hooks. Nation shall not lift up sword against nation, neither shall they learn war any more.

O house of Jacob, come, and let us walk in the light of the Lord."

The law of God, from Zion, in the top of the mountains, when taught to the nations, will provide the means for every female to answer the end of their creation; to be protected in honor and virtue; and to become a happy wife and mother, so far as they are capacitated and inclined. While every man who stoops from his Godlike majesty to a level with the brute creation so far as to trifle with the fountain of life, (female virtue) will atone for the same with his blood.

And thus adultery, and fornication, with all their attendant train of disease, despair, shame, sorrow and death will cease from our planet, and joy, love, confidence, and all the pure kindred affections, and family endearments be cherished in every bosom of man.

Spiritual Communication.
A Sermon Delivered by Elder P. P. Pratt, Senr,
Before the Conference at Salt Lake City, April 7, 1853

(San Francisco? 1853?)

I was led to reflection on this subject, not only by my acquaintance with the present state of the world, and the movements and powers which seem new to many, but because this text, written by Isaiah so many centuries since, and copied by Nephi ages before the birth of Jesus Christ, seemed as appropriate, and as directly adapted to the present state of things, as if written but yesterday, or a year since.

"Should not a people seek unto their God, for the living to hear from the dead?" is a question by the Prophet, and at a time when they shall invite you to seek unto those familiar with spirits, and to wizards, &c., or in other words to magnetizers, rappers, clairvoyants, writing mediums, &c. When they shall say these things unto you, then is the time to consider the question of that ancient Prophet—"Should not a people seek unto their God, for the living to hear from the dead?"

We hear much, of late, about visions, trances, clairvoyance, mediums of communication with the spirit world, writing mediums, &c. by which the world of spirits is said to have found means to communicate with spirits in the flesh. They are not working in a corner. The world is agitated on these subjects. Religious ministers are said to preach, editors to write and print, judges to judge, &c., from this kind of inspiration. It is brought into requisition to develop the sciences, to detect crime, and in short to mingle in all the interests of life.

In the first place, what are we talking about, when we touch the question of the living hearing from the dead? It is a saying, that "dead men tell no tales." If this is not in the Bible, it is somewhere else, and if it be true, it is just as good as if it were in the Bible.

The Sadducees in the time of Jesus, believed there were no such things as angels or spirits, or existence in another sphere; that when an individual was dead, it was the final end of the workings of his intellectual being, that the elements were dissolved, and mingled with the great fountain from which they emanated, which was the end of individuality, or conscious existence.

Jesus, in reply to them, took up the argument from the scriptures, or history of the ancient fathers, venerated by reason of antiquity, in

172

hopes, by this means, to influence the sadducees, or at least the Pharisees and others, by means so powerful, and so well adapted to the end in view.

Said He, God has declared himself the God of Abraham, Isaac, and Jacob. Now God is not the God of the dead, but of the living. As much as to say that Abraham, Isaac, and Jacob were not dead, but living that they had never been dead at all, but had always been living; that they never did die, in the sense of the word that these Sadducees supposed, but were absolutely alive.

Now, if intelligent beings, who once inhabited flesh, such as our fathers, mothers, wives, children, &c., have really died, and are now dead in the sense of the word, as understood by the ancient Sadducees, or modern Atheist, then it is in vain to talk of converse with the dead. All controversy in that case is at an end on the subject of correspondence with the dead, because an intelligence must exist before it can communicate. If these individuals are dead, in the sense that the human body dies, we have never known of a single instance of any intelligence communicated therefrom.

Jesus, in his argument with the Sadducees, handled the subject according to the strictest principles of ancient and modern theology, and true philosophy. He conveyed the idea in the clearest terms, that an individual intelligence, or identity could never die.

The outward tabernacle, inhabited by a spirit, returns to the element from which it emanated. But the thinking being, the individual, the active agent or identity that inhabited that tabernacle, never ceased to exist, to think, act, live, move, or have a being: never ceased to exercise those sympathies, affections, hopes, and aspirations which are founded in the very nature of intelligences, being the inherent and invaluable principles of their eternal existence.

No, they never cease. They live, move, think, act, converse, feel, love, hate, believe, doubt, hope, and desire.

But what are they, if they are not flesh and bones? What are they if they are not tangible to our gross organs of sense? Of what are they composed, that we can neither see, hear, nor handle them, except we are quickened, or our organs touched by the principles of vision, clairvoyance, or spiritual sight? What are they? Why, they are organized intelligences. What are they made of? They are made of the element which we call Spirit, which is as much an element of material existence as earth, air, electricity, or any other tangible substance recognized by man but so subtle, so refined is its nature, that it is not tangible to our gross organs. It is invisible to us unless we are quickened by a portion of the same element; and like electricity, and several other substances, it is only known or made manifest to our senses by its effects. For instance, electricity is not always visible to us, but its existence is made manifest by its operations upon the wire, or upon the nerves. We cannot see the air, but we feel its effects, and without it we cannot breathe.

If a wire were extended in connection with the equatorial line of our globe in one entire circle of 25,000 miles in extent, the electric fluid would convey a token from one intelligence to another, the length of the entire circle, in a very small portion of a second, or, we will say, in the twinkling of an eye. This, then, proves that the spiritual fluid, or element called electricity is an actual, physical, and tangible power, and is as much a real and tangible substance, as the ponderous rocks which were laid on yesterday in the foundation of our contemplated Temple.

It is true that this subtle fluid or spiritual element, is endowed with the powers of locomotion in a far greater degree than the more gross and solid elements of nature; that its refined particles penetrate amid the other elements with greater ease, and meet with less resistance from the air or other substances, than would the more gross elements. Hence its speed, or superior powers of motion.

Now let us apply this philosophy to all the degrees of spiritual element, from electricity, which may be assumed to be one of the lowest or more gross elements of spiritual matter, up through all the gradations of spiritual fluids, till we arrive at a substance so holy, so pure, so endowed with intellectual attributes, and sympathetic affections, that it may be said to be on a par, or level, in its attributes, with man.

Let a given quantity of this element, thus endowed or capacitated, be organized in the size and form of man, let every organ be developed, formed, and endowed, precisely after the pattern or model of man's outward or fleshy tabernacle—what would we call this individual, organized portion of the spiritual element?

We would call it a spiritual body, an individual intelligence, an agent endowed with life, with a degree of independence, or inherent with, with the powers of motion, of thought, and with the attributes of moral, intellectual and sympathetic affections and emotions.

We would conceive of it as possessing eyes to see, ears to hear, hands to handle. As in possession of the organs of taste, of smelling and of speech.

Such beings are we, when we have laid off this outward tabernacle of flesh. We are in every way interested, in our relationships, kindred ties, sympathies, affections, and hopes, as if we had continued to live, but had stepped aside, and were experiencing the loneliness of absence for a season. Our posterity, our ancestors, to the remotest ages of antiquity, or of future time, are all brought within the circle of our sphere of joys, sorrows, interests, or expectation. Each forms a link in the great chain of life, and in the science of mutual salvation, improvement, and exaltation through the blood of the Lamb.

Our prospects, hopes, faith, charity, enlightenment, improvement, in short, all our interests are blended, and more or less influenced by the acts of each.

Is this the kind of being that departs from our sight when its earthly tabernacle is laid off, and the veil of eternity is lowered between us? Yes, verily. Where then does it go?

"To heaven," says one. "To the eternal world of glory," says another. "To the celestial kingdom, to inherit thrones and crowns, in all the fulness of the presence of the Father, and of Jesus Christ," says a third.

Now, my dear hearers, these things are not so. Nothing of the kind. Throne, kingdoms, crowns, principalities, and powers, in the celestial and eternal worlds, and the fullness of the presence of the Father, and of His Son Jesus Christ, are reserved for resurrected beings, who dwell in immortal flesh. The world of resurrected beings and the world of spirits, are two distinct spheres, as much so as our own sphere is distinct from that of the Spirit world.

Where then does the spirit go, on its departure from its earthly tabernacle! It passes to the next sphere of human existence called the world of spirits, a veil being drawn between us in the flesh and that world of spirits. Well, says one, is there no more than one place in the Spirit world! Yes, there are many places and degrees in that world, as in this. Jesus Christ, when absent from his flesh, did not ascend to the Father, to be crowned and enthroned in power. Why! Because He had not yet a resurrected body, and had therefore a mission to perform in another sphere. Where then did he go. To the world of spirits, to wicked, sinful spirits, who died in their sins, being swept on by the flood of Noah. The Thief on the cross, who died at the same time, also went to the same world, and to the same particular place in the same world, for he was a sinner, and would of course go to the prison of the comdemned, there to await the ministry of that Gospel which had failed to reach his case while on the earth. How many other places Jesus might have visited while in the Spirit world, is not for me to say, but there was a moment in which the poor, uncultivated ignorant thief, was with him in that world. And as he commenced, though late to repent while on the earth, we have reason to hope that that moment was improved by our Saviour, in ministering to him that gospel which he had no opportunity to teach to him while expiring upon the cross. "This day shalt thou be with me in Paradise," said Jesus, or, in other words, this day shalt thou be with me in the next sphere of existence—the world of spirits.

Now mark the difference. Jesus was there as a preacher of righteousness, as one holding the keys of Apostleship, or priesthood, appointed to preach glad tidings to the meek, to bind up the broken-hearted, to preach liberty to the captive, and the opening of the prison to them that were bound. What did the thief go there for? He went there in a state of ignorance, and sin, being uncultivated, unimproved, and unprepared for salvation. He went there to be taught, and to complete that repentance, which in a dying moment he commenced on the earth. He had beheld Jesus expire on the cross and he had implored him to remember him when he should come into possession of his kingdom. The Saviour, under these extreme circumstances, did not then teach him the Gospel, but referred him to the next opportunity; when they should meet in the Spirit world. If the thief thus favored continued to improve, he is no doubt waiting in hope for the signal to be given, at the sound of the next trump, for him to leave the Spirit world and re-enter the fleshly tabernacle, and to ascend to a higher degree of felicity. Jesus Christ, on the other hand, departed from the Spirit world on the third day, and re-entered his fleshly tabernacle, in which he ascended, and was crowned at the right hand of the Father. Jesus Christ, then, and the thief on the cross, have not dwelt together in the same kingdom or place for this eighteen hundred years, nor have we proof that they have seen each other during that time.

To say that Jesus Christ dwells in the world of Spirits, with those whose bodies are dead, would not be the truth. He is not there. He only staid there until the third day. He then returned to his tabernacle, and ministered among the sons of earth for forty days, where he ate, drank, talked, preached, reasoned out of the scriptures, commissioned, commanded, blessed, &c. Why did he do this? Because he had ascended on high, and been crowned with all poor in heaven and on earth, therefore he had authority to do all these things.

So much then for that wonderful question that has been asked by our Christian neighbors, so many thousand times, in the abundance of their charity for those who, like the thief on the cross, die in their sins, or without baptism and the other gospel ordinances. The question naturally arises, do all the people who die without the Gospel hear it as soon as they arrive in the world of spirits? To illustrate this, let us look at the dealings of God with the people of this world. "What can we reason but from what we know?" We know and understand the things of this world, in some degree, because they are visible, and we are daily conversant with them. Do all the people in this world hear the gospel as soon as they are capable of understanding? No, indeed, but very few in comparison, have heard it at all.

Ask the poor Lamanites who have with their fathers before them, inhabited these mountains for a thousand years, whether they have ever heard the Gospel, and they will tell you nay. But why not? Is it not preached on the earth? Yea, verily, but the earth is wide, and circumstances differ very greatly among its different inhabitants.

The Jews once had the Gospel, with its Apostleship, powers and blessings offered unto them, but they rejected it as a people, and for this reason it was taken from them, and thus many generations of them have been born, and have lived and died without it. So with the gentiles, and so with the Lamanites. God has seen proper to offer the Gospel with its priesthood and powers, in different ages and countries, but it has been as often rejected, and therefore withdrawn from the earth. The consequence is that the generations of men have, for many ages, come and gone in ignorance of its principles, and the glorious hopes they inspire.

Now these blessings would have continued on the earth, and would have been enjoyed in all the ages and nations of man, but for the agency of the people. They chose their own forms of government, laws, institutions, religions, rulers and priests, instead of yielding to the influence and guidance of the chosen vessels of the Lord, who were appointed to instruct and govern them.

Now, how are they situated in the Spirit world? If we reason from analogy, we should at once conclude that things exist there after the same pattern. I have not the least doubt but there are spirits there who have dwelt there a thousand years, who, if we could converse with them face to face, would be found as ignorant of the truths, the ordinances, powers, keys, priesthood, resurrection and eternal life of the body, in short, as ignorant of the fulness of the Gospel, with its hopes and consolations, as is the Pope of Rome, or the Bishop of Canterbury, or as are the Chiefs of the Indian tribes of Utah.

And why this ignorance in the Spirit world? Because a portion of the inhabitants thereof are found unworthy of the consolations of the Gospel, until the fulness of time, until they have suffered in hell, in the dungeons of darkness, or the prisons of the condemned, amid the buffetings of fiends, and malicious and lying spirits. As in earth, so in the Spirit world. No spirit can enter into the privileges of the Gospel, until the keys are turned and the gospel opened by those in authority, for all which there is a time, according to the wise dispensations of justice and mercy.

It was many, many centuries before Christ lived in the flesh, that a whole generation, eight souls excepted, were cut off by the flood. What became of them? I do not know exactly all their history in the Spirit world. But this much I know — they have heard the Gospel from the lips of a crucified Redeemer, and have the privilege of being judged according to men in the flesh. As these persons were ministered to by

Jesus Christ, after he had been put to death, it is reasonable to suppose that they had waited all that time, without the knowledge or privileges of the gospel.

How long did they wait? You may reckon for yourselves. The long ages, centuries, thousands of years which intervened between the flood of Noah and the death of Christ. Oh! the weariness, the tardy movement of time! the lingering ages for a people to dwell in condemnation, darkness, ignorance and despondency, as a punishment for their sins. For they had been filled with violence while on the earth in the flesh, and had rejected the preaching of Noah, and the Prophets which were before him.

Between these two dispensations, so distant from each other in point of time they were to linger without hope, and without God, in the Spirit world; and similar has been the fate of the poor Jew, the miserable Lamanite, and many others in the flesh. Between the commission and ministry of the Former and the Latter-day-Saints, and Apostles, there has been a long and dreary night of darkness. Some fifteen to seventeen centuries have passed away, in which the generations of men have lived without the keys of the gospel.

Whether in the flesh, or in the Spirit world, is this not hell enough? Who can imagine a greater hell than before our eyes, in the circumstances of the poor, miserable, degraded Indian, and his ancestors, since the keys of the Gospel were taken from them some fifteen hundred years ago? Those who had the Gospel in the former dispensations, and were made partakers of its spirit, its knowledge and powers, and then turned away and became the enemies of God, and of His saints, the malicious and wilful opposers of that which they knew to be true, have no forgiveness in this world, neither in the Spirit world which is the world next to come. Such apostates seek, in all dispensations, to bring destruction on the innocent, and to shed innocent blood, or consent thereto. For such, I again repeat, I know no forgiveness. Their children, who, by the conduct of such fathers, have been plunged into ignorance and misery for so many ages, and have lived without the privileges of the Gospel, will look, down upon such a parentage with mingled feelings of horror, contempt, reproach, and pity, as the agents who plunged their posterity into the depths of misery and woe.

Think of those swept away by the flood in the days of Noah. Did they wait a long time in prison? Forty years! Oh! what a time to be imprisoned! What do you say to a hundred, a thousand, two thousand, three or four thousand years to wait? Without what? Without even a clear idea or hope of a resurrection from the dead, without the broken heart being bound up, the captive delivered, or the door of the prison opened. Did not they wait? Yes they did, until Christ was put to death in the flesh.

Now what would have been the result, if they had repented while in the flesh at the preaching of Noah? Why, they would have died in hope of a glorious resurrection, and would have enjoyed the society of the redeemed, and lived in happiness in the Spirit world, till the resurrection of the son of God. Then they would have received their bodies, and would have ascended with him, amid thrones, principalities, and powers, in heavenly places.

I will suppose, in the Spirit world, a grade of spirits of the lowest order, composed of murderers, robbers, thieves, adulterers, drunkards, and persons ignorant, uncultivated, etc., who are in prison, or in hell, without hope, without God, and unworthy, as yet, of Gospel instruction. Such spirits, if they could communicate, would not tell you of the resurrection, or of any of the Gospel truths, for they knew nothing about them. They would not tell you about heaven or priesthood, for in all their meanderings in the world of Spirits, they have never been privileged with the ministering of a holy Priest. If they should tell all the truth they possessed they could not tell much.

Take another class of spirits — pious, well disposed men; for instance, the honest Quaker, Presbyterian, or other sectarian, who, although honest, and well disposed, had not, while in the flesh, the privilege of the Priesthood and Gospel. They believed in Jesus Christ, but died in ignorance of his ordinances, and had not clear conceptions of his doctrines, and of the resurrection. They expected to go to that place called heaven, as soon as they were dead, and that their doom would then and there be fixed, without any further alteration or preparation. Suppose they should come back, with liberty to tell all they know? How much light could we get from them? They could only tell you about the nature of things in the world in which they live. And even that world you could not comprehend, by their description thereof, any more than you can describe colors to a man born blind, or sounds to those who have never heard.

What, then, could you get from them? Why, common chit chat, in which there would be a mixture of truth, error, and mistakes, in mingled confusion; all their communications would betray the same want of clear and logical conceptions, and sound sense and philosophy, as would characterize the same class of Spirits in the flesh.

Who, then, is prepared among the spirits in the Spirit world, to communicate the truth on the subject of salvation, to guide the people, to give advice, to confer consolation, to heal the sick, to administer joy, and gladness, and hope of immortality and eternal life, founded on manifest truth?

All that have been raised from the dead, and clothed with immortality—all that have ascended to yonder heavens, and been crowned as Kings and Priests; all such are our fellow servants, and of our brethren the Prophets, who have the testimony of Jesus; all such are waiting for the work of God among their posterity upon the earth. They could declare glad tidings if we were only prepared to commune with them. What else? Peter, James, Joseph, Hyrum, Father Smith,—any or all of those ancient or modern Saints who have departed this life, who are clothed upon with the powers of the eternal Apostleship or Priesthood; who have gone to the world of Spirits, not to sorrow, but as joyful messengers, bearing glad tidings of eternal truth to the spirits in prison— could not these teach us good things? Yes, if they were permitted so to do.

But suppose all spirits were honest, and aimed at truth, yet each one could only converse of the things he is privileged to know, or comprehend, or which have been revealed to his understanding, or brought within the range of his intellect.

If this be the case, what then do we wish, in communicating with the eternal world, by visions, angels, or ministering spirits? Why, if a person is sick, they would like to be visited, comforted or healed by an angel or spirit! If a man is in prison, he would like an angel to visit him, and comfort or deliver him. A man shipwrecked would like to be instructed in the way of escape for himself and fellows from a watery grave. In case of extreme hunger a loaf of bread brought by an angel would not be unacceptable.

If a man were journeying and murderers were lying in wait for him in a certain road, an angel would be useful to him in telling him of the circumstance, and to take another road.

If a man were journeying to preach the Gospel, an angel would be useful to tell the neighbors of his high and holy calling, as in the case of Peter and Cornelius. Or would you not like to have angels all around you, to guard, guide, and advise you in every emergency?

The Saints would like to enter a holy temple, and have their President and his assistants administer for their dead. They love their fathers, although they had once almost forgotten them. Our fathers have forgotten to hand down to us their genealogy. They have not felt sufficient interest to transmit to us their names, and the time and place of birth, and in many instances they have not taught us when and where ourselves were born or who were our grandparents, and their ancestry. Why is all this? It is because of the veil of blindness which is cast over the earth, because there has been no true Church, Priesthood, or Patriarchal Order, no holy place for the deposit or preservation of the sacred archives of antiquity, no knowledge of the eternal kindred ties, relationship, or mutual interests of eternity. The hearts of the children had become estranged from the fathers, and the hearts of the fathers from the children, until one came in the spirit and power of Elijah, to turn the keys of these things, to open communication between worlds, and to kindle in our bosoms that glow of eternal affection which lay dormant.

Suppose our temple was ready, and we should enter there to act for the dead, we could only act for those whose names are known to us. And these are few with the most of us Americans. And why is this? We have never had time to look to the heavens, or to the past or future, so busy have we been with the things of the earth. We have hardly had time to think of ourselves, to say nothing of our fathers.

It is time that all this stupidity and indifference should come to an end, and that our hearts were opened and our charities extended, and that our bosoms expanded, to reach forth after whom? Those whom we consider dead! God has condescended so far to our capacity, as to speak of our fathers as if they were dead, although they are all living spirits, and will live forever. We have no dead. Only think of it! Our fathers are all living, thinking, active agents; we have only been taught that they are dead! Shall I speak my feelings, that I had on yesterday, while were were laying these corner stones of the temple? Yes, I will utter them if I can.

It was not with my eyes not with the power of actual vision, but by my intellect, by the natural faculties inherent in man, by the exercise of my reason, upon known principles, or by the power of the Spirit, that it appeared to me that Joseph Smith, and his associate Spirits, the Latter-day Saints, hovered about us on the brink of that foundation, and with them all the angels and spirits from the other world, that might be permitted, or that were not too busy elsewhere. Why should I think so? In the first place, what else on this earth have they to be interested about? Where would their eyes be turned in the wide earth if not centered here? Where would their hearts and affections be, if they cast a look or a thought towards the dark speck in the heavens that we inhabit, unless to the people of these valleys and mountains? Are there others who have the keys for the redemption of the dead? Is any one else preparing a sanctuary for the holy conversation and ministrations pertaining to their exaltation? No, verily. No other people have opened their hearts to conceive ideas so grand. No other people have their sympathies drawn out to such an extent toward the fathers.

No. If you go from this people, to hear the doctrines of others, you will hear the doleful sayings—"As the tree falls, so it lyeth. As death leaves you, so judgment will find you. There is no work, nor device, nor knowledge in the grave, etc. etc. There is no change after death, but you are fixed, irretrievably fixed, for all eternity. The moment the breath leaves the body, you must go to an extreme of heaven or hell, there to rejoice with Peter on thrones of power, in the presence of Jesus Christ in the third heavens, or, on the other hand, to roll in the flames of hell, with murderers and devils. Such are the doctrines of our Sectarian brethren, who profess to believe in Christ, but who know not the mysteries of godliness, and the boundless resources of eternal charity, and of that mercy which endureth forever.

It is here that the Spirit world would look, with an intense interest, it is here that the nations of the dead (if I may so call them,) would concentrate their hopes of ministration on the earth in their behalf. It is here that the countless millions of the Spirit world would look for the ordinances of redemption, so far as they have been enlightened by the preaching of the Gospel, since the keys of the former dispensation were taken away from the earth.

Why, if they looked upon the earth at all, it would be upon those Corner Stones that we laid yesterday. If they listened at all, it would be to hear the sounds of voices and instruments, and the blending of sacred and martial music in honor of the commencement of a temple for the redemption of the dead. With what intensity of interest did they listen to the songs of Zion, and witness the feelings of their friends. They were glad to behold the glittering bayonets of the guards around the Temple ground, and they longed for the day when there would be a thousand where there is now but one. They wish to see a strong people, gathered and united, in sufficient power to maintain a spot on earth where a baptismal font might be erected for the baptism for the dead. It was here that all their expectations were centered. What cared they for all the golden palaces, marble pavements, or gilded halls of state on earth? What cared they for all the splendor, equipage, titles, and empty sounds of the self-styled great of this world; which all pass away as the dew of the morning before the rising sun? What cared they for the struggles, the battles, the victories, and numerous other worldly interests that vibrate the bosoms of men on either side? None of these things would interest them. Their interests were centred here, and thence extended to the work of God among the nations of the earth.

Did Joseph, in the Spirit world, think of anything else yesterday but the doings of his brethren on the earth? He might have been necessarily employed, and so busy as to be obliged to think of other things. But if I were to judge from the acquaintance I had with him in his life, and from my knowledge of the spirit of Priesthood, I would suppose him to be so hurried as to have little or no time to cast an eye or a thought after his friends on the earth. He was always busy while here, and so are we. The spirit of our holy ordination and anointing will not let us rest.

The spirit of his calling will never suffer him to rest, while Satan, sin, death or darkness, possesses a foot of ground on this earth, — while the spirit world contains the spirit of one of his friends, or the grave holds captive one of their bodies, he will never rest or slacken his labors.

You might as well talk of Saul, King of Israel, resting while Israel was oppressed by the Canaanites or Philistines, after Samuel had anointed him to be king. At first he was like another man, but when occasion called into action the energies of a king, the spirit of his anointing came upon him. He slew an ox, divided it into twelve parts, and sent a part to each of the twelve tribes of Israel, with this proclamation: — "So shall it be done to the ox of the man who will not come up to the help of the Lord of Hosts."

Ye Elders of Israel! you will find that there is a spirit upon you which will urge you to continued exertion, and will never suffer you to feel at ease in Zion while a work remains unfinished in the great plan of the redemption of our race. It will inspire the Saints to build, plant, improve, cultivate, make the desert fruitful, in short, to use the elements, send missions abroad, build up States and Kingdoms and Temples at home and send abroad the light of a never-ending day to every people and nation of the globe.

You have been baptised, you have had the laying on of hands, and some have been ordained, and some anointed with a holy anointing. A spirit has been given you; and you will find if you undertake to rest, it will be the hardest work you ever performed. I came home here from a foreign mission. I presented myself to our President, and inquired what I should do next. "Rest," said he.

If I had been set to turn the world over, to dig down a mountain, to go to the ends of the earth, or traverse the deserts of Arabia, it would have been easier than to have undertaken to rest, while the Priesthood was upon me. I have received the holy anointing, and I can never rest till the last enemy is conquered, death destroyed, and truth reigns triumphant. May God bless you all. Amen.

{17}

"Keys of the Mysteries of the Godhead"

(from *Key to the Science of Theology:
Designed as An Introduction to the First Principles
of Spiritual Philosophy; Religion; Law and Government;
as Delivered by the Ancients, and as Restored in this Age,
for the Final Development of Universal Peace, Truth and Knowledge*
[Liverpool: F. D. Richards, 1855])

> Eternal Father, Being without end!
> Thy glorious fulness who can comprehend!
> Thine own infinitude alone is fraught
> With attributes to swell a human thought,
> To grasp thy knowledge, or thy nature scan.
> As Father of the endless race of man.

"This is life eternal: to know the only true and living God, and Jesus Christ whom he hath sent."

Since the decline of the science of Theology, a mystery, dark and deep, has shrouded the human mind, in regard to the person and nature of the Eternal Father, and of Jesus Christ, His son.

Councils of the fathers, and wise men of Christendom, have assembled again and again, in order to solve the mystery of Godliness, and fix some standard or creed upon which all parties might rest and be agreed.

This, however, was not in their power. It is impossible for the world by its wisdom to find out God. *"Neither knoweth any man the Father save the son, and he to whomsoever the son will reveal him."*

The key to the science of Theology, is the key of divine revelation. Without this key, no man, no assemblage of men, ever did, or ever will know the Eternal Father, or Jesus Christ.

When the key of revelation was lost to man, the knowledge of God was lost. And as life eternal depended on the knowledge of God, of course the key of eternal life was also lost.

Oh the mysteries, the absurdities, the contentions, the quarrels, the bloodshed, the infidelity, the senseless and conflicting theories, which have grown and multiplied among sectaries on this subject!

Among these theories, we will notice one, which is, perhaps, more extensively received by different sects than any other. The language runs thus — *"There is one only living and true God, without body, parts, or passions; consisting of three persons — the Father, Son, and Holy Ghost."*

It is painful to the human mind to be compelled to admit, that such wonderful inconsistencies of language or ideas, have ever found place in any human creed. Yet, so it is.

It is but another way of saying, that there is a God who does not exist, a God who is composed of nonentity, who is the negative of all existence, who occupies no space, who exists in no time, who is composed of no substance, known or unknown, and who has no powers or properties in common with any thing or being known to exist, or which can possibly be conceived of, as existing either in the heavens or on the earth.

Such a God could never be seen, heard, or felt, by any being in the universe.

There never has been a visible idol worshipped among men, which was so powerless as this *"God without body, parts, or passions."*

The god of Egypt, the crocodile, could destroy.

The images of different nations could be felt and seen.

The Peruvian god, the Sun, could diffuse its genial warmth, light, and influence.

But not so with the God without *"body, parts, or passions."*

That which has no parts, has no whole.

Beings which have no passions, have no soul.

Before we can introduce the keys and powers of practical Theology to the understanding of men in this age, we must, of necessity, place within their comprehension some correct ideas of the true God.

It is written that, *"without faith it is impossible to please Him."* Those who do not please Him, can never partake of the powers and gifts of the science of Theology, because the keys and powers of this science emanate from Him as a free gift, but they are never given to those with whom He is not well pleased. The individual who would partake of this power, must therefore have faith in Him. But how can he believe in a being of whom he has no correct idea?

So vague, so foreign from the simple plain truth, are the ideas of the present age, so beclouded is the modern mind with mysticism, spiritual nonentity, or immateriality in nearly all of its ideas of the person or persons of the Deity, that we are constrained to use the language of an ancient apostle, as addressed to the learned of Athens — *"Whom therefore ye ignorantly worship, Him declare I unto you."*

Although there are facts in our *own* existence, which are beyond our present comprehension or capacity, which is true, in a higher sense, in relation to the Godhead, still the limited knowledge we are able to comprehend in relation to ourselves, may at least be rational, and be as clearly conveyed and understood as any other subject. So with our knowledge of Deity. Although there are facts beyond our reach in relation to His existence, attributes, and power, yet that which we may know and comprehend or express of Him, should be divested of all mystery, and should be as clearly conceived, expressed, and conveyed as any other item of truth or of science.

Jesus Christ, a little babe like all the rest of us have been, grew to be a man, was filled with a divine substance or fluid, called the Holy Spirit, by which he comprehended and spake the truth in power and authority; and by which he controlled the elements, and imparted health and life to those who were prepared to partake of the same.

This man died, being put to death by wicked men.

He arose from the dead the third day, and appeared to his disciples. These disciples, on seeing him, supposed him to be a spirit only.

They may have possessed some of the vague ideas of men in more modern times, in regard to an immaterial existence beyond the grave: an existence unconnected with any real or tangible matter, or substance.

But their risen Lord adopted the most simple means of dispersing their *mysticism*, their *spiritual vagaries* or *immateriality*. He called upon them to handle him and see, *"For,"* said he, *"a spirit hath not flesh and bones, as ye see me have."*

They accordingly handled him, examined the prints of the nails in his hands and feet, and the mark of the spear in his side. But, as if this was not enough in order to familiarize them still more with the facts of a material or tangible immortality, he ate and drank with them — partaking of a broiled fish and an honey-comb.

In short, he was with them for forty days, in which he walked, talked, ate, drank, taught, prophesied, commanded, commissioned, reasoned with and blessed them, thus familiarizing to them that immortality and eternal life which he wished them to teach in all the world.

He then ascended up in their presence, toward that planet where dwelt his Father and their Father, his God and their God.

While he was yet in sight in the open firmament, and they stood gazing upward, behold! two men stood by them in white raiment, and said —

"Ye men of Galilee why stand ye gazing up into heaven? This same Jesus which is taken up from you into heaven shall so come in like manner as ye have seen him go into heaven."

Here, then, we have a sample of an immortal God — a God who is often declared in the Scriptures to be like his father, *"being the brightness of his glory, and the express image of his person,"* and possessing the same attributes as his Father, in all their fulness; a God not only possessing body and parts, but flesh and bones, and sinews, and all the attributes, organs, senses, and affections of a perfect man.

He differs in nothing from his Father, except in age and authority, the Father having the seniority, and, consequently, the right, according to the Patriarchal laws of eternal Priesthood, to preside over him, and over all his dominions, for ever and ever.

While on the one hand, this God claims affinity and equality, as it were, with his Father, he claims, on the other hand, affinity and equality with his brethren, on the earth, with this difference, however, that his person is a specimen of Divine, eternal Humanity, immortalized, and with attributes perfected; while his brethren who dwell in mortal flesh, although children of the same royal Parent in the heavens, are not yet immortalized, as it regards their fleshly tabernacles, and are not perfected in their attributes; and although joint heirs, are younger, he being the first born among many brethren in the spiritual world. They are therefore subject to him.

But every man who is eventually made perfect — raised from the dead, and filled or quickened, with a fulness of celestial glory, will become like them in every respect, physically, and in intellect, attributes or powers.

The very germs of these Godlike attributes, being engendered in man, the offspring of Deity, only need cultivating, improving, developing, and advancing by means of a series of progressive changes, in order to arrive at the fountain "Head," the standard, the climax of Divine Humanity.

The difference between Jesus Christ and his Father is this — one is subordinate to the other, does nothing of himself, independently of the Father, but does all things in the name and by the authority of the Father, being of the same mind in all things. The difference between Jesus Christ and another immortal and celestial man is this — the man is subordinate to Jesus Christ, does nothing in and of himself, but does all things in the name of Christ, and by his authority, being of the same mind, and ascribing all the glory to him and his Father.

On account of the double relationship of Jesus Christ — with God the Father on one hand, and with man on the other, many have adopted the creed, that "Two whole and perfect natures" were blended in the person of Jesus Christ; that he was every way a God, and every way a man; as if God and man were two distinct species. This error came by reason of not knowing ourselves. For just in proportion as we comprehend ourselves in our true light, and our relationships and affinities with the past, present and future, with time and eternity, with Gods, angels, spirits and men, who have gone before us, and who will come after us, so, in proportion, we may be able to benefit by the keys of the mysteries of the Godhead, or, in other words, to know and comprehend Jesus Christ and his Father.

Gods, angels and men, are all of one species, one race, one great family widely diffused among the planetary systems, as colonies, kingdoms, nations, &c.

The great distinguishing difference between one portion of this race and another, consists in the varied grades of intelligence and purity, and also in the variety of spheres occupied by each, in the series of progressive being.

An immortal man, possessing a perfect organization of spirit, flesh, and bones, and perfected in his attributes, in all the fulness of celestial glory, is called *a God.*

An immortal man, in progress of perfection, or quickened with a lesser degree of glory, is called *an angel.*

An immortal spirit of man, not united with a fleshly tabernacle, is called a spirit.

An immortal man, clothed with a mortal tabernacle, is called a man.

It may then consistently enough be said, that there are, in a subordinate sense, a plurality of Gods, or rather of the sons of God; although there is one Supreme Head, who is over all, and through all, and in all His sons, by the power of His Spirit.

Jesus Christ and his Father are two persons, in the same sense as John and Peter are two persons. Each of them has an organized, individual tabernacle, embodied in material form, and composed of material substance, in the likeness of man, and possessing every organ, limb, and physical part that man possesses.

There is no more mystery connected with their oneness, than there is in the oneness of Enoch and Elijah, or of Paul and Silas.

Their oneness consists of a oneness of spirit, intelligence, attributes, knowledge, or power.

If Enoch, Elijah, Abraham, Peter, Paul, and millions of others ever attain to the immortal life, and their fleshly tabernacles be quickened by a fulness of celestial life, intelligence and power, then it can be said of them, *they are one, as the Father and Son are one.*

It could then be said of each of them, in him dwells all the fulness of the powers and attributes of the Eternal God, or, in other words, he possesses endless life, together with all intelligence, knowledge, light, and power. He therefore has the same mind as all the others—is in communication and in perfect union with each and all of them.

All these are Gods, or sons of God—they are the Kings, Princes, Priests and Nobles of Eternity. But over them all there is a Presidency or Grand Head, who is the Father of all. And next unto him is Jesus Christ, the eldest born, and first heir of all the realms of light.

Every person knows, by reflection, that intelligence may be imparted without diminishing the store possessed by the giver. Therefore it follows, that millions of individual beings may each receive all the attributes of eternal life, and light, and power.

Again it follows, that in the use of this power, by consent and authority of the head, any one of these Gods, may create, organize, people, govern, control, exalt, glorify and enjoy worlds on worlds, and the inhabitants thereof; or, in other words, each of them can find room in the infinitude of space, and unoccupied chaotic elements in the boundless storehouse of eternal riches, with which to erect for himself thrones, principalities, and powers, over which to reign in still increasing might, majesty and dominion, for ever and ever.

All these are kingdoms which, together with their Kings, are in subordination to the great Head and Father of all, and to Jesus Christ the first born, and first heir, among the sons of God.

All these kingdoms, with all their intelligences, are so many acquisitions to *His* dominion who is Lord of lords, and King of kings, and of whom it is written, by the Prophet Isaiah, "Of the increase of his kingdom there shall be no end."

All these are so many colonies of our race, multiplied, extended, transplanted, and existing for ever and ever, as occupants of the numberless planetary systems which do now exist, or which will roll into order, and be peopled by the operations of the Holy Spirit, in obedience to the mandates of the sons of God.

These kingdoms present every variety and degree in the progress of the great science of life, from the lowest degradation amid the realms of death, or the rudimental stages of elementary existence, upward through all the ascending scale, or all the degrees of progress in the science of eternal life and light, until some of them in turn arise to thrones of eternal power.

Each of these Gods, including Jesus Christ and his Father, being in possession of not merely an organized spirit, but a glorious immortal body of flesh and bones, is subject to the laws which govern, of necessity, even the most refined order of physical existence.

All physical element, however embodied, quickened, or refined, is subject to the general laws necessary to all existence.

Some of these laws are as follows —

First. Each atom, or embodiment of atoms, necessarily occupies a certain amount of *space*.

Second. No atom, or embodiment of atoms, can occupy the identical space occupied by other atoms or bodies.

Third. Each individual organized intelligence must possess the power of self motion to a greater or less degree.

Fourth. All voluntary motion implies an inherent will, to originate and direct such motion.

Fifth. Motion, of necessity, implies that a certain amount of time is necessary, in passing from one portion of space to another.

These laws are absolute and unchangeable in their nature, and apply to all intelligent agencies which do or can exist.

They, therefore, apply with equal force to the great, supreme, eternal Father of the heavens and of the earth, and to His meanest subjects.

It is, therefore, an absolute impossibility for God the Father, or Jesus Christ, to be everywhere personally present.

The omnipresence of God must therefore be understood in some other way than of His bodily or personal presence.

This leads to the investigation of that substance called the Holy Spirit.

As the mind passes the boundaries of the visible world, and enters upon the confines of the more refined and subtle elements, it finds itself associated with certain substances in themselves invisible to our gross organs, but clearly manifested to our intellect by their tangible operations and effects.

The very air we breathe, although invisible to our sight, is clearly manifested to our sense of feeling. Its component parts may be analyzed. Nay more, the human system itself is an apparatus which performs a chemical process upon that element. It is received into the system by the act of respiration, and there immediately undergoes the separation of its component parts.

The one part, retained and incorporated in the animal system, diffuses life and animation, by supplying the necessary animal heat, &c., while the other part, not adapted to the system, is discharged from the lungs to mingle with its native element.

There are several of these subtle, invisible substances but little understood as yet by man, and their existence is only demonstrated by their effects. Some of them are recognized under the several terms, electricity, galvanism, magnetism, animal magnetism, spiritual magnetism, essence, spirit, &c.

The purest, most refined and subtle of all these substances, and the one least understood, or even recognized, by the less informed among mankind, is that substance called the Holy Spirit.

This substance, like all others, is one of the elements of material or physical existence, and therefore subject to the necessary laws which govern all matter, as before enumerated.

Like the other elements, its whole is composed of individual particles. Like them, each particle occupies space, possesses the power of motion, requires time to move from one part of space to another, and can in no wise occupy two spaces at once. In all these respects it differs nothing from all other matter.

This substance is widely diffused among the elements of space. This Holy Spirit, under the control of the Great Eloheim, is the grand moving cause of all intelligences, and by which they act.

This is the great, positive, controlling element of all other elements. It is omnipresent by reason of the infinitude of its particles, and it comprehends all things.

It is the controlling agent or executive, which organizes and puts in motion all worlds, and which, by the mandate of the Almighty, or of any of His commissioned agents, performs all the mighty wonders, signs and miracles, ever manifested in the name of the Lord—the turning of the earth backward on its axis, the dividing of the sea, the removing of a mountain, the raising of the dead, or the healing of the sick.

It penetrates the pores of the most solid substances, pierces the human system to its most inward recesses, discerns the thoughts and intents of the heart. It has power to move through space with an inconceivable velocity, far exceeding the tardy motions of electricity, or of physical light.

It comprehends the past, present, and future, in all their fulness. Its inherent properties embrace all the attributes of intelligence and affection.

It is endowed with knowledge, wisdom, truth, love, charity, justice, and mercy, in all their ramifications.

In short, it is the attributes of the eternal power and Godhead.

Those beings who receive of its fulness are called sons of God, because they are perfected in all its attributes and powers, and being in communication with it, can, by its use, perform all things.

Those beings who receive not a fulness, but a measure of it, can know and perform some things, but not all.

This is the true light, which in some measure illuminates all men. It is, in its less refined particles, the physical light which reflects from the sun, moon, and stars, and other substances; and by reflection on the eye, makes visible the truths of the outward world.

It is, also, in its higher degrees, the intellectual light of our inward and spiritual organs, by which we reason, discern, judge, compare, comprehend and remember the subjects within our reach.

Its inspiration constitutes instinct in animal life, reason in man, vision in the Prophets, and is continually flowing from the Godhead throughout all His creatures.

Such is the Godhead, as manifested in His words, and in His works. He dwells in His own eternal palaces of precious stones and gold, in the Royal City of the heavenly Jerusalem.

He sits enthroned in the midst of all His creations, and is filled and encircled with light unapproachable by those of the lower spheres.

He associates with myriads of His own begotten sons and daughters who, by translation or resurrection, have triumphed over death.

His ministers are sent forth from his presence to all parts of His dominions.

His Holy Spirit centres in His presence, and communicates with, and extends to the utmost verge of His dominions, comprehending and controlling all things under the immediate direction of His own will, and the will of all those in communication with Him, in worlds without end!

{18}

"Origin of the Universe"

(from *Key to the Science of Theology:*
Designed as An Introduction to the First Principles
of Spiritual Philosophy; Religion; Law and Government;
as Delivered by the Ancients, and as Restored in this Age,
for the Final Development of Universal Peace, Truth and Knowledge
(Liverpool: F. D. Richards, 1855)

Boundless infinitude of time, and space,
And elements eternal! Who can trace
Earth with its treasures, Heaven with its spheres,
Time's revolutions, eternity's years?
But what are all these, when measured by thee,
But marks on thy dial, or motes on thy sea!

The idea of a God without "body, parts, or passions," is not more absurd or inconsistent than that modern popular doctrine, that all things were created from nonentity, or in other words, that something originated from nothing.

It is a self-evident truth, which will not admit of argument, that nothing remains nothing. Nonentity is the negative of all existence. This negative possesses no property or element upon which the energies of creative power can operate.

This mysticism must, therefore, share the fate of the other mysteries of false Theology and philosophy, which have for ages shrouded the world in the sable curtains of a long and dreary night. It must evaporate and disappear as a mere creation of fancy, while, in its place, are introduced the following self-evident and incontrovertible facts—

First. There has always existed a boundless infinitude of space.

Second. Intermingled with this space there exists all the varieties of the elements, properties, or things of which intelligence takes cognizance; which elements or things taken altogether compose what is called the Universe.

Third. The elements of all these properties or things are eternal, uncreated, self-existing. Not one particle can be added to them by creative power. Neither can one particle be diminished or annihilated.

Fourth. These eternal, self-existing elements possess in themselves certain inherent properties or attributes, in a greater or less degree; or, in other words, they possess intelligence, adapted to their several spheres.

These elements have been separated, by philosophers, into two grand divisions, viz. —

"PHYSICAL AND SPIRITUAL."

To a mind matured, or quickened with a fulness of intelligence, so as to be conversant with all the elements of nature, there is no use for the distinction implied in such terms.

To speak more philosophically, all the elements are spiritual, all are physical, all are material, tangible realities. Spirit is matter, and matter is full of spirit. Because all things which do exist are eternal realities, in their elementary existence.

Who then can define the precise point, in the scale of elementary existence, which divides between the physical and spiritual kingdoms? There are eyes which can discern the most refined particles of elementary existence. There are hands and fingers to whose refined touch all things are tangible.

In the capacity of mortals, however, some of the elements are tangible, or visible, and others invisible. Those which are tangible to our senses, we call physical; those which are more subtle and refined, we call spiritual.

Spirit is intelligence, or the light of truth, which filleth all things.

Its several emotions or affections, such as love, joy, &c., are but so many actions or motions of these elements, as they operate in their several spheres.

By these actions or emotions the elements manifest their eternal energies, attributes, or inherent powers.

In contemplating the works of creation, then, the student must not conceive the idea that space, or time, or element, or intelligence, was originated, but rather, that these are eternal, and that they constitute the energies which act, and the things acted upon, including the place and time of action.

The whole vast structure of universal organized existence, presents undeniable evidence of three facts, viz. —

First. The eternal existence of the elements of which it is composed.

Second. The eternal existence of the attributes of intelligence, and wisdom to design.

Third. The eternal existence of power, to operate upon and control these eternal elements, so as to carry out the plans of the designer.

It will be recollected that the last chapter recognizes a family of Gods, or, in other words, a species of beings, who have physical tabernacles of flesh and bones, in the form of man, but so constructed as to be capable of eternal life; that these tabernacles are quickened, or animated by a fulness of that holiest of all elements, which is called the Holy Spirit, which element or spirit, when organized, in individual form, and clothed upon with flesh and bones in the highest possible refinement, contains, in itself, a fulness of the attributes of light, intelligence, wisdom, love, and power; also that there are vast quantities of this spirit or element not organized in bodily forms, but widely diffused among the other elements of space.

A General Assembly, Quorum, or Grand Council of the Gods, with their President at their head, constitute the designing and creating power.

The motive power, which moves to action this grand creative power, is wisdom, which discovers a use for all these riches, and inspires the carrying out of all the designs in an infinite variety of utility and adaptation.

Wisdom inspires the Gods to multiply their species and to lay the foundation for all the forms of life, to increase in numbers, and for each to enjoy himself in the sphere to which he is adapted, and in the possession and use of that portion of the elements necessary to his existence and happiness.

In order to multiply organized bodies, composed of spiritual element, worlds and mansions composed of spiritual element would be necessary as a home, adapted to their existence and enjoyment. As these spiritual bodies increased in numbers, other spiritual worlds would be necessary, on which to transplant them.

Again. In order to enable these organized spirits to take upon them a fleshly tabernacle, physical worlds, with all their variety and fulness, would be necessary for their homes, food, clothing, &c., that they might be begotten, sustained, and born, that they might live, die, and rise again to receive their inheritances on their respective earths.

Hence the great work of regeneration of worlds, or the renovation and adaptation of the elements to the resurrection and eternal state of man, would also be endless, or eternally progressive.

Through every form of life, and birth, and change, and resurrection, and every form of progress in knowledge and experience, the candidates for eternal life must look upon the elements as their home; hence the elements, upon the principle of adaptation, must keep pace with the possessors who use them, in all the degrees of progressive refinement.

While room is found in infinite space:

While there are particles of unorganized element in Nature's storehouse:

While the trees of Paradise yield their fruits, or the Fountain of Life its river:

While the bosoms of the Gods glow with affection:

While eternal charity endures, or eternity itself rolls its successive ages, the heavens will multiply, and new worlds and more people be added to the kingdoms of the Fathers.

Thus, in the progress of events, unnumbered millions of worlds, and of systems of worlds, will necessarily be called into requisition, and be filled by man, and beast, and fowl, and tree, and all the vast varieties of beings, and things which ever budded and blossomed in Eden, or thronged the hills and valleys of the celestial Paradise.

When, in the endless progression of events, the full time had arrived for infinite wisdom to organize and people this globe which we inhabit, the chaotic elements were arranged in order. It appears at the commencement of this grand work, that the elements, which are now so beautifully arranged and adapted to vegetable and animal life, were found in a state of chaos, entirely unadapted to the uses they now serve.

There was one vast mixture of elements. Earth, water, soil, atmosphere — in short, the entire elements of which this mass was composed, seem to have been completely compounded, or mingled into one vast chaos, and the whole overwhelmed with a darkness so dense as to obscure the light of heaven.

Let us turn from the contemplation of scenes so sublimely fearful. Suffice it to say, the mandate came, darkness fled, the veil was lifted, light pierced the gloom, and chaos was made visible. Oh what a scene! A world without landscape, without vegetation, without animal life, without man, or animated beings. No sound broke on the stillness, save the voice of the moaning winds, and of dashing, foaming waters. Again, a voice comes booming over the abyss, and echoing amid the wastes, the mass of matter hears and trembles, and lo! the sea retires, the muddy shapeless mass lifts its head above the waters.

Molehills to mountains grow. Huge islands next appear, and continents at length expand to view, with hill and vale, in one wide dreary waste, unmeasured and untrodden.

The surface, warmed and dried by the cheering rays of the now resplendent sun, is prepared for the first seeds of vegetation.

A Royal Planter now descends from yonder world of older date, and bearing in his hand the choice seeds of the older Paradise, he plants them in the virgin soil of our new born earth. They grow and flourish there, and, bearing seed, replant themselves, and thus clothe the naked earth with scenes of beauty, and the air with fragrant incense. Ripening fruits and herbs at length abound. When, lo! from yonder world is transferred every species of animal life. Male and female, they come, with blessings on their heads; and a voice is heard again, *"Be fruitful and multiply."*

Earth—its mineral, vegetable and animal wealth—its Paradise, prepared, down comes from yonder world on high, a son of God, with his beloved spouse. And thus a colony from heaven, it may be from the sun, is transplanted on our soil. The blessings of their Father are upon them, and the first great law of heaven and earth is again repeated, "*Be fruitful and multiply.*"

Hence, the nations which have swarmed our earth.

In after years, when Paradise was lost by sin; when man was driven from the face of his heavenly Father, to toil, and droop, and die; when heaven was veiled from view; and, with few exceptions, man was no longer counted worthy to retain the knowledge of his heavenly origin; then, darkness veiled the past and future from the heathen mind; man neither knew himself, from whence he came, nor whither he was bound. At length a Moses came, who knew his God, and would fain have led mankind to know Him too, and see Him face to face. But they could not receive His heavenly laws, or bide His presence.

Thus the holy man was forced again to veil the past in mystery, and, in the beginning of his history, assign to man an earthly origin.

Man, moulded from earth, as a brick!

A Woman, manufactured from a rib!

Thus, parents still would fain conceal from budding manhood, the mysteries of procreation, or the sources of life's ever flowing river, by relating some childish tale of new born life, engendered in the hollow trunk of some old tree or springing with spontaneous growth, like mushrooms, from out the heaps of rubbish. O Man! When wilt thou cease to be a child in knowledge?

Man, as we have said, is the offspring of Deity. The entire mystery of the past and future, with regard to his existence, is not yet solved by mortals.

We first recognise him, as an organized individual or intelligence, dwelling with his Father in the eternal mansions. This organized spirit we call a body, because, although composed of the spiritual elements, it possesses every organ after the pattern, and in the likeness or similitude of the outward or fleshly tabernacle it is destined eventually to inhabit. Its organs of thought, speech, sight, hearing, tasting, smelling, feeling,&c., all exist in their order, as in the physical body; the one being the exact similitude of the other.

This individual, spiritual body, was begotten by the heavenly Father, in His own likeness and image, and by the laws of procreation.

It was born and matured in the heavenly mansions, trained in the school of love in the family circle, and amid the most tender embraces of parental and fraternal affection.

In this primeval probation, in its heavenly home, it lived and moved as a free and rational intelligence independent in its own sphere. It was placed under certain laws, and was responsible to its great Patriarchal Head.

This had been called a "First Estate." And it is intimated that, of the spirits thus placed upon their agency, one-third failed to keep their first estate, and were thrust down, and reserved in chains of darkness, for future judgment. As these are not permitted to multiply their species, or to move forward in the scale of progressive being, while in this state of bondage and condemnation, we will trace them no further, as their final destiny is not revealed to mortals.

The spirits which kept their first estate, were permitted to descend below, and to obtain a tabernacle of flesh in the rudimental existence in which we find them in our present world, and which we will call a second estate.

In passing the veil which separates between the first and second estates, man becomes unconscious, and, on awakening in his second estate, a veil is wisely thrown over all the past.

In his mortal tabernacle he remembers not the scenes, the endearing associations, of his first, primeval childhood in the heavenly mansions. He therefore commences anew in the lessons of experience, in order to start on a level with the new born tabernacle, and to re-develop his intellectual faculties in a progressive series, which keep pace with the development of the organs and faculties of the outward tabernacle.

During his progress in the flesh, the Holy Spirit may gradually awaken his faculties; and in a dream, or vision, or by the spirit of prophecy, reveal, or rather awaken the memory to, a partial vision, or to a dim and half defined recollection of the intelligence of the past. He sees in part, and he knows in part; but never while tabernacled in mortal flesh will he fully awake to the intelligence of his former estate. It surpasses his comprehension, is unspeakable, and even unlawful to be uttered.

Having kept his second estate, and filled the measure of his responsibilities in the flesh, he passes the veil of death, and enters a third estate, or probationary sphere. This is called the world of spirits, and will be treated on more fully under its appropriate head.

Filling the measure of his responsibilities in the world of spirits, he passes, by means of the resurrection of the body, into his fourth estate, or sphere of human existence. In this sphere he finds himself clothed upon with an eternal body of flesh and bones, with every sense, and every organ, restored and adapted to their proper use.

He is thus prepared with organs and faculties adapted to the possession and enjoyment of every element of the physical or spiritual worlds, which can gratify the senses, or conduce to happiness of intelligences. He associates, converses, loves, thinks, acts, moves, sees, hears, tastes, smells, eats, drinks and possesses.

In short, all the elements necessary to his happiness being purified, exalted, and adapted to the sphere in which he exists, are placed within his lawful reach, and made subservient to his use.

{19}

"Destiny of the Universe"

(from *Key to the Science of Theology:
Designed as An Introduction to the First Principles
of Spiritual Philosophy; Religion; Law and Government;
as Delivered by the Ancients, and as Restored in this Age,
for the Final Development of Universal Peace, Truth and Knowledge*
[Liverpool: F. D. Richards, 1855])

> The mystic future, with its depths profound,
> For ages counted as forbidden ground,
> Now lifts its veil, that man may penetrate
> The secret springs, the mysteries of fate;
> Know whence he is, and whither he is bound,
> And why the spheres perform their ample round.

The Grand Council having developed the vast structure of the heavens and the earth, with all their fulness, with the evident design of utility and adaptation to certain definite uses, it well becomes us to watch their progress, and to study with diligence their future and final destiny.

From a general traditional belief in an immaterial hereafter, many have concluded that the earth and all material things would be annihilated as mere temporary structures; that the material body, and the planets it occupies, make no part of eternal life and being; in short, that God, angels and men, become at last so lost, dissolved, or merged in spirituality, or immateriality, as to lose all adaptation to the uses of the physical elements; that they will absolutely need no footstool, habitation, possession, mansion, home, furniture, food, or clothing; that the whole vast works and beautiful designs of the visible creation are a kind of necessary evil or clog on the spiritual life, and are of no possible use except to serve for the time being, for the home and sustenance of beings in their grosser, or rudimental state.

What a doleful picture! With what gloom and melancholy must intelligences comtemplate the vast structure, as viewed in this light!

What a vastness of design!

What a display of wisdom!

What a field of labour in execution, do the works of creation present to the contemplative mind!

Yet all this wisdom of design, all this labour of execution, after serving a momentary purpose, to be thrown away as an incumbrance to real existence and happiness.

All these "spiritual," "immaterial" vagaries have no foundation in truth.

The earth and other systems are to undergo a variety of changes, in their progress towards perfection. Water, fire, and other elements are the agents of these changes. But it is an eternal, unchangeable fact, a fixed law of nature, easily demonstrated and illustrated by chemical experiment, that neither fire nor any other element can annihilate a particle of matter, to say nothing of a whole globe.

A new heaven and a new earth are promised by the sacred writers. Or, in other words, the planetary systems are to be changed, purified, refined, exalted and glorified, in the similitude of the resurrection, by which means all physical evil or imperfection will be done away.

In their present state they are adapted to the rudimental state of man. They are, as it were, the nurseries for man's physical embryo formation. Their elements afford the means of nourishing and sustaining the tabernacle, and of engendering and strengthening the organ of thought and mind, wherein are conceived and generated thoughts and affections which can only be matured and consummated in a higher sphere — thoughts pregnant with eternal life and love.

As the mind enlarges, the aspirations of an eternal being, once ennobled and honoured in the councils of heaven, among the sons of God, reach forth too high, and broad, and deep, to be longer adapted to the narrow sphere of mortal life. His body is imprisoned, chained to the earth, while his mind would soar aloft, and grasp the intelligence, wisdom and riches of the boundless infinite.

His rudimental body must therefore pass away, and be changed, so as to be adapted to a wider and more glorious sphere of locomotion, research, action and enjoyment.

When the planet on which he dwells has conceived, brought forth, and nourished the number of tabernacles assigned to it in its rudimental state, by infinite wisdom it must needs be acted upon by a chemical process. The purifying elements; for instance, fire, must needs be employed to bring it through an ordeal, a refinement, a purification, a change commensurate with that which had before taken place in the physical tabernacle of its inhabitants. Thus renovated, it is adapted to resurrected man.

When man, and the planet on which he lives, with all its fulness, shall have completed all their series of progressive changes, so as to be adapted to the highest glories of which their several characters and species are capable, then, the whole will be annexed to, or numbered with the eternal heavens, and will there fulfil their eternal rounds, being another acquisition to the mansions, or eternally increasing dominions of the great Creator and Redeemer.

Worlds are mansions for the home of intelligences.

Intelligences exist in order to enjoy.

Joy, in its fulness, depends on certain principles, viz. —

Life Eternal. Love Eternal. Peace Eternal. Wealth Eternal. &c.

Without the first, enjoyment lacks durability.

Without the second, it can hardly be said to exist.

Without the third, it would not be secure.

Without the fourth, it must be limited, &c.

Eternal life, in its fulness, implies a spiritual intelligence, embodied in the likeness of its own species and clothed upon with an outward tabernacle of eternal, incorruptible flesh and bones. This state of existence can only be attained by the resurrection of the body, and its eternal re-union with the spirit.

Eternal life thus attained, and endowed with the eternal attributes of intelligence and love, could never exercise, or derive enjoyment from the affections of the latter, unless associated with other beings endowed with the same attributes.

Hence the object, or necessity of eternal kindred ties, associations, and affections, exercised as the attributes of that charity which never ends.

The third proposition, viz. —

Eternal Peace, could never be secured without the development of Eternal Law and government, which would possess in itself the attributes of infinite truth, goodness and power.

Any government short of this, could never guarantee *Eternal Peace*. It would be liable to be overthrown, by the lack of truth to discern, disposition to execute, or power to enforce, the measures necessary to insure peace.

The fourth proposition, viz. —

Eternal Wealth, must, of necessity, consist of an everlasting inheritance or title, defined and secured by this eternal government, to portions of the organized elements, in their pure, incorruptible and eternal state.

In order to be wealthy, eternal man must possess a certain portion of the surface of some eternal planet, adapted to his order or sphere of existence.

This inheritance, incorruptible, eternal in the heavens, must be sufficiently extensive for his accommodation, with all his family dependencies. It must also comprise a variety of elements, adapted to his use and convenience. Eternal gold, silver, precious stones, and other precious materials would be useful in the erection and furnishing of mansions, and of public and private dwellings or edifices.

These edifices combined, or arranged in wisdom, would constitute eternal cities. Gardens, groves, walks, rivulets, fountains, flowers and fruits, would beautify and adorn the landscape, please the eye, the taste, the smell; and thus contribute gladness to the heart of man.

Silks, linens, or other suitable materials would be necessary to adorn his person, and to furnish and beautify his mansions.

In short, eternal man, in possession of eternal worlds, in all their variety and fulness, will eat, drink, think, converse, associate, assemble, disperse, go, come, possess, improve, love and enjoy. He will increase in riches, knowledge, power, might, majesty and dominion, in worlds without end.

Every species of the animal creation ever organized by creative goodness, or that ever felt the pangs of death, or uttered a groan while subject to the king of terrors, or exulted in the joys of life and sympathy, and longed for the redemption of the body, will have part in the resurrection, and will live for ever in their own spheres, in the possession of peace, and a fulness of joy, adapted to their several capacities.

> O Child of earth, conceived in corruption!
> Brought forth in pain and sorrow! sojourning
> In a world of mourning, mid sighs and tears,
> And groans, and awaiting in sadness thy home
> In the gloomy grave, as food for worms;
> Lift up thy head, cast thine eyes around thee,
> Behold yon countless hosts of shining orbs,
> Yon worlds of light and life. Then turn to earth,
> Survey the solid globe, its mineral wealth,
> Its gems, its precious stones, its gold, its springs;
> Its gardens, forests, fruits, and flowers;
> Its countless myriads of breathing life,
> From *Mote* to *Man*, through all the varied scale
> Of animated being.
> Visit the gloomy caverns of the dead,
> The ancient sepulchre, where e'en the worm
> Of death himself, has died for want of food,
> And bones disjointed are crumbled fine, and
> Mingled with the dust.
> Nay, deeper still, descend the fathomless
> Abyss of souls condemned, in darkness chained
> Or thrust in gloomy dungeons of despair —
> Where the very names of Mercy, of Hope,

And of death's conqueror remain unknown.
Observe with care the whole, indulge in tears,
But hope, believe, and clothed with charity
Which never fails, thine eyes enlightened,
Thy person clad in light ethereal,
Time fades, and opens on eternity.
Again review the scene beheld before.
You startle, seem surprised! confused! o'erwhelmed!
Death is conquered, corruption is no more,
All is *life*, and the word ETERNITY
Is inscribed in characters indelible,
On every particle and form of life.

Socrates, Plato, Confucius, and many other philosophers and divines have written largely on the immortality of the *soul* or spirit of man.

Some of these have suffered, with joy and cheerfulness, imprisonment, torture, and even death, with only this limited view of eternal existence.

Could these martyrs to a portion of truth so limited, and yet so full of hope and consolation, have handled immortal flesh and bones in the persons of Enoch or Elijah translated, or of Jesus raised from the dead; could they have learned from their sacred lips, and realized the full import of that joyful sentence —

"Behold! I make all things new;"

could they have contemplated eternal worlds, of matter in all its elements and forms of animal life, indissoluble and everlasting; could they have beheld eternal man, moving in the majesty of a God, amid the planetary systems, grasping the knowledge of universal nature, and with an intellect enlightened by the experience and observations of thousands and even millions of years; could they have had a glimpse of all this, and heard the promise —

"There shall be no more death,"

issuing from the fountain of truth, prompted by infinite benevolence and charity, re-echoing amid the starry worlds, reaching down to earth, vibrating, with a thrill of joy, all the myriads of animated nature, penetrating the gloomy vaults of death, and the prisons of the spirit world, with a ray of hope, and causing to spring afresh, the well-springs of life, and joy, and love, even in the lonely dungeons of despair! O! how would their bosoms have reverberated with unutterable joy and triumph, in view of changing worlds.

Could the rulers of this world have beheld, or even formed a conception of, such riches, such nobility, such an eternal and exceeding weight of glory, they would have accounted the wealth, pleasures, honors, titles, dignities, glories, thrones, principalities and crowns of this world as mere toys — the play-things of a day, dross, not worth the strife and toil of acquiring, or the trouble of maintaining, except as a duty, or troublesome responsibility.

With this view of the subject, what man so base, so grovelling, so blind to his own interests, as to neglect those duties, self-denials, sacrifices, which are necessary in order to secure a part in the *first* resurrection, and a far more exceeding and eternal weight of glory in that life which never ends?

{20}

The Autobiography of Parley Parker Pratt,
One of the Twelve Apostles of the Church of Jesus Christ
of Latter-day Saints, Embracing His Life, Ministry and Travels,
with Extracts, in Prose and Verse, from His Miscellaneous
Writings. Edited by His Son, Parley P. Pratt.

(New York: Published for the Editor and Proprietor
by Russell Brothers, 1874.)

CHAPTER XXII.

October 31, 1838. — In the afternoon we were informed that the Governor had ordered this force against us, with orders to exterminate or drive every "*Mormon*" from the State. As soon as these facts were ascertained we determined not to resist anything in the shape of authority, however abused. We had now nothing to do but to submit to be massacred, driven, robbed or plundered, at the option of our persecutors.

Colonel George H. Hinkle, who was at that time the highest officer of the militia assembled for the defence of Far West, waited on Messrs. J. Smith, S. Rigdon, Hyrum Smith, L. Wight, George Robinson and myself, with a request from General Lucas that we would repair to his camp, with the assurance that as soon as peaceable arrangements could be entered into we should be released. We had no confidence in the word of a murderer and robber, but there was no alternative but to put ourselves into the hands of such monsters, or to have the city attacked, and men, women and children massacred. We, therefore, commended ourselves to the Lord, and voluntarily surrendered as sheep into the hands of wolves. As we approached the camp of the enemy General Lucas rode out to meet us with a guard of several hundred men.

The haughty general rode up, and, without speaking to us, instantly ordered his guard to surround us. They did so very abruptly, and we were marched into camp surrounded by thousands of savage looking beings, many of whom were dressed and painted like Indian warriors. These all set up a constant yell, like so many bloodhounds let loose upon their prey, as if they had achieved one of the most miraculous victories that ever graced the annals of the world. If the vision of the infernal regions could suddenly open to the mind, with thousands of malicious fiends, all clamoring, exulting, deriding, blaspheming, mocking, railing, raging and foaming like a troubled sea, then could some idea be formed of the hell which we had entered.

In camp we were placed under a strong guard, and were without shelter during the night, lying on the ground in the open air, in the midst of a great rain. The guards during the whole night kept up a constant tirade of mockery, and the most obscene blackguardism and abuse. They blasphemed God; mocked Jesus Christ; swore the most dreadful oaths; taunted brother Joseph and others; demanded miracles; wanted signs, such as: "Come, Mr. Smith, show us an angel." "Give us one of your revelations." "Show us a miracle." "Come, there is one of your brethren here in camp whom we took prisoner yesterday in his own house, and knocked his brains out with his own rifle, which we found hanging over his fireplace; he lays speechless and dying; speak the word and heal him, and then we will all believe." "Or, if you are Apostles or men of God, deliver yourselves, and then we will be Mormons." Next would be a volley of oaths and blasphemies; then a tumultuous tirade of lewd boastings of having defiled virgins and wives by force, etc., much of which I dare not write; and, indeed language would fail me to attempt more than a faint description. Thus passed this dreadful night, and before morning several other captives were added to our number, among whom was brother Amasa Lyman.

We were informed that the general officers held a secret council during most of the night, which was dignified by the name of court martial; in which, without a hearing, or, without even being brought before it, we were all sentenced to be shot. The day and hour was also appointed for the execution of this sentence, viz.: next morning at 8 o'clock, in the public square at Far West. Of this we were informed by Brigadier-General Doniphan, who was one of the council, but who was so violently opposed to this cool blooded murder that he assured the council that he would revolt and withdraw his whole brigade, and march them back to Clay County as soon as it was light, if they persisted in so dreadful an undertaking. Said he, "It is cold blooded murder, and I wash my hands of it." His firm remonstrance, and that of a few others, so alarmed the haughty murderer and his accomplices that they dare not put the decree in execution.

Thus, through a merciful providence of God our lives were spared through that dreadful night. It was the common talk, and even the boast in the camp, that individuals lay here and there unburied, where they had shot them down for sport. The females they had ravished; the plunder they had taken; the houses they had burned; the horses they had stolen; the fields of grain they had laid waste, were common topics; and were dwelt on for mere amusement, or, as if these deeds were a stepstone to office; and it is a fact that such deeds were so considered.

No pen need undertake to describe our feelings during that terrible night, while there confined—not knowing the fate of our wives and children, or of our fellow Saints, and seeing no way for our lives to be saved except by the miraculous power of God. But, notwithstanding all earthly hopes were gone, still we felt a calmness indescribable. A secret whispering to our inmost soul seemed to say: "Peace, my sons, be of good cheer, your work is not yet done; therefore I will restrain your enemies, that they shall not have power to take your lives."

While thus confined, Wm. E. McLellin, once my fellow laborer in the gospel, but now a *Judas*, with hostile weapon in hand to destroy the Saints, came to me and observed: "Well, Parley, you have now got where you are certain never to escape; how do you feel as to the course you have taken in religion?" I answered, "that I had taken that course which I should take if I had my life to live over again." He seemed thoughtful for a moment, and then replied: "Well—I think, if I were you, I should die as I had lived; at any rate, I see no possibility of escape for you and your friends."

Next morning Gen. Lucas demanded the Caldwell militia to give up their arms, which was done. As soon as the troops who had defended the city were disarmed, it was surrounded by the enemy and all the men detained as prisoners. None were permitted pass out of the city— although their families were starving for want of sustenance; the mills and provisions being some distance from the city.

The brutal mob were now turned loose to ravage, steal, plunder and murder without restraint. Houses were rifled, women ravished, and goods taken as they pleased. The whole troop, together with their horses, lived on the grain and provisions. While cattle were shot down for mere sport, and sometimes men, women and children fared no better. On the third morning after our imprisonment we were placed in a wagon, in order for removal. Many of the more desperate then crowded around, cocked their rifles, and singling us out presented them to our breasts, and swore they would blow us through. Some guns were snapped, but missed fire, and the rest were in a small degree restrained by the officers, and we still lived.

We were now marched to Far West, under the conduct of the whole army; and while they halted in the public square, we were permitted to go with a guard for a change of linen and to take final leave of our families, in order to depart as prisoners to Jackson County, a distance of sixty miles.

This was the most trying scene of all. I went to my house, being guarded by two or three soldiers; the cold rain was pouring down without, and on entering my little cottage, there lay my wife sick of a fever, with which she had been for some time confined. At her breast was our son Nathan, an infant of three months, and by her side a little girl of five years. On the foot of the same bed lay a woman in travail, who had been driven from her house in the night, and had taken momentary shelter in my hut of ten feet square—my larger house having been torn down. I stepped to the bed; my wife burst into tears; I spoke a few words of comfort, telling her to try to live for my sake and the children's; and expressing a hope that we should meet again though years might separate us. She promised to try to live. I then embraced and kissed the little babes and departed.

Till now I had refrained from weeping; but, to be forced from so helpless a family, who were destitute of provisions and fuel, and deprived almost of shelter in a bleak prairie, with none to assist them, exposed to a lawless banditti who were utter strangers to humanity, and this at the approach of winter, was more than nature could well endure.

I went to Gen. Moses Wilson in tears, and stated the circumstances of my sick, heart-broken and destitute family in terms which would have moved any heart that had a latent spark of humanity yet remaining. But I was only answered with an exultant laugh, and a taunt of reproach by this hardened murderer.

As I returned from my house towards the troops in the square, I halted with the guard at the door of Hyrum Smith, and heard the sobs and groans of his wife, at his parting words. She was then near confinement; and needed more than ever the comfort and consolation of a husband's presence. As we returned to the wagon we saw S. Rigdon taking leave of his wife and daughters, who stood at a little distance, in tears of anguish indescribable. In the wagon sat Joseph Smith, while his aged father and venerable mother came up overwhelmed with tears, and took each of the prisoners by the hand with a silence of grief too great for utterance.

In the meantime, hundreds of the brethren crowded around us, anxious to take a parting look, or a silent shake of the hand; for feelings were too intense to allow of speech. In the midst of these scenes orders were given and we moved slowly away, under the conduct of Gen. Wilson and his whole brigade. A march of twelve miles brought us to Crooked River, where we camped for the night. Here Gen. Wilson began to treat us more kindly; he became very sociable; conversing very freely on the subject of his former murders and robberies committed against us in Jackson. He did not pretend to deny anything; but spoke upon the whole as freely as if he had been giving the history of other ages or countries, in which his audience had no personal concern. Said he:

"We Jackson County boys know how it is; and, therefore, have not the extremes of hatred and prejudice which characterize the rest of the troops. We know perfectly that from the beginning the Mormons have not been the aggressors at all. As it began in '33 in Jackson County, so it has been ever since. You Mormons were crowded to the last extreme, and compelled to self-defence; and this has been construed into treason, murder and plunder. We mob you without law; the authorities refuse to protect you according to law; you then are compelled to protect yourselves, and we act upon the prejudices of the public, who join our forces, and the whole is legalized, for your destruction and our gain. Is not this a shrewd and cunning policy on our part, gentlemen?

"When we drove you from Jackson County, we burned two hundred and three of your houses; plundered your goods; destroyed your press, type, paper, books, office and all—tarred and feathered old Bishop Partridge, as exemplary an old man as you can find anywhere. We shot down some of your men, and, if any of you returned the fire, we imprisoned you, on your trial for murder, etc. Damn'd shrewdly done, gentlemen; and I came damn'd near kicking the bucket myself; for, on one occasion, while we were tearing down houses, driving families, and destroying and plundering goods, some of you good folks put a ball through my son's body, another through the arm of my clerk, and a third pierced my shirt collar and marked my neck. No blame gentlemen; we deserved it. And let a set of men serve me as your community have been served, and I'll be damn'd if I would not fight till I died.

"It was repeatedly insinuated, by the other officers and troops, that we should hang you prisoners on the first tree we came to on the way to Independence. But I'll be damn'd if anybody shall hurt you. We just intend to exhibit you in Independence, let the people look at you, and see what a damn'd set of fine fellows you are. And, more particularly, to keep you from that G-d damn'd old bigot of a Gen. Clark and his troops, from down country, who are so stuffed with lies and prejudice that they would shoot you down in a moment."

Such was the tenor of the conversation addressed by Gen. Wilson to his prisoners. Indeed, it was now evident that he was proud of his prey, and felt highly enthusiastic in having the honor of returning in triumph to Independence with his prisoners, whom his superstition had magnified into something more than fellow citizens—something noble or supernatural, and worthy of public exhibition.

As we arose and commenced our march on the morning of the 3d of November, Joseph Smith spoke to me and the other prisoners, in a low, but cheerful and confidential tone; said he: *"Be of good cheer, brethren; the word of the Lord came to me last night that our lives should be given us, and that whatever we may suffer during this captivity, not one of our lives should be taken."* Of this prophecy I testify in the name of the Lord, and, though spoken in secret, its public fulfilment and the miraculous escape of each one of us is too notorious to need my testimony. In the after part of the day we came to the Missouri River, which separated us from Jackson County. Here the brigade was halted and the prisoners taken to a public house, where we were permitted to shave, change our linen, and partake of some refreshment. This done, we were hurried to the ferry and across the river with the utmost haste, in advance of the troops. This movement was soon explained to us. The truth was, Gen. Clark had now arrived near the scene of action, and had sent an express to take us from Gen. Wilson and prevent us from going to Jackson County — both armies being competitors for the honor of possessing the wonderful, or, in their estimation, royal prisoners.

Clark and his troops, from a distance, who had not arrived in the city of Far West till after our departure, were desirous of seeing the strange men whom it was said had turned the world upside down and of possessing such a wonderful trophy of victory, or of putting them to death themselves. On the other hand, Wilson and his brigade were determined to exhibit us through the streets of Independence as a visible token of their own achievements. Therefore, when demanded by Gen. Clark's express, they refused to surrender us; and hurried us across the ferry with all possible despatch. Marching about a mile, we encamped for the night in the wilderness, with about fifty troops for our guard — the remainder not crossing the ferry till the next morning.

Some of the neighboring citizens visited us next morning — it being Sunday. One of the ladies came up and very candidly inquired of the troops which of the prisoners the "Mormons" worshipped? One of the guards pointing to Mr. Smith with a significant smile, said, "This is he." The woman, then turning to Mr. Smith, inquired whether he professed to be the Lord and Saviour?

Do not smile, gentle reader, at the ignorance of these poor innocent creatures, who, by the exertions of a corrupt press and pulpit, are kept in ignorance and made to believe in every possible absurdity in relation to the Church of the Saints. Mr. Smith replied, that he professed to be nothing but a man, and a minister of salvation, sent by Jesus Christ to preach the gospel. After expressing some surprise, the lady inquired what was the peculiar nature of the gospel, as held by himself and his Church? At this the visitors and soldiers gathered around, and Mr. Smith preached to them faith in the Lord Jesus Christ, repentance towards God, reformation of life, immersion in water, in the name of Jesus Christ, for remission of sins, and the gift of the Holy Ghost by the laying on of hands.

All seemed surprised, and the lady, in tears, went her way, praising God for the truth, and praying aloud that the Lord would bless and deliver the prisoners.

At ten o'clock the brigade had all crossed the river, and come up with us. We were then marched forward in our carriages, while the troops were formed into a front and rear guard, with quite a martial appearance. As we passed along through the settlements hundreds of men, women and children flocked to see us. General W. often halted the whole brigade to introduce us to the populace, pointing out each of us by name. Many shook us by the hand, and, in the ladies at least, there appeared some feelings of human compassion and sympathy.

In this way we proceeded till we arrived at Independence. It was now past noon, and in the midst of a great rain; but hundreds crowded to witness the procession, and to gaze at us as we were paraded in martial triumph through the principal streets, the bugles sounding a blast of triumphant joy.

CHAPTER XXIII

This ceremony being finished, a vacant house was prepared for our reception, into which we were ushered through the crowd of spectators which thronged every avenue.

The troops were then disbanded. In the meantime we were kept under a small guard, and were treated with some degree of humanity, while hundreds flocked to see us day after day. We spent most of our time in preaching and conversation, explanatory of our doctrines and practice. Much prejudice was removed, and the feelings of the populace began to be in our favor, notwithstanding their former wickedness and hatred. In a day or two we were at liberty to walk the streets without a guard. We were finally removed from our house of confinement to a hotel, where we boarded at the public table, and lodged on the floor, with a block of wood for a pillow. We no longer had any guard; we went out and came in when we pleased—a certain keeper being appointed merely to watch over us, and look to our wants.

With him we walked out of town to the westward, and visited the desolate lands of the Saints, and the place which, seven years before, we had dedicated for the building of a Temple. This was a beautiful rise of ground, about half a mile west of Independence centre. When we saw it last it was a noble forest, but our enemies had since robbed it of every vestige of timber, and it now lay desolate, or clothed with grass and weeds.

O, how many feelings did this spot awaken in our bosoms! Here we had often bowed the knee in prayer, in bygone years. Here we had assembled with hundreds of happy Saints in the solemn meeting, and offered our songs, and sacraments, and orisons. But now all was solemn and lonely desolation. Not a vestige remained to mark the spot where stood our former dwellings. They had long since been consumed by fire, or removed and converted to the uses of our enemies.

While at Independence we were once or twice invited to dine with General Wilson and some others, which we did.

While thus sojourning as prisoners at large, I arose one morning when it was very snowy, and passed silently and unmolested out of the hotel, and as no one seemed to notice me, or call me in question, I thought I would try an experiment. I passed on eastward through the town; no one noticed me. I then took into the fields, still unobserved. After travelling a mile I entered a forest; all was gloomy silence, none were near, the heavens were darkened and obscured by falling snow, my track was covered behind me, and I was free. I knew the way to the States eastward very well, and there seemed nothing to prevent my pursuing my way thither; thoughts of freedom beat high in my bosom; wife, children, home, freedom, peace, and a land of law and order, all arose in my mind; I could go to other States, send for my family, make me a home and be happy.

On the other hand, I was a prisoner in a State where all law was at an end. I was liable to be shot down at any time without judge or jury. I was liable to be tried for my life by murderous assassins, who had already broken every oath of office and trampled on every principle of honor or even humanity. Hands already dripping with the blood of aged sires, and of helpless women and children, were reaching out for my destruction. The battle of Crooked River had already been construed into *murder* on the part of the brave patriots who there defended their lives and rescued their fellow citizens from kidnappers and land pirates, while the pirates themselves had been converted into loyal militia.

To go forward was freedom, to go backward was to be sent to General Clark, and be accused of the highest crimes, with murderers for judge, jury and executioners.

"Go free!" whispered the tempter.

"No!" said I, "never, while brother Joseph and his fellows are in the power of the enemy. What a storm of trouble, or even of death, it might subject them to."

I turned on my heel, retraced my steps, and entered the hotel ere they had missed me. As I shook the snow off my clothes the keeper and also brother Joseph inquired where I had been. I replied, just out for a little exercise. A walk for pleasure in such a storm gave rise to some pleasantries on their part, and there the matter ended.

There was one thing which buoyed up our spirits continually during our captivity: it was the remembrance of the word of the Lord to brother Joseph, saying, that our lives should all be given us during this captivity, and not one of them should be lost. I thought of this while in the wilderness vacillating whether to go or stay, and the thought struck me: "*He that will seek to save his life shall lose it; but he that will lose his life for my sake shall find it again, even life eternal.*" I could now make sure of my part in the first resurrection, as I had so intensely desired when about eleven years old. But, O, the path of life! How was it beset with trials!

At length, after repeated demands, we were sent to General Clark, at Richmond, Ray County. Generals Lucas and Wilson had tried in vain for some days to get a guard to accompany us. None would volunteer, and when drafted they would not obey orders; for, in truth, they wished us to go at liberty. At last a colonel and two or three officers started with us, with their swords and pistols, which were intended more to protect us than to keep us from escaping. On this journey some of us rode in carriages and some on horseback. Sometimes we were sixty or eighty rods in front or rear of our guards, who were drinking hard out of bottles which they carried in their pockets.

At night, having crossed the Missouri River, we put up at a private house. Here our guards all got drunk, and went to bed and to sleep, leaving us their pistols to defend ourselves in case of any attack from without, as we were in a very hostile neighborhood. Next morning we rode a few miles, and were met by an express from General Clark, which consisted of one Colonel Sterling Price and a guard of soldiers. This company immediately surrounded us with poised pieces, in regular military order, as if we had been Buonaparte and staff on the way to St. Helena; thinking, perhaps, that if we should escape, the whole United States and Europe would be immediately overthrown.

In this manner we were escorted to Richmond, the headquarters of General Clark and his army of three or four thousand men. Here, as usual, we had to endure the gaze of the curious, as if we had been a caravan of animals for exhibition. Troops were paraded to receive us, which, as we approached, opened to the right and left, thus forming a long avenue, through which we passed into a block house, and were immediately put in chains, under a strong guard, who stood over us continually with poised pieces, cocked and primed. Colonel Price continued in the superintendence of the prisoners and the guards.

General Clark at length called to see us. He seemed more haughty, unfeeling, and reserved than even Lucas or Wilson had been when we first entered their camp. We inquired of the general what were his intentions concerning us. I stated to him that we had now been captives for many days, and we knew not wherefore, nor whether we were considered prisoners of war or prisoners of civil process, or "*prisoners of hope.*" At the same time remarking, that all was wrapt in mystery; for, as citizens of the United States and of Missouri, in time of peace, we could in nowise be considered as prisoners of war; and, without civil process, we were not holden by civil authority; and as to being "prisoners of hope," there was not much chance to hope, from our present appearances!

He replied that *"we were taken to be tried."*

"Tried? By what authority?"

"By court martial."

"What! Ministers of the gospel tried by court martial! Men who sustain no office in military affairs, and who are not subject by law to military duty; such men to be tried by court martial! And this in time of peace, and in a republic where the constitution guaranteed to every citizen the right of trial by jury?"

"Yes. This is in accordance with the treaty of stipulations entered into at Far West at the time of the surrender, and as agreed to by Colonel Hinkle, your commanding officer."

"Colonel Hinkle, our commanding officer! What had he to do with our civil rights? He was only a colonel of a regiment of the Caldwell County Militia."

"Why! was he not the commanding officer of the fortress of Far West, the headquarters of the *Mormon forces*?"

"We had no *'fortress'* or *'Mormon forces,'* but were part of the State militia."

At this the general seemed surprised, and the conversation ended.

We were astonished above measure at proceedings so utterly ignorant and devoid of all law or justice. Here was a Major-General, selected by the Governor of Missouri, and sent to banish or exterminate a religious society. And then, to crown the whole with inconceivable absurdity, said religious society is converted by this officer and his associates into an independent government, or foreign nation. And last, and equally absurd, the State of Missouri assumed her independence of the Federal Government so far as to *treat* with this imaginary *"Mormon Empire,"* or foreign nation. A colonel of militia, subordinate to the general then in the field, is converted into a foreign minister, an envoy extraordinary, in behalf of the "Mormon Empire," to enter into treaty stipulations with his Missouri majesty's forces, under Generals Lucas, Wilson and Clark!

The City of Far West, the capital of *"Mormonia,"* is the *"Ghent,"* where this treaty of peace is ratified. The standing army of the conquered nation stack their arms, which are carried in triumph to Richmond. Preachers of the gospel are converted into *"noble"* or *"royal prisoners"* chained to the car of the victorious champions to be led captive as sport for the Philistines, or to be shot or hung at pleasure, while the residue of the inhabitants of the fallen empire—men, women and children—are to have their real estate and all other goods confiscated, and themselves banished the State on pain of death. A few, however, are selected from among these exiles to be imprisoned or executed at the mere dictation of a Nero or a Nicholas.

Was this in America, in the nineteenth century? Were these scenes transacted in a constitutional republic? Yes, verily, and worse, — a tale of horror, of woe, of long years of lawless outrage and tyranny is yet to be told, of which this is a mere stepping stone or entering wedge. . . .

CHAPTER XXVI.

I must not forget to state that when we arrived in Richmond as prisoners there were some fifty others, mostly heads of families, who had been marched from Caldwell on foot (distance 30 miles), and were now penned up in a cold, open, unfinished court house, in which situation they remained for some weeks, while their families were suffering severe privations.

The next morning after our dialogue with General Clark he again entered our prison and informed us that he had concluded to deliver us over to the civil authorities for an examining trial. He was then asked why he did not do away with the unlawful decree of *banishment*, which was first ordered by General Lucas, in compliance with the Governor's order, and which compelled thousands of citizens to leave the State. Or upon what principle the military power aided the civil law against us, while at the same time it caused our families and friends to be murdered, plundered and driven, contrary to all law?

He replied that he approved of all the proceedings of General Lucas, and should not alter them. I make this statement because some writers have commended Clark for his heroic, merciful, and prudent conduct towards our society, and have endeavored to make it appear that Clark was not to be blamed for any of the measures of Lucas.

The Court of Inquiry now commenced, before Judge Austin A. King. This continued from the 11th to 28th of November, during which we were kept most of the time in chains, and our brethren, some fifty in number, were penned up in the cold, dreary court house. It was a very severe time of snow and winter weather, and we suffered much. During this time Elder Rigdon was taken very sick, from hardship and exposure, and finally lost his reason; but still he was kept in a miserable, noisy and cold room, and compelled to sleep on the floor with a chain and padlock round his ankle, and fastened to six others. Here he endured the constant noise and confusion of an unruly guard, the officer of which was Colonel Sterling Price, since Governor of the State.

These guards were composed generally of the most noisy, foul-mouthed, vulgar, disgraceful rabble that ever defiled the earth. While he lay in this situation his son-in-law, George W. Robinson, the only male member of his family, was chained by his side. Thus Mrs. Rigdon and her daughters were left entirely destitute and unprotected. One of his daughters, Mrs. Robinson, a young and delicate female, with her little infant, came down to see her husband, and to comfort and take care of her father in his sickness. When she first entered the room, amid the clank of chains and the rattle of weapons, and cast her eyes on her sick and dejected parent and sorrow worn husband, she was speechless, and only gave vent to her feelings in a flood of tears. This faithful lady, with her little infant, continued by the side of her father till he recovered from his sickness, and till his fevered and disordered mind resumed its wonted powers.

In one of those tedious nights we had lain as if in sleep till the hour of midnight had passed, and our ears and hearts had been pained, while we had listened for hours to the obscene jests, the horrid oaths, the dreadful blasphemies and filthy language of our guards, Colonel Price at their head, as they recounted to each other their deeds of rapine, murder, robbery, etc., which they had committed among the "*Mormons*" while at Far West and vicinity. They even boasted of defiling by force wives, daughters and virgins, and of shooting or dashing out the brains of men, women and children.

I had listened till I became so disgusted, shocked, horrified, and so filled with the spirit of indignant justice that I could scarcely refrain from rising upon my feet and rebuking the guards; but had said nothing to Joseph, or any one else, although I lay next to him and knew he was awake. On a sudden he arose to his feet, and spoke in a voice of thunder, or as the roaring lion, uttering, as near as I can recollect, the following words:

"*SILENCE, ye fiends of the infernal pit. In the name of Jesus Christ I rebuke you, and command you to be still; I will not live another minute and hear such language. Cease such talk, or you or I die THIS INSTANT !*"

He ceased to speak. He stood erect in terrible majesty. Chained, and without a weapon; calm, unruffled and dignified as an angel, he looked upon the quailing guards, whose weapons were lowered or dropped to the ground; whose knees smote together, and who, shrinking into a corner, or crouching at his feet, begged his pardon, and remained quiet till a change of guards.

I have seen the ministers of justice, clothed in magisterial robes, and criminals arraigned before them, while life was suspended on a breath, in the Courts of England; I have witnessed a Congress in solemn session to give laws to nations; I have tried to conceive of kings, of royal courts, of thrones and crowns; and of emperors assembled to decide the fate of kingdoms; but dignity and majesty have I seen but *once*, as it stood in chains, at midnight, in a dungeon in an obscure village of Missouri.

In this mock Court of Inquiry the Judge could not be prevailed on to examine the conduct of the murderers and robbers who had desolated our society, nor would he receive testimony except against us. By the dissenters and apostates who wished to save their own lives and secure their property at the expense of others, and by those who had murdered and plundered us from time to time, he obtained abundance of testimony, much of which was entirely false. Our Church organization was converted by such testimony into a temporal kingdom, which was to fill the whole earth and subdue all other kingdoms.

This Court of Inquisition inquired diligently into our belief of the seventh chapter of Daniel concerning the kingdom of God, which should subdue all other kingdoms and stand forever. And when told that we believed in that prophecy, the Court turned to the clerk and said: *"Write that down; it is a strong point for treason."* Our lawyer observed as follows: "Judge, you had better make the Bible treason." The Court made no reply.

These texts and many others were inquired into with all the eagerness and apparent alarm which characterized a Herod of old in relation to the babe of Bethlehem, the King of the Jews.

The ancient Herod, fearing a rival in the person of Jesus, issued his exterminating order for the murder of all the children of Bethlehem from two years old and under, with a view to hinder the fulfilment of a prophecy which he *himself* believed to be true.

The modern Herod (Boggs), fearing a rival kingdom in *"the people of the Saints of the Most High,"* issued his exterminating order for the murder of the young children of an entire people, and of their mothers as well as fathers, while this Court of Inquisition inquired as diligently into the one prophecy as his predecessor did into the other. These parallel actions go to show a strong belief in the prophecies on the part of the actors in both cases. Both were instigated by the devil to cause innocent blood to be shed. And marvellously striking is the parallel in the final result of the actions of each.

The one slew many young children, but failed to destroy the infant King of the Jews.

The other slew many men, women and children, but failed to destroy the Kingdom of God.

The one found a timely refuge in Egypt.

The other in Illinois.

Jesus Christ fulfilled his destiny, and will reign over the Jews, and sit on the throne of his father, David, forever.

The Saints are growing into power amid the strongholds of the mountains of Deseret, and will surely take the Kingdom, and the greatness of the Kingdom, under the whole Heaven.

Who can withstand the Almighty, or frustrate his purposes? Herod died of a loathsome disease, and transmitted to posterity his fame as a tyrant and murderer. And Lilburn W. Boggs is dragging out a remnant of existence in California, with the mark of Cain upon his brow, and the fear of Cain within his heart, lest he that findeth him shall slay him. He is a living stink, and will go down to posterity with the credit of a wholesale murderer.

The Court also inquired diligently into our missionary operations. It was found, on investigation, that the Church had sent missionaries into England and other foreign countries. This, together with our belief in the Bible, was construed into treason against the State of Missouri, while every act of defence was set down as murder, etc. The Judge, in open court, while addressing a witness, proclaimed, that if the members of the Church remained on their lands to put in another crop they should be destroyed indiscriminately, and their bones be left to bleach on the plains without a burial. Yes, reader, the cultivation of lands held by patents issued by the United States land office, and signed by the President of the Republic, was, by Judge Austin A. King, in open court, pronounced a capital offence, for which a whole community were prejudged and sentenced to death. While those who should be the instruments to execute this sentence were called by the dignified name of citizens, and these *good* citizens afterwards elected that same Judge for Governor of the State.

The Judge inquired of the prisoners if they wished to introduce any witnesses for the defence. A list of names was supplied by the prisoners, when, who should be selected to go to Far West to obtain and bring them before the Court, but the identical bandit, Bogart, and his gang, who were defeated by us in the battle of Crooked River, after they had become famous for kidnapping, plundering and murdering!

Of course, every man in Caldwell would flee from such a gang if they could; but he succeeded in capturing a few of our friends, whose names were on the list, and bringing them before the Court, when, instead of being sworn, they were immediately ordered to prison to take their trial. Others were sent for, and, as far as found, shared the same fate. This manoeuvre occupied several days, during which the Court was still in session, and the fate of the prisoners suspended.

At length the Judge exclaimed to the prisoners: "If you have any witnesses bring them forward; the Court cannot delay forever—it has waited several days already." A member of the Church, named Allen, was just then seen to pass the window. The prisoners requested that he might be introduced and sworn. He was immediately called in and sworn. He began to give his testimony, which went to establish the innocence of the prisoners, and to show the murders, robberies, etc., committed by their accusers. But he was suddenly interrupted and cut short by cries of *"Put him out;" "Kick him out;" "G-d d—n him, shoot him;" "Kill him, d—n him, kill him;" "He's a d——d Mormon."*

The Court then ordered the guard to put him out, which was done amid the yells, threats, insults and violence of the mob who thronged in and around the court house. He barely escaped with his life. Mr. Doniphan, attorney for the defence, and since famed as a general in the Mexican war, finally advised the prisoners to offer no defence; "for," said he, "though a legion of angels from the opening heavens should declare your innocence, the Court and populace have decreed your destruction." Our Attorney offered no defence, and thus the matter of our trials was finally submitted.

By the decision of this mock Court some twenty or thirty of the accused were dismissed, among whom was Amasa Lyman. Some twenty others were suffered to be bailed out, and themselves and bail both forced to leave the State, thus forfeiting the bail bonds, while Joseph Smith, Hyrum Smith, Sidney Rigdon, Lyman Wight, Caleb Baldwin and Alexander McRay (all heads of families) were committed to the jail of Clay County on the charge of treason; and Morris Phelps, Lyman Gibbs, Darwin Chase, Norman Shearer and myself were committed to the jail of Richmond, Ray County, for the alleged crime of murder, said to be committed in the act of dispersing the bandit, Bogart, and his gang.

This done, the civil and military authorities dispersed, and the troubled waters became a little more tranquil.

As our people were compelled by the memorable *"Treaty of Far West"* to leave the State by the following spring, they now commenced moving by hundreds and by thousands to the State of Illinois, where they were received in the most humane and friendly manner by the authorities, and by the citizens in general. In the meantime bands of murderers, thieves and robbers were roaming unrestrained among the unarmed and defenceless citizens, committing all manner of plunder, and driving off cattle, sheep and horses, abusing and insulting women.

My wife and children soon came to me in prison, and spent a portion of the winter in the cold, dark dungeon, where myself and fellow prisoners were frequently insulted and abused by our dastardly guards, who often threatened to shoot us on the spot, and who made murder, robbery and whoredoms with negro slaves their daily boast. . . .

CHAPTER XXIX.

On the 17th of March, 1839, my wife took leave of the prison with her little children, and, with a broken heart, returned to Far West, in order to get passage with some of the brethren for Illinois. She tarried in Far West a month. All the Society had gone from the State, but a few of the poor and widows, and the Committee who tarried behind to assist them in removing. About the middle of April a gang of robbers entered Far West armed, and ordered my wife, and the Committee, and the others to be gone by such a time, or they would murder them. This gang destroyed much furniture and other property.

Thus my wife was driven away according to the Governor's previous order, while I was still detained in a filthy dungeon. My family were conveyed to Quincy, Illinois, distance two hundred and eighty miles, by David W. Rogers of New York, who is a descendant of the celebrated martyr, John Rogers, of Smithfield celebrity, England.

On the 20th of April, 1839, the last of the Society departed from Far West. Thus had a whole people, variously estimated at from ten to fifteen thousand souls, been driven from houses and lands and reduced to poverty, and had removed to another State during one short winter and part of a spring. The sacrifice of property was immense — including houses, lands, cattle, sheep, hogs, agricultural implements, furniture, household utensils, clothing, money and grain. One of the most flourishing counties in the State and part of several others were reduced to desolation, or inhabited only by marauding gangs of murderers and robbers.

On the 24th of April our cases came before the Grand Jury of the county of Ray; which Grand Jury, the reader is aware, would be naturally composed of our persecutors and their accessories; and at whose head was the same Judge King who had presided in the former mock trial and Inquisition which committed us to prison. . . .

CHAPTER XXXI.

. . . At the end of this extraordinary mock trail or inquisition, which lasted over two weeks, I was unchained from Joseph and Hyrum Smith, and the others, and being separated from them, was conducted to a gloomy, dark, cold and filthy dungeon in Richmond, Ray County, where I was doomed to spend the winter and spring, and await a further trial; while they shared a similar fate in a place called Liberty, in Clay County.

When I first entered the dungeon there were some twenty men, mostly heads of families, who had been torn from their families in those awful times, and thrust into prison. It was not only crowded to suffocation, without a chair, stool, bench, bed, furniture or window light, but just then completely filled with smoke by a fire which was lighted in a stove without a pipe, or any conductor for the smoke to pass out, except at the crevices between the timbers, where the winter storm was passing in. When my guard conducted me to the door of this miserable cell it grated on its huge hinges and opened like the pit yawning to receive me; a volume of thick smoke issued forth and seemed to forbid my entrance; but, urged in my rear by bayonets and loaded pistols in the hands of savage beings, I endeavored to enter, but was forced to retreat again outside of the door to breathe for a moment the free air. At this instant several pistols were cocked and presented at my head and breast, with terrible threats and oaths of instant death if I did not go in again. I told them to fire as soon as they pleased, for I must breathe a moment or die in the attempt. After standing a few moments, I again entered the prison, and threw myself down, my face to the floor, to avoid the smoke. Here I remained for some time, partly in a state of insensibility; my heart sickened within me, and a deathlike feeling came over me, from which I did not wholly recover for several days.

I arose, however, as soon as I was able, and began to speak to and recognize my fellow prisoners—most of whom were my neighbors and acquaintances. The door was now locked, bolted and barred, and several guards placed before it. The fire died away, and the smoke gradually cleared away from the dungeon; but the floor formed a hard and cold winter lodging.

In a few days all those in our prison, except five, were released on bail, and themselves and bail banished from the State, with the rest of the Society; thus compelling them to forfeit their bail bonds, which amounted in all to many thousand dollars. The five who remained were Morris Phelps, Darwin Chase, Norman Shearer, Luman Gibbs and myself. Two of these were finally dismissed—being boys scarcely out of their teens. But another was soon added by the name of King Follet.

This made our final number four. One of this number viz.: Luman Gibbs, denied the faith and turned a traitor to the others; becoming their most inveterate enemy. This was in order to save his life and gain his liberty. However, he was still kept in prison as a spy upon us, lest it should be said that it was wholly a religious persecution; but he was treated very well, and went out to dine with the Sheriff or others, or to spend a day with his wife whenever it pleased him to do so. Our food was of the most unwholesome kind, and scant at that; consisting of bones and remnants of meat, coarse corn bread, and sometimes a little coffee. We generally partook of our meals in a standing position, using our fingers instead of knives, forks or plates. A tin cup served us for our coffee. We were guarded very strictly, both by night and day, by two or three men with loaded pistols.

These consisted of the most unprincipled, profligate villains that could be found anywhere. They would swear, drink, gamble, and sing the most obscene and disgusting songs. They would boast of shooting the *Mormons*; robbing and plundering them; committing rapes, etc. They would also insult every female slave or black woman who might happen to come within hearing, and then boast of their criminal connections with them. The blasphemy; the noisy grumbling; the blackguard chit chat; doleful lullaby and vulgar songs of these guards grating daily upon our ears, seemed like the howls and wailings of the damned, or like wandering spirits and demons hovering around to torment us. What greatly added to our affliction, as if to complete our hell, the old apostate, Gibbs, became very quarrelsome and noisy—not only to us, but with his wife also, who sometimes came into the prison to spend a few days with him. He was a hard faced, ill formed man, of about fifty years of age; full of jealousy, extremely selfish, very weak minded, and, withal, a little love cracked; and, I may say, that he seemed not to possess one redeeming quality.

His wife was about the same age, and withal, a coarse, tall, masculine looking woman, and one of whom he had no reason to complain or be jealous. True, she did not love him—for no female could possibly do that; but then no one else would love her, nor was she disposed to court their affections. However, he was jealous of her, and, therefore, abused her; and this kept a constant and noisy strife and wrangling between them whenever she was present.

Whole nights were spent in this way, during which no one in or about the prison slept. After a quarrel of some two or three days and nights between them, he would attempt to regain her love, and a conversation like the following would ensue. Luman, drawing down his face and drawling his words with a loud and doleful tone, commenced as follows:

"Now, Phila, won't you love me? Come; here's my watch, and here's all the money I've got!" Then turning to us he would exclaim: "Boys, I'll tell you all about it; the fact is, she never did love me; she only married me out of pity—we being members of the Baptist church together in Vermont." Then again addressing his wife: "Come now, Phila; won't you love me? O, that I had been born a rich man! I would give you a dollar a minute to love me."

Phila would then laugh and call him "a silly old fool." Whereupon he would turn away in a rage, and exclaim: "Go along away, you — —-, you! Nobody wants your love, no how!"

On one occasion they had quarreled and kept us awake all night, and just at break of day we heard a noise like a scuffle and a slamming against the wall; next followed a woman's voice, half in a laugh and half in exultation: — "Te-he-he-he, Luman, what's the matter? What's the matter, Luman?" Then a pause, and afterwards a man's voice in a grum, sorry, and rather a whining tone was heard at a distance from the bed, exclaiming: "Now, I swan, Phila, that's tu bad."

The truth of the matter was this: She had braced her back against the wall, and with both her feet placed against his body, had kicked him out of bed, and landed him upon the opposite side of the room.

Such scenes as these and all the folly of the guards served to enhance the misery of imprisonment, and to render our sufferings complete. We tried to keep them quiet, but tried in vain. Neither threats nor persuasion, coaxing nor reasoning had any influence over them. This miserable specimen of humanity was a peculiar favorite of the Sheriff and guards, and other citizens of Richmond. He was considered by them as the only honest, good, deserving man in the prison. They often expressed pity for him, and wished he was at liberty. He, in turn, watched our movements closely, and was ready to betray us on the least show, on our part, of any meditated plan of escape.

Under these painful circumstances we spent a long and dreary winter. Our whole community, who were not in prison, were forced out of the State, with the loss of homes, property, and many lives. They fled by thousands to Illinois.

My wife visited me several times in prison; but at length the period expired that the State authorities had stipulated for every Mormon to be gone, and my wife and children, and a few others who remained behind, were obliged to fly or be exterminated, as bands of armed men were roaming amid the deserted settlements, robbing, plundering, destroying property, and threatening all who remained.

My fellow prisoners, who had been separated from me and sent to the prison at Liberty, had also effected their escape, and had fled to Illinois to join their families. In short, all were gone, except King Follett, Morris Phelps and myself, and the old apostate, who was left to torment us.

Alone in a State which was wholly governed by an open banditti of murderers and robbers, we seemed abandoned to our fate, and doomed to suffer that full weight of vengeance and fury which seemed in reserve for an entire people; but that people were now beyond their reach; all the fury of the storm, therefore, seemed now to beat upon our heads. We were daily threatened with assassination, without the form of a trial; and were repeatedly told that we never should escape alive from the State. Our guards were doubly vigilant, while the Sheriff took every possible precaution. Luman, the apostate, was also in constant watchfulness, and busy in forming plans for escape; then accusing us and pretending to reveal wonderful things to our keepers in regard to our plans; which, in fact, only existed in his lying brain. This increased the severity of our confinement, and seemed to preclude the possibility of escape.

To be tried without friends or witnesses, or even with them, by a set of "Gadianton robbers" and murderers, who could drive out and murder women and children, was but to be condemned and executed; to tarry there and drag out a miserable life, while our wives and children wandered abroad in a land of strangers, without the protection of husbands and fathers, was worse than to die ten thousand deaths.

Under these circumstances, and half way between hope and despair, I spent several days in fasting and prayer, during which one deep and all absorbing inquiry, one only thought, seemed to hold possession of my mind. It seemed to me that if there was a God in Heaven who ever spake to man on earth I would know from him the truth of this one question. It was not how long shall I suffer; it was not when or by what means I should be delivered; but it was simply this: Shall I ever, at any time, however distant it may be, or whatever I may suffer first; shall I ever be free again in this life, and enjoy the society of my dear wife and children, and walk abroad at liberty, dwell in society and preach the gospel, as I have done in bygone years?

Let me be sure of this and I care not what I suffer. To circumnavigate the globe, to traverse the deserts of Arabia, to wander amid the wild scenes of the Rocky Mountains to accomplish so desirable an object, would seem like a mere trifle if I could only be sure at last. After some days of prayer and fasting, and seeking the Lord on the subject, I retired to my bed in my lonely chamber at an early hour, and while the other prisoners and the guard were chatting and beguiling the lonesome hours in the upper apartment of the prison, I lay in silence, seeking and expecting an answer to my prayer, when suddenly I seemed carried away in the spirit, and no longer sensible to outward objects with which I was surrounded. A heaven of peace and calmness pervaded my bosom; a personage from the world of spirits stood before me with a smile of compassion in every look, and pity mingled with the tenderest love and sympathy in every expression of the countenance. A soft hand seemed placed within my own, and a glowing cheek was laid in tenderness and warmth upon mine. A well known voice saluted me, which I readily recognized as that of the wife of my youth, who had for near two years been sweetly sleeping where the wicked cease from troubling and the weary are at rest. I was made to realize that she was sent to commune with me, and answer my question.

Knowing this, I said to her in a most earnest and inquiring tone: Shall I ever be at liberty again in this life and enjoy the society of my family and the Saints, and preach the gospel as I have done? She answered definitely and unhesitatingly: "YES!" I then recollected that I had agreed to be satisfied with the knowledge of *that one* fact, but now I wanted more.

Said I: Can you tell me how, or by what means, or when I shall escape? She replied: "THAT THING IS NOT MADE KNOWN TO ME YET." I instantly felt that I had gone beyond my agreement and my faith in asking this last question, and that I must be contented at present with the answer to the first.

Her gentle spirit then saluted me and withdrew. I came to myself. The doleful noise of the guards, and the wrangling and angry words of the old apostate again grated on my ears, but Heaven and hope were in my soul.

Next morning I related the whole circumstance of my vision to my two fellow prisoners, who rejoiced exceedingly. This may seem to some like an idle dream, or a romance of the imagination; but to me it was, and always will be a reality, both as it regards what I then experienced and the fulfilment afterwards.

In order to show some pretence of respect for some of the forms of law, Judge Austin A. King now entered our prison and took our testimony, preparatory to a change of venue. I shall never forget this interview. There stood our Judge, face to face with those who, by his cruelty and injustice, had lived a cold half year in a dungeon. He refused to look us in the eye; hung his head and looked like a culprit before his betters about to receive his doom. The looks of guilt and misery portrayed in his countenance during that brief interview bespoke more of misery than we had suffered during our confinement. I actually pitied him in my heart. With an extraordinary effort and a voice scarcely audible, he administered the oaths and withdrew.

By means of this change we were finally to be removed one hundred miles down the country, and confined in the prison at Columbia, Boone County, to await a final trial.

A long, dreary winter and spring had now passed away, and the time drew near for our removal. We looked forward to the change with some degree of hope and expectation, for it could not be for the worse, and might, perhaps, be for the better. At any rate, the journey would give us a chance to leave our dark and loathsome dungeon, and look upon the light of day, the beauties of nature, and to breathe the untainted air.

The morning of the departure at length arrived. Mr. Brown, the Sheriff, entered our prison with a fierce and savage look and, bidding us hold out our hands, coupled us together in pairs, with irons locked on our wrists, and marched us out; and, amid a throng of people, placed us in a carriage. Accompanied with four guards on horseback, with loaded pistols, we bid farewell to Richmond.

It was a pleasant morning in early summer, when all the freshness and beauty of spring seemed blended in rich profusion, with the productions peculiar to the season as it advanced towards maturity. The leaves on the trees were full grown, and the forest presented a freshness of beauty and loveliness which reminded me of Paradise. The plains were covered with a coat of green, and the wild flowers of the prairie, blooming in all their variety, sent forth a perfume which mingled with every zephyr, and wafted sweet odors on every breeze. To prisoners who had breathed only a tainted air for half a year the very ground itself seemed to send forth a sweetness which was plainly perceptible to the senses. We enjoyed our ride through that delightful country more than any being could who had never been confined for weary months in a dreary dungeon.

The day at length closed, and we were taken into a house and stretched upon our backs on the floor, all fastened together with wrist and ankle irons in such a manner that we could not turn nor change our position. The doors and windows were then made fast, and the sentinels on duty guarded us by turns until morning. This was our night's rest after forty miles travel.

The next day proved extremely rainy, with heavy thunder; but still we travelled. In the course of the day we came to a stream which was swollen by the rains to that degree that we had to swim over it and stem a swift current. This hindered us for some hours — in crossing over with horses, wagons, baggage, etc.; and as all of us were engaged in this business, our chains were taken off for the time.

When we had crossed over, put on our clothes, and replaced the baggage, saddles, arms, etc., ready for a start, it was night, and we were very weary and hungry, having had no refreshments during the day. The rain was also pouring in torrents, and the night setting in extremely dark. Four miles of wild country, partly covered with forests and underwood, still lay between us and the nearest house. Through the hurry of the moment, or for some other reason, they neglected to replace our irons, and our limbs were free. The carriage drove through a thick forest during the extreme darkness, and was several times on the eve of upsetting. This caused us to assume a position for saving ourselves by rising upon our feet ready to jump out in case of the carriage upsetting.

The Sheriff and guards seeing this, road close on each side, and, cocking their pistols, swore they would shoot us dead if we attempted to leave the carriage, and that if it upset they would shoot us anyhow, for fear we might attempt to escape.

After two days more of rain, hail and travel, we arrived at Columbia, where we were immediately thrust into a gloomy dungeon filled with darkness, filth and cobwebs; the naked floor was our lodging. We had travelled hard, through rain and fatigue, for several days, and on the last day had rode till sundown without refreshment. We were extremely hungry and weary, but received no refreshment, not even a drink of water, till late in the evening, when our new keeper, Mr. John Scott, visited us with some buttermilk and bread; but we were now too much exhausted and too low spirited to eat. We thanked him for his kindness, and sank down exhausted on the floor, where we rested as well as we could till morning. We saw no more of Sheriff Brown or his guards, and will now take final leave of them, merely observing that they made it a point to insult every black woman they met on the way, frequently turning aside with them into the woods and fields. On returning to the company they would boast and glory in their criminal intercourse with them.

After spending one night in our new dungeon we were called on by the Sheriff to come up into a more comfortable apartment, and were treated with some degree of humanity. We were no longer troubled with guards, and even Luman and Phila behaved much better. We had been in our new situation something like a month, when we were visited by some friends from Illinois, from whom we learned the fate or our families and friends.

The wife of Mr. Phelps rode one hundred and sixty miles on horseback, accompanied by her brother, a young man named Clark. They arrived in Columbia and paid us a visit in prison about the 1st day of July. My brother Orson also arrived on horseback about the same time. With these friends we had a good visit for some days — they being permitted to stay in the prison with us. They also brought a letter from my wife, by which I learned that she made her escape from Far West to Quincy, Illinois, with her children and some of her goods, by the aid of Mr. David Rogers, of New York. During this journey they were much exposed to hardships and trouble, having to camp by the way, in company with other women and children who were in a like condition. On crossing a swollen stream, Mrs. Pratt had left the carriage to cross on a foot bridge, leaving the children to ride through it. She had just crossed over and turned to look back, to see whether the carriage came through in safety, when she discovered a little girl's bonnet floating down the stream, and, on examination, as the carriage rose the bank, her daughter, a girl of six years old, was missing from the carriage. The next moment she saw her floating down the swift current. She gave the alarm to Mr. Rogers, the driver, who instantly dropped the reins and sprang after her into the stream.

At this instant the horses, being high spirited and active, began to run, and would probably have dashed themselves and the carriage, goods, and the other child to pieces but for the timely interference of a large prong of a tree, which caught the carriage with such a strong hold that all was brought to a stand. In the meantime Mr. Rogers succeeded in rescuing the child and bringing her safe to shore.

She had, as she stated, pitched head foremost out of the carriage into the water. One of the wheels ran over her, and crushed her fast into the mud at the bottom of the stream; but as it rolled over she caught the spokes with her hands, and by this means the same weight that crushed her down brought her to the surface and saved her life. On examination the marks of the wheel was distinctly seen on both her thighs, which were seriously injured and nearly broken.

After a wearisome journey and various toils and dangers, they at length arrived at Quincy, Illinois, where Mrs. Pratt rented a small house, and by the sale of a few books, with the use of her two cows, which some of the brethren had brought from Missouri for her, she was making shift to live from day to day. She still expressed some faint hopes of seeing her husband again in a land of liberty, although at present there was little ground to hope, and she was sometimes nearly in despair.

Such was the news brought us by the arrival of our friends in the prison at Columbia on the 1st of July, 1839, after eight months of weary confinement. Previous to their arrival the Lord had shown me in a vision of the night the manner and means of escape. And, like Pharaoh's dream, the thing had been doubled — that is shown to me on two occasions in the same manner.

Mrs. Phelps had the same thing shown to her in a vision previous to her arrival; my brother, Orson Pratt, also came to us with a firm impression that we were about to be delivered. He even predicted that we should go to Illinois, when he should return there. As we sat pondering upon these things, and comparing our visions and manifestations of the spirit on this subject, my brother Orson opened the Book of Mormon, when the first sentence that caught his eye was the words of Ammon to King Lamoni: "Behold, my brother and my brethren are in prison, in the land of Middoni, and I go to deliver them!" This was indeed a similar instance to ours. Ammon, on that occasion had an own brother in prison, and also brethren in the ministry, and did deliver them. Our case was exactly similar, not in Middoni, but in Missouri. And, what was still more strange, in a book of six hundred pages, this was the only sentence which would have fitted our case.

He now began in earnest to make arrangements for our escape. If there had been no strong bolts and bars to overcome, still there was one serious obstacle which a miracle alone could immediately remove, which was this: I was then very sick and scarcely able to stand on my feet, or to go up and down from the upper room, where we were in the day time, to the dungeon where we slept.

It was the second of July, and our friends could only make an excuse for staying to spend the great national holiday with us (the 4th) before they must leave or excite the suspicions and ill will of the people; and, as that day had been a lucky one for our fathers and our nation, we had determined on that time as the proper one to bid farewell to bondage and gain our liberty. In short, we had determined to make that notable day a jubilee to us, or perish in the attempt. We, therefore, prayed earnestly to the Lord, that if he had determined to favor our plan, he would heal and strengthen me, and give us all courage to act well our part. Through the ministration of the ordinance appointed for healing, I was instantly healed, and from that moment began to feel as strong and fearless as a lion.

Our plan was this: My brother, Orson Pratt, was to wait on the Judge and Attorney, and obtain various papers and arrangements for summoning witnesses from Illinois to attend our trial, which had just been adjourned for some months to come. He was also to procure an order from the Court to take affidavits in Illinois, in case the witnesses should object to come to the State from which they had been banished, in order to attend the trials.

These active preparations on our part to defend our case, together with engaging a lawyer or two, and paying a part of their fees before hand, served as a sufficient blindfold to cover our real intentions. This done, and the papers all prepared in the hands of my brother, he and Mrs. Phelps and her brother were to stay with us until the 4th, and after celebrating the day with a dinner in the prison (which we obtained leave to do), he and the young Mr. Clark were to take leave with their horses, and also with the horse and saddle on which Mrs. Phelps had ridden, on pretence of taking him home with them to Illinois, while she stayed with her husband a few weeks in the prison; in the meantime engaging her board in the family of the keeper, who occupied part of the building in connection with the prison.

This measure, on the part of Mrs. Phelps, served the double purpose of lulling them into serenity, and also of furnishing a third horse; as there were three of us. These three horses were to be stationed in a thicket, or forest, about half a mile from the prison, and there the two friends were to await, in readiness for us to mount, should we be so fortunate as to reach the thicket alive.

Sundown, on the evening of the fourth, was the moment agreed upon, and if we did not then appear they were to give us up for lost, and make the best of their way to Illinois and inform our friends that we had gone to Paradise in attempting to come to them. The reason for appointing this hour was this: Our door would be opened at sundown to hand in our supper, and we must then make the attempt as our only chance; for it was customary to lock us up in the lower dungeon as soon as the shades of evening began to appear.

This plan all matured, and the arrangements completed with the court and the lawyers, the fourth of July dawned upon us with hope and expectation. While the town and nation were alive with the bustle of preparation for the celebration of the American Jubilee, and while guns were firing and music sounding without, our prison presented a scene of scarcely less life and cheerfulness; for we were also preparing to do proper honors to the day. We had prevailed on the keeper to furnish us with a long pole, on which to suspend a flag, and also with some red stripes of cloth. We then tore a shirt in pieces, and took the body of it for the ground work of a flag, forming with the red stripes of cloth an eagle and the word "*Liberty,*" in large letters. This rude flag of red and white was suspended on the pole from the prison window, directly in front of the public square and court house, and composed one of the greatest attractions of the day. Hundreds of the people from the country, as well as villagers who were there at the celebration, would come up and stare at the flag, and reading the motto, would go swearing or laughing away, exclaiming, "Liberty! Liberty! What have the Mormons to do with celebrating *liberty* in a damned old prison?"

In the meantime active preparations were in progress for our public dinner; and with the contributions of our friends who were to partake with us, and a portion served from the public table of the citizens of the town, we had a plentiful supply. And, as we considered it was to be a day of release, we partook of our feast with much cheer, and with thankful as well as social feelings, which I think have been seldom if ever surpassed.

O ye sons of Columbia, at home and abroad! Think back to the fourth of July, 1839; call to mind your feast in honor of national freedom, and ask yourselves the question, whether in all your pomp and show of joy and social glee, you felt anything compared with *our* feelings, or the interest excited during that feast.

Eight months and four days we had been deprived of the sweets of that liberty which a whole nation was then engaged in celebrating; and we felt that:

> Now's the day, and now's the hour,
> To trample on a tyrant's power;
> To burst at once the prison's gloom,
> Or find a martyr'd hero's tomb.

The dinner over, our brethren took a final leave of us and our prison, loaded with love, respects, compliments and messages to our families and friends in Illinois. All these, together with the goodbyes and farewells, were heard and witnessed by the keeper's family, and served the purpose for which they were intended, viz.: To lull them into security, and to remove all possible ground of suspicion as to our intentions.

After riding out of town a mile or two in the forest, on the road towards Illinois, they turned off into the thick leaved wilderness, and made their way in secret, as best as they could, to the thicket agreed upon, within about half a mile of the prison; where, with horses saddled and bridle reins in hand, they awaited in anxious suspense the slow progress of the setting sun.

CHAPTER XXXII.

The prison at Columbia was situated in the same square with the court house, being on the north edge of the town. Between it and the wilderness, where our friends held the horses in waiting, there were several fields and fences, say for the distance of half a mile, consisting of meadow and pasture land, and all in full view of the town. The prison consisted of a block house, two stories high, with two rooms below and two above. The keeper and his family occupied one end, and the other was used as the prison—the only entrance being through the lower room of the dwelling part, which was occupied by the family, and then up a steep flight of stairs, at the head of which was a heavy oaken door, ironed, locked and bolted as if to secure a Bonaparte or a Samson. On the inside of this was still another door, which was but slender, with a square hole near the top, of sufficient size to hand in the food and dishes of the prisoners.

The large, heavy door had always to be opened when food, drink, or other articles were handed in; and while open, the inner door served as a temporary guard to prevent prisoners from escaping, and was not always opened on such occasions, the food being handed through the hole in the top of the door, while the door itself remained locked. However, as a fortunate circumstance for us, the coffee pot when filled would not easily slip through the hole in the door, and, rather than spill the coffee and burn his fingers, the keeper would sometimes unlock and open the inner door, in order to set in this huge and obstinate pot; and once in, the door would immediately close, and the key be turned, while the outer door would perhaps stand open till the supper was finished, and the dishes handed out.

Now, our whole chance of escape depended on the question, whether the inner door would be opened that evening, or the coffee pot squeezed in at the hole in the top. Mrs. Phelps and Mrs. Gibbs were in the upper room of the keeper's apartment, near the head of the stairs, and only a log or timber partition between us and them, and several open crevices in the same, so that we could easily communicate with them. One of them was waiting the issue of the great scene about to be enacted with almost breathless interest and feverish anxiety, as on the good or ill success of that moment depended her future hopes through life, while the other was totally ignorant of the whole affair. In a far corner of our prison sat Luman, the old apostate, entirely ignorant of the whole plan, and with no other anxiety than a slight wish for the sun to go down, that he might enjoy his supper and the society of his dear "Phila" in his curtained bed in the upper room, while we were locked in the dungeon below to sleep on an oak floor, amid cobwebs and filth.

The citizens of the town were now some of them gathering in small groups outside of their doors to enjoy the quiet of a summer evening, to smoke a cigar or chat over the merits of the celebration; while others were on horseback, to enjoy an evening's ride or to return to their homes. Bands of music, or rather an occasional beat of the drum, or blast of the bugle, was still to be heard in the distance; while a few soldiers, or rather militia in uniform, were hurrying to and fro. Groups of boys were playing about the square, and last, though not least, our flag was still on high, with "Liberty" and the eagle in bold colors waving to the night breeze. This had so attracted the attention of the little fellows that once and again they begged of us to make them a present of it; but we told them we could not spare it till the next morning—the fact is, we were not willing to surrender our castle before the time, or till we made good our retreat.

As the sun began to decline behind the long range of forest which bounded the western horizon, and the lengthened shadows of the tall trees were thrown over our prison, we called upon the Lord to prosper us and open our way, and then sang aloud the following lines:

> Lord, cause their foolish plans to fail,
>   And let them faint or die:
> Our souls would quit this poor old jail,
>   And fly to Illinois—
>
> To Join with the embodied Saints,
>   Who are with freedom blest:
> That only bliss for which we pant,
>   With them awhile to rest.

233

Give joy for grief—give ease for pain,
    Take all our foes away;
But let us find our friends again
    In this eventful day.

These lines were sung several times over, with the spirit and with the understanding also, and very loud and distinct—being heard by the old apostate and his wife, and by the keepers of the prison; but the doctrine of spiritualizing had become so prevalent that neither this, nor the flag of liberty, nor any other Scripture seemed to them to have any literal meaning, till they found too late the true interpretation by the fulfilment.

The sun was now setting, and the footsteps of the old keeper were heard on the stairs—the key turned, the outer door grated on its huge hinges, while at the same moment we sprang upon our feet, hats and coats on (rather an unusual dress for a hot day in July—for, by the bye, my hat proved to be a fur cap, which I wore when first taken in November previous), and stood by the door to act the part of waiters in receiving the dishes and food for supper, and placing them on the table. Dish after dish was handed in through the small aperture in the door, and duly received and placed upon the table by us, with as much grace and as calm countenances as if we thought of nothing else but our suppers. And I will now venture to say that famishing men never watched the movements of a coffee pot with more anxiety than we did on this occasion. At length the other dishes all being handed in, the huge pot made its appearance in the hole in the top of the door, but one of us cried out to the keeper—"Colonel, you will only spill the coffee by attempting to put it through, besides, it burns our fingers; it will be more convenient to unlock and hand it in at the door." With this it was lowered down again, and the key turned on the inner door.

In this, as in most other fields of battle, where liberty and life depend on the issue, every one understood the part assigned to him and exactly filled it. Mr. Follett was to give the door a sudden pull, and fling it wide open the moment the key was turned. Mr. Phelps being well skilled in wrestling was to press out foremost, and come in contact with the jailer; I was to follow in the centre, and Mr. Follett, who held the door, was to bring up the rear, while sister Phelps was to pray.

No sooner was the key turned than the door was seized by Mr. Follett with both hands; and with his foot placed against the wall, he soon opened a passage, which was in the same instant filled by Mr. Phelps, and followed by myself and Mr. Follett. The old jailer strode across the way, and stretched out his arms like Bunyan's Apollion, or like the giant Despair in Doubting Castle, but all to no purpose. One or

234

two leaps brought us to the bottom of the stairs, carrying the old gentleman with us headlong, helter skelter, while old Luman sat and laughed in his corner of the prison, and Mrs. Phelps exclaimed "O Lord God of Israel, thou canst help." Old Mrs. Gibbs looked on in silent amazement, while the jailer's wife acted the part of the giant Despair's wife, Diffidence, and not only assisted in the scuffle, but cried out so loud that the town was soon alarmed. In the mean time we found ourselves in the open air, in front of the prison and in full view of the citizens, who had already commenced to rally, while Mr. Phelps and the jailer still clinched fast hold of each other like two mastiffs. However, in another instant he cleared himself, and we were all three scampering off through the fields towards the thicket. By this time the town was all in motion. The quietness of the evening was suddenly changed into noise and bustle, and it was soon evident that the thrilling scenes of the great drama of the 4th of July, and of the Columbian celebration of liberty were yet to be enacted. The streets on both sides of the fields where we were running were soon thronged with soldiers in uniform, mounted riflemen, footmen with fence stakes, clubs, or with whatever came to hand, and with boys, dogs, etc., all running, rushing, screaming, swearing, shouting, bawling and looking, while clouds of dust rose behind them. The cattle also partook of the general panic and ran bellowing away, as if to hide from the scene. The fields behind us also presented a similar scene. Fences were leaped or broken down with a crash; men, boys and horses came tumbling over hedge and ditch, rushing with the fury of a whirlwind in the chase; but we kept our course for the thicket, our toes barely touching the ground, while we seemed to leap with the fleetness of a deer, or as the young hart upon the mountains.

Our friends who had stood waiting in the thicket, had watched the last rays of the sun as they faded away, and had observed the quiet stillness of the evening as it began to steal over the distant village where we were confined; and had listened with almost breathless anxiety for the first sound which was to set all things in commotion, and which would say to them in language not to be misunderstood, that the struggle had commenced. For some moments after the last golden beam had disappeared they listened in vain. The occasional lowing of a cow as she came home from the woodland pasture, impatient for her calf and the milkmaid to ease her of her rich burthen; the mingled sound of human voices in the distance in common conversation, the merry laugh of the young beaux and their sweethearts, the quiet song of the whippoorwill, mingled with the merry notes of the violin, the thrill of the bugle, or the soft and plaintive notes of the flute, stole upon the silence of the evening, and were occasionally interrupted by the clatter of hoofs, as a few of the citizens were retiring from the enjoyments of a public day to their own peaceful homes in the country. These, and the beatings of their anxious and almost bursting hearts, were the only sounds which fell upon their ear, till suddenly they heard a rumbling and confused noise, as of footsteps rushing down the stairs of a prison, then a shrill cry of alarm from Mrs. Diffidence, the giantess, and soon followed by the shouts and rush of men, dogs, horses and prisoners towards the spot where they were located. They then sprang forward to the edge of the fields and ran back again to the horses, and again returned, as if the using of their own limbs would serve to add nimbleness to those of the prisoners, and to quicken their speed.

As soon as the prisoners drew near, they were hailed by their friends, and conducted to the horses. They were breathless and nearly ready to faint; but in a moment they were assisted to mount, and a whip and the reins placed in their hands, while the only words interchanged were—"Fly quickly, they are upon you!" "Which way shall we go?" "Where you can; you are already nearly surrounded." "But what will you do? they will kill you if they cannot catch us." "We will take care of ourselves; fly, fly, I say, instantly." These words were exchanged with the quickness of thought, while we were mounting and reining our horses; in another instant we were all separated from each other, and each one was making the best shift he could for his own individual safety.

I had taken about the third jump with my horse when I encountered a man rushing upon me with a rifle, and, taking aim at my head, he said "G-d d—n you, stop, or I'll shoot you." He was then only a few paces from me, and others were rushing close in his rear, but I turned my horse quickly in another direction, and rushed with all speed into the thickest of the forest, followed for some minutes by him and his dog; but I soon found myself alone, while I could only hear the sound of distant voices, the rushing of horsemen in every direction, with the barking of dogs. What had become of my companions or our friends I knew not. I rode on at full speed for a full mile or more, when the woods terminated, and no alternative was left for me but to go either to the right or to the left into one of the public highways where I would be every moment exposed to my pursuers, or go over the fence and pass through the open fields to the wilderness beyond, or, on the other hand, to turn back into the heart of the forest, partly towards the town and prison from whence I had escaped. As horse's feet and men's voices were already heard along the highways which lay on each side of me, I determined upon the latter. I, therefore, changed my course, took my back track, and plunged into the depth of the forest. I then dismounted, tied my horse in a thicket, walked some distance from him and climbed a tree—intending to wait in this situation amid the concealment of the thick foliage till the darkness of evening would enable me to proceed with safety. Seating myself in one of its forked branches, and placing my arms in two other similar forks, I was supported from falling, although in a moment after I had ceased my exertions I fainted away. In this situation I remained for some time, without the least power to change my position or help myself; my breath was gone through over exertion, and my mouth and throat parched with a burning thirst, my stomach sickened, and as I began again to breathe I was seized with vomiting, and threw up nearly all the food which my stomach contained. I then gradually recovered my strength till I could speak, when I began to call on the Lord, saying, "O Lord, strengthen me this once, deliver me from my persecutors and bring me in safety to a land of liberty, and I will praise thy name and give thee all the glory, and the remnant of my days shall be wholly devoted to thy service; for surely my life is now at stake, and if preserved, it is thy gift, therefore I shall owe it all to thee."

The darkness of evening was now fast setting in, and every moment seemed to increase my safety and security from immediate discovery, although I could still hear the distant sound of tramping horses, and the voices of men and dogs in pursuit, and sometimes so near that I could distinguish some of their words. It was a dark and moonless evening, the sky was only lighted by the glimmer of a few stars partly obscured by the clouds, and the thick foliage of the forest increased the gloom, and served to render the darkness nearly complete. I now came down from the tree and felt my way to the place where I had tied my horse, but as good or ill luck would have it, he had loosed himself and gone, leaving me to my fate. I then groped my way amid the dark shades of the forest to a small stream of warm, muddy water, and, stooping down, partly quenched my thirst. I then made my way to the highway and commenced my journey on foot, carefully watching on either hand lest I should be surprised and taken.

I was an entire stranger to the country—having no guide but the polar star. My road lay nearly northward and upwards of a hundred miles of a wild country, peopled only by enemies, still lay between me and a State where the principles of freedom yet prevailed in a sufficient degree to insure my safety. If I could make my way through this wilderness of enemies, on foot, after the weakness and debility caused by eight months' confinement, and after the fatigues of my evening's race, and neither inquire the way nor make my appearance at any house for entertainment and refreshment, then I should still have the great Mississippi River to ferry over, and be liable to be discovered and retaken in the act, while in sight of liberty. The thoughts of these dangers, the anxious inquiries of my mind as to what had become of my fellow prisoners and friends, which I had no means of satisfying, and the hopes and expectation of soon meeting my family and friends in a land of liberty, alternately occupied my mind as I slowly pursued my solitary way during that dark and, to me, eventful night.

[Publisher's note: Parley Pratt subsequently escaped to Quincy, Illinois, where he was reunited with his wife and family. Morris Phelps also escaped unharmed, but King Follett was captured, held a few months, then released. Orson Pratt and the Clark boy escaped after hiding in a ravine. The women were taunted but not imprisoned. All eventually helped settle the new Mormon headquarters in Nauvoo, Illinois.]

Index

A

Aaronic priesthood, 27

Adam, 52, 107, 197

adoption, laws of in Kingdom of God, 5, 8, 9

affections, destruction of civilization if not governed, 127; increase with intelligence, 123; not devilish, 124

after life, *see* spirit world

alcohol, Smith and devil drink together, 139-40

America, destruction of, 23-24, 142-43; discovery, 92

"Angel Caught," 41

angels, 16, 187, 188

animal magnetism, relation to Holy Spirit, 190

apostates, those who have gospel and turn away, 178

apostles, 152: chosen in Judea, America, and among ten tribes, 163; New Testament system, 153-54; preach in spirit world, 180; succession, 154

atheism, 26

authority, government analogy, 70-71

B

Babylon, kingdom of, 87-89

Baldwin, Caleb, 220

baptism for dead, 182

Bible, 1, 29; and scriptures, 26, 162; Apocrypha, 74; Mormons and, 80-81

Boggs, Lilburn W., 219

Book of Mormon, 16, 26-27, 30; account to Indians, 158-60; compass, 36, 38; criticism because similar to the Bible, 35-36, 76; defense of, 72-73, 81-82; description of to Queen Victoria, 92-93; evidence for truth of, 164; its translation, 21-22; Joseph Smith's defense against the devil, 135; proved false if Gentiles not scourged and overthrown within five or ten years, 24; significance of, 161-62; Sunderland on, 24-26, 36-44; typographical errors, 35

books, relation to knowledge, 97-99

Boudinot, Elias, 38-39

brass plates, 25, 39-40

Bush, Rev. C. S., 74-82

C

Caldwell County Militia, 208, 215

Campbell, Alexander, 28, 42

celibacy, condemned by the Lord, 125

Chase, Darwin, at Richmond jail, 220, 222

chemistry, 110

children, blessing and giving names, 168

Chile, Book of Mormon people land there, 158

Christianity, charges Mormons are not 79-80; plunges America into degradation, 170

Clark, General, 211, 214

Columbia prison, Boone County, moved to prison there, 226-28; plan by Orson Pratt for escape of prisoners, 229-31; last night in jail, 233-34; escape on July 4, 232-38

Cornelius, 8

Cowdery, Oliver, 43

Creation, account of, 49-50, 51-52, 106-107, 196-97

Crooked River, 209, 213

D

Daniel, and last days, 88-89

death, how fits with eternality of matter, 110-11

devil, dialogue with Joseph Smith, 131-40; command to depart, 168

Doniphan, Mr., 207, 220

E

earth, its future changes, 64-68, 90, 115, 201-202

eight witnesses, 76

electricity, analogy to Holy Spirit, intelligence, 174, 190

Elijah, and resurrection, 60-61

England, 89, 95

Enoch, and resurrection, 60-61

eternal progression, 195, 196

Europe, in Daniel's vision, 89

Eve, 52, 107, 197

F

Fall, 53–55, 111

family, eternal, 202

Far West, 206, 207, 215, 221

first estate, 148, 197–98

Follet, King, Richmond jail, 222, 224, 234, 238

fourth estate, resurrection, 198–99

French Prophets, 18, 19

G

gathering of Israel, 90

general conference, during Millennium, 144

Gentile, not one unbelieving fifty years hence, 24

geology, 108

Gibbs, Luman, at Richmond jail, 220, 222, 223–24

gifts of spirit, 4, 84–85, 153

Gilbert, Sidney, 32

God, difference God and Christ and man, 115, 156, 187, 188, 189; each one can create kingdoms, 189; family of Gods, species of beings, 194–95; General Assembly, Quorum or Grand Council of Gods, 195; Godhead, 191–92; man to become like Christ and Father, 187; multiply species, 195; plurality of Gods, 188; same race as angels and man, 187; sectarian God, 35, 109, 184–85, 193; subject to law, 50, 189

gold plates, 21–22, 38

gospel, offered and rejected by various peoples, 177

government, 166–68

grace, salvation by, 57

great and abominable church, 23

H

healing of sick, 19, 168

Himes (Boston), 28

Hinkle, George H., 206, 215

Holy Spirit, 4–5; attributes of the eternal power and Godhead, 191; composed of particles, 190; connection to electricity, galvanism, magnetism, animal magnetism, spiritual magnetism, 190–91; controlling agent of motion of the worlds, 191; moving cause of all intelligences, 191

Howe, Eber D., 28, 42, 135

Hurlbut, Philastus, 42, 44, 135

I

Illinois, saints commence moving there, 220

Independence, prisoners there, 212–13

Indians, 23; address to "red man," 158–60; and Hebrew, 39; as descendants of Ten Tribes, 39; Book of Mormon and, Sutherland's critique, 38–39; first land in what is now Chile, 158; reject the gospel, 177

infant baptism, 31, 93

intelligence, 21–23, 121–30, 173–74, 188, 194, 202

J

Jared, 21

Jehovah, and Jesus, 45, 100

Jerusalem, 71

Jesus Christ, 31, 152, 162–63, 186–87; as material being, 116–17; as pattern of resurrection, 58–61; before resurrected, 175–76; commissions officers of the kingdom, 2; differs from Father only in seniority, 186; double relationship, to man and to God, 187; his life, 2–4; his model as king, 129–30; his work, 55–58; in Zion, 142, 144; Mormons believe in Christ, 79–80; on communication with the dead, 173; preach to those from Noah's time in spirit world, 177–78; records written by those who receive testimony of him, in many places, 164

Jews, 29, 48; address to, 157–58; and Jesus, 157; and New Testament, 157; last days, 157; reject the gospel, 177; restoration of Israel, 154

John, 7, 58–59

judgment day, 66–67

K

King, Judge Austin A., 216, 221, 226

Kingdom of God, 2–13

L

Laban, his murder, 39

language, God's communication through, 69

last days, 14, 87, 90–91, 171

laws, omnipotent and unalterable, 107; outline of laws of space, intelligence, etc., 189–90

Liberty jail, 221, 224

Lucas, General, 206

Lucifer, in the pre-existence, 149

Lyman, Amasa, 220

M

man, same race as gods and angels, 187

Smith, Hyrum, 206, 209, 220

Smith, Joseph, Jr., 43, 220; at Far West, 206, 207; dialogue with the devil, 131–40; Parley Pratt, feel present at laying cornerstone of Salt Lake Temple, 181; rebuke guards at Richmond, 217; reply to woman who asked if Mormons worship him, preach gospel, 211; speech to prisoners, 210–11; stories circulating against him, 41, 136–37; work in the spirit world, 182–83

Smith, Joseph, Sr., 209

Smith, Lucy, 209

space, 193

Spaulding theory, 42–44, 135–36

spirit, and matter, 48, 116, 194; intelligent beings with personal identity and embodiment, 116; not united with fleshly tabernacle, 188; spirit body, 197; spiritualism, mediums, etc., 172; third estate, 198

spirit world, after life of spirits, 128–29, 174–75, 182, 200; from Bible, 173; grades there, 179; hearing the gospel there, 176–79; Joseph Smith's work there, 182–83; those raised from the dead and with apostleship preach the gospel, 180

Sunderland, La Roy, 15ff.; God will smite him dumb, 24

Swedenborg, 18, 19

T

technology, improvements follow freedom's triumphs and conquests, 167

temples, 27-28, 174; in Millennium, 141; laying cornerstone in Salt Lake City, feel Joseph and others there, 181–82; prisoners visit temple site at Independence, 212; work for dead, 180–82

ten tribes, records to come, twelve apostles chosen among, 163

third estate, probationary sphere, world of spirits, 198

three witnesses, 76, 159–60

U

universalism, 57

Urim and Thummim, 145

V

vengeance, 150

W

Washington, D.C., 69

wealth, and Christianity, 84, 85; eternal, 202–203

West, as refuge, 17

Whitmer, Peter, 43

Wight, Lyman, 206, 220

Wilson, General Moses, 209–10

witnesses, 164

women, 125, 146–51, 171

works, salvation by, 57

Y

Young, Brigham, and his wives, 169

Z

Zion, 141, 147

Zion's Watchman, 15, 16